MOTHERS IN PUBLIC AND POLITICAL LIFE

Funded by the Government of Canada
Financé par la gouvernement du Canada |  Canada

Demeter Press
140 Holland Street West
P. O. Box 13022
Bradford, ON L3Z 2Y5
Tel: (905) 775-9089
Email: info@demeterpress.org
Website: www.demeterpress.org

Demeter Press logo based on the sculpture "Demeter" by Maria-Luise Bodirsky, www.keramik-atelier.bodirsky.de

Printed and Bound in Canada

Front cover artwork: Gioia Albano, "Whatever it is that makes you happy," 2015, ink, acrylic colour, pencils, and marker pen on paper, 25 x 25 cm. www.albanogioia.com.

Library and Archives Canada Cataloguing in Publication

     Mothers in public and political life / edited by Simone Bohn and Pınar Melis Yelsalı Parmaksız.

Includes bibliographical references.
ISBN 978-1-77258-105-8 (softcover)

     1. Working mothers. 2. Women politicians. 3. Mothers--Employment. 4. Mothers--Social conditions. I. Bohn, Simone, 1973-, editor II. Yelsali Parmaksiz, Pinar Melis, 1977-, editor

HQ759.48 M68 2017   306.874'3   C2017-904670-5

MOTHERS IN PUBLIC AND POLITICAL LIFE

EDITED BY
Simone Bohn and
Pınar Melis Yelsalı Parmaksız

DEMETER

DEMETER PRESS

To our children:
Cecilia, Julian, and Eric Bohn
and
Dora Parmaksız

Table of Contents

Acknowledgements

The Editors would like to thank all the contributors for their work, and especially Andrea O'Reilly for the opportunity and for her efforts to promote matricentric studies.

1.
Researching Mothers in Public and Political Life

An Introduction

SIMONE BOHN AND PINAR MELIS YELSALI PARMAKSIZ

HOW DOES POLITICAL POWER—in its multiple forms—constrain or enable mothers' agency? How do mothers engage with consolidated and traditional political spaces, or challenge them to modify how they work and create new ones? What types of political solidarity does mothering forge? What kinds of "collective action" problems (Olson) do mothers need to overcome in order to put their "repertoires of contention" (Tilly) in motion? What sorts of political claims do they put forward, and how do they (re)define what political is?

Drawing on distinct research traditions across a variety of disciplines, this volume aims at adding a "matricentric" perspective (O'Reilly, *Matricentric*) to the study of political power in its different configurations. Its chapters' common thread is the analysis of mothers' claim-making capacity and activity both inside and outside of arenas of political power. The ultimate goal is to understand how formal as well as informal political institutions limit or catalyze mothers' ability to contribute to the *res publica*, or "the public affairs," and to have their otherwise unacknowledged claims noticed and addressed by the political system and society at large.

Several of these matricentric politically related queries are essentially empirical in nature, which means that the answers to them are largely context specific. Nevertheless, one needs to recognize that political systems everywhere share some degree of similarity, as they set the boundaries in which political actors, including mothers, operate. In any given country, political power manifests itself through a set of formal and informal institutions. Formal institutions, in the case of the political realm, refer to a set of organized, ritualized, and procedural praxes, which in liberal representative democracies are crystallized in specific organizations (such as legislatures, executive bodies, and judicial courts) whose *modus procedendi* is regulated by written, formalized codes. From this perspective, as rules and structures that absorb and process social conflict, political institutions create a system of incentives that advantages some social actors, demands and behaviour, and disadvantages others (North). It is thus incumbent upon matricentric scholars to understand which particular institutional configurations benefit mothers operating within the limits established by a specific political system and which ones hinder the attainment of their tactical and strategic interests. In addition, it bears mentioning that since institutions are long-term historical developments (Weber; de Tocqueville; Pierson), the way that they are created and evolve strongly affects mothers' ability to have their political voice heard and to have their specific demands addressed.

Chapters two, three, and four of this volume centre on mothers' interactions with formal political institutions. In chapter two, "Mothers and Electoral Politics: A Research Agenda," Simone Bohn analyzes mothers' engagement in electoral politics in contemporary democracies. The author emphasizes that this topic has been underresearched and that the small number of existing studies have opposing stances. Although some consider that the current functioning of electoral politics noticeably disadvantages mothers as political actors, others deem that motherhood confers upon women valuable political expertise that can generate considerable electoral dividends. In other words, although mothers face substantial difficulties at the ballot box, electoral politics is not totally impenetrable to them. Bohn concludes her chapter with suggestions on how to address this paucity of scholarly output on mothers and elections.

Chapter three, "Motherhood and Public Service: An Exploration of School Board Trustees," clearly sides with the literature that sees motherhood as an electoral asset. Using in-depth interviews with past and present school board trustees in the Southwest United

States, Rebecca E. Deen and Beth Ann Shelton provide evidence that instead of hindering women's electoral ambition, motherhood actually propels women into political activism and leads to successful participation in electoral politics at the local level.

Moving slightly away from electoral politics, chapter four—"The Marriage and Children Gap? Marital Status, Parenthood, and Social Welfare Attitudes"—highlights how motherhood decisively shapes women's views on state's responses to models of social welfare. Using survey analysis, Shirley Adelstein shows that motherhood strongly affects political attitudes and the perceived social role of formal political institutions. In particular, single women who experience motherhood are more drawn to espouse views that advocate for heightened societal responsibility over human care and for state involvement in attenuating the problems stemming from socioeconomic exclusion.

Whereas those chapters address, in distinct ways, mothers' relationship with formal institutions, the next four chapters focus on informal institutions, which refer to "socially shared rules, usually unwritten, that are created, communicated, and enforced outside of officially sanctioned channels" (Helmke and Levistky 727). That is to say, that these are societal norms that strongly affect individual behaviour as well as the ability of groups—particularly those who are socially or political marginalized—to form solidarities, to build a collective identity, and, especially, to have their demands absorbed by the political system and addressed by public policies. For instance, societal narratives on what constitutes mothering and good motherhood (Ladd-Taylor and Umansky; O'Reilly, *Toni Morrison*) are deeply political and are imbued with power ramifications, as they can strongly constrain mothers' ability to engage in political activism and public life. Patriarchal normativity can also have a negative effect on mothers' ability to exercise their citizenship rights within a nation state (Bobel). Interestingly, nation states themselves designate patriarchal normativity; as a consequence, women are perceived primarily as the biological and cultural reproducers—as mothers of the nation (Anthias and Yuval-Davis). Nation, on the other hand, is imagined as a family in nationalist ideology; family becomes one of the strongest analogies to refer to the nation. In this framework, the traditional nuclear family, with the assumed roles and functions for its members, serves as the legitimate model for sustaining power relations within the nation.

Chapter five, "Shared Advice for Political Marriages: The Espistolary Dialogues between Mothers and Daughters," highlights how mothers themselves have been instrumental in the maintenance of certain informal political institutions. It examines the narratives that three royal mothers carefully crafted in order to advise their daughters on the best ways of obtaining and maintaining successful political marriages in the seventeenth and eighteenth centuries. In this piece, Mary T. Duarte magisterially weaves together "epistolary dialogues" between mothers and daughters, which rather than questioning prevailing patriarchal normativity further reinforced it, with the goal of guaranteeing the continuity in power of particular royal families. Motherhood is, thus, portrayed as a tool used by the nobility to socialize its younger generations into the duties, sacrifices, and (perhaps most important) interests associated with being royalty.

Chapter six, "Motherliness and Women's Emancipation in the Published Articles of Ika Freudenberg: A Discursive Approach," resumes this type of discursive analysis and focuses on the ideas of a nineteenth-century German activist, Ika Freudenberg, who questioned the then-prevailing notions of women and womanhood, and especially their relationship to motherhood. In this chapter, Mirjam Höfner shows how Freudenberg advocated for a specific project of women's emancipation, which was seen as a possibility when the idea of motherliness (and not necessarily the reality of motherhood) would become dominant in society. Interestingly, Freudenberg saw childbearing as a detriment (possibly temporary) to the full realization of the superior goal of womanhood and to women's participation in the public realm.

Chapter seven, "Women and the Paternal State: A Maternalist Frame for Gender Equality," reflects on the state's use of maternal discourse as part of a conservative political outlook in Turkey and the impact of the mobilization of mothers and women to reclaim gender equality. In this piece, Pınar Melis Yelsalı Parmaksız focuses on mothers' participation in the 2013 Gezi protest, which addressed the antiabortion debate, violence against women, and gender-related disputes. In this process, maternalist frames were redefined as plausible sources for symbolic action in the face of symbolic violence. This reconceptualization can potentially challenge gendered notions of power (or certain prevalent informal institutions) and its practice at the state level.

As mothers from several different historical contexts questioned patriarchal normativity, motherhood became an important springboard for activism. Women appealed to their maternal roles to justify their demands—for instance, for suffrage as well as for education and civic liberties starting from the nineteenth and early twentieth centuries. Afterward, mothers' activism evolved to include campaigns, environmental activism, and peace movements (Hayden 196).

The implications of mothers' activism from the angle of gender theory, however, are somewhat contentious. On the one hand, Jean Bethke Elshtain and Sara Ruddick acknowledge the maternal values of care and altruism, and endorse this normativity as the virtues that should prevail in society as a whole (qtd. in Reiger 312). Others hold very different views. Cynthia Cockburn, for example, investigates the role of women in general and that of mothers in particular in antiwar movements in different contexts and disputes that the role of motherhood necessarily reinforces the biological understanding of mothering. Socio-biological understanding of the role of motherhood, Cockburn argues, reflects nothing but the stereotypical role of mothers as the reproducers of social and national entities, which contributes to realizing the nationalistic and militaristic expectations from women in a patriarchal society (210). Thus, authors, such as Cockburn see an important role for motherhood in rejecting the exploitation of "love power," which is embodied in the sociobiological relations and in the practices of motherhood (211).

There is no intention here of discussing the utility of the conceptualization of motherhood; it cannot unify all women around a given set of practices, as mothers differ substantially in their experiences of mothering. For example, when heteronormativity-based discourses are prevalent, they complicate the lives of lesbian mothers in ways that are different than the hurdles experienced by other mothers (Lewin). Instead, the question here is whether motherhood-based activism is favourable to any form of gender politics.

Some case studies illustrate the potential of motherhood-based activism. Amy Swerdlow, for example, discusses "Strike for Peace," which was a group of mothers organized to protest the Vietnam War, and the author notes that members' activism eventually led to the development of a "feminist consciousness" (qtd. in Hayden 197). Another example is *Zene u Crnom* (Women in Black) in Serbia. It was formed in 1991 as an antimilitarist, feminist organization bringing together feminists of the former Tito era, peace activists, and the antiwar mothers; it showed a strong position against nationalism and militarism (Cockburn qtd. in Daşlı et.al. 19). Similarly, motherhood activism appears as the "ethical reference" in many different but relevant social and political contexts for creating what is called "the maternal memory" and for "coming to terms with the past" (Burchianti 135). An inspirational example of motherhood activism comes from the case of the mothers of the Plaza de Mayo in Argentina and that inspiration has spread across countries to mobilize mothers in such places as the countries of the former Yugoslavia and Turkey. As these cases—and the ones presented in this volume—illustrate, the maternal feelings of care or mourning or the maternal memory come into prominence not as a "rhetorical trope" but as a form of political mobilization out of the mythical paradigm of motherhood (Aretxaga qtd. in Burchianti 142). In other words, mothers' political consciousness and collective activity are likely to bring about political activism based on motherhood, which is relevant for gender politics. Nevertheless, maternal politics is partial, as any other politics is—it is limited by its context (Hayden 212).

The next section of chapters follows up on this discussion, and introduces important examples of political activism through motherhood. Chapter eight, "On *Andariegas, Carishinas,* and Bad Mothers: Challenges to the Political Participation of Indigenous Women in the Ecuadorian Andes," studies the indigenous women of Cotacachi, Ecuador, who have taken leadership positions in their local communities and have played important roles in the indigenous political movement. In this chapter, María Moreno shows how indigenous women are seen as the symbolic reproducers of their culture. Although their participation in politics is valued, their autonomous political activities require strong efforts from them to accommodate sometimes conflicting role expectations. Moreno analyzes in detail the experiences of these women, and debates how and to what extent ideas about motherhood are associated with their political activism as mothers.

In chapter nine, "Between the Private and the Public: Paradoxes of Motherhood and Politics in Brazil," Nathalie Reis Itaboraí focuses on the political participation of women in Brazil to examine how motherhood impacts both the decision to participate into politics and the level of engagement with it. Her chapter is based on participatory observation during political events and conferences as well as on interviews. Itaboraí's research not only reflects the focal feminist methodological principles but also successfully reveals that power intersects at various social positions. In other words, differences among mothers and the duties of motherhood no doubt matter for their political participation.

In chapter ten, "Before Boston's Busing Crisis: Operation Exodus, Grassroots Organizing, and Motherhood, 1965-1967," Julie de Chantal brings into light the somewhat less-known activist Ellen Jackson—a thirty-year-old, working-class Black mother who launched the first volunteering busing service as part of the struggle against de facto racial segregation of public schools in Boston. De Chantal demonstrates that Black mothers played a significant political role in civil rights organizations in Boston, rendering practical matters into political action.

In a similar vein, chapter eleven, "On the Margins of Politicized Motherhood: Mothers' Human Rights Activism Revisited in Turkey from the 1970s to the 1990s," unearths the role played by mothers in the human rights movement in Turkey. Its author, Tuba Demirci-Yılmaz, focuses on the life stories of three women, who represent dissimilar political ideologies, but were mobilized as mothers and hence contributed to the institutionalization of human rights activism, despite the risk of oppression and violence. The chapter also shows that the activism of mothers can make a change in informal politics, as it can transform normative stereotypes of mothers and mothering.

Chapter twelve, "The Mothers at Home to the Mothers on the Streets: Caring, Politics, and the Right to Have Rights," also depicts mothers' intense activism. Rosamaria Carneiro analyzes different instances of protest involving groups of mothers; she demonstrates their great capacity of mobilization and of making their claims socially visible by taking them to the streets. Carneiro shows that mothers' platform of action ranges widely—from the defense of their reproductive rights, to the fight against violence against women, to the struggle against racism, and to the protection of democracy.

Chapter thirteen, "The Disappearing of the Disappeared in the Plaza de Mayo: Who Will Hold the Space of the Madres Once They Are Gone?," centres on mothers engaged in street protest as well. Sarah A. Schoellkopf's chapter provides a renewed interest in the widely known and inspiring Mothers of the Plaza de Mayo, and evokes the question about the endurance of their maternal activism. Schoellkopf makes an assessment about the present-day activism of the Mothers of the Plaza de Mayo, which is less known outside Argentina. In doing so, she opens up a debate about the relevance of the maternal activism and evaluates the legacy of the particular movement. She concludes by pondering who will carry their torch into the future.

Mothers mobilize around issues related to the needs of their children and issues that include coming to terms with the past. The activism of mothers as exemplified in chapter fourteen— "'Black Protest': Abortion Law in Poland in the Context of Division into Private and Public Sphere"—also raises claims regarding the issue of reproductive rights. Edyta Pietrzak and Anna Fligel analyze the recent mobilization of Polish women, known as "the Black Protest," against the radicalization of abortion law in Poland in 2016. The authors put the women's protests against the radicalization of reproductive rights in the framework of a public and private divide in order to promote an effective civil society.

All in all, these chapters show that, paradoxically, although formal and informal political institutions do constrain mothers' agency, they also catalyze it. In different historical contexts, mothers have overcome collective action problems and forged solidarities, have pressed the state to deliver particular public policies, have tried to enter the electoral system, and have fought against the illegal killings committed by dictators. The chapters in this volume also provide unequivocal evidence that motherhood is a launch pad for groups of women to fight against societal values and norms that are gender oppressive.

WORKS CITED

Bobel, Chris. *The Paradox of Natural Mothering*. Temple University Press, 2001.

Burchianti, Margaret E. "Building Bridges of Memory: The Mothers of the Plaza de Mayo and the Cultural Politics of Maternal Memories." *History and Anthropology*, vol. 15, no. 2, 2004, pp. 133-150.

Cockburn, Cynthia. *From Where We Stand: War, Women's Activism and Feminist Analysis*. Zed Books, 2007.

Daşlı, Güneş, et al. *Kadınların Barış Mücadelesinde Dünya Deneyimleri, Sırbistan, Kosova, Sri Lanka, Suriye*. Demos, 2017.

de Tocqueville, Alexis. *Democracy in America*. 1835. Vintage Books, 1990.

Hayden, Sara. "Family Metaphors and the Nation: Promoting a Politics of Care through the Million Mom March." *Quarterly Journal of Speech*, vol. 89, no. 3, 2002, pp. 196-215.

Helmke, G., and S. Levistky. "Informal Institutions and Comparative Politics: A Research Agenda." *Perspective on Politics*, vol. 2, no. 4, 2004, pp. 725-40.

Ladd-Taylor, M. and L. Umansky. "Introduction." *Bad Mothers: The Politics of Blame in Twentieth-Century America*, edited by M. Ladd-Taylor and L. Umansky, *Bad Mothers: The Politics of Blame in Twentieth-Century America*, New York University Press, 1998, pp. 1-29.

Lewin, Ellen. *Lesbian Mothers: Accounts of Gender in American Culture*. Cornell University Press, 1993.

North, Douglass. *Institutions, Institutional Change and Economic Performance*. Cambridge University Press, 1990.

Olson, Mancur. *The Logic of Collective Action*. Harvard University Press, 1971.

O'Reilly, Andrea. *Matricentric Feminism. Theory, Activism and Practice*. Demeter Press, 2016.

O'Reilly, Andrea. *Toni Morrison and Motherhood: A Politics from the Heart*. State University of New York Press, 2004.

Reiger, Kerreen. "Reconceiving Citizenship: The Challenge of Mothers as Political Activists." *Feminist Theory* vol. 1, no. 3, 2000, pp. 309-27.

Pierson, Paul. *Politics in Time.* Princeton: Princeton University Press, 2004.

Tilly, Charles. *Regimes and Repertoires.* University of Chicago Press, 2006.

Weber, Max. *Economy and Society.* University of California Press, 1978.

Yuval-Davis, Nira, and Floya Anthias, editors. *Woman, Nation, State.* Palgrave Macmillan, 1989.

MOTHERS IN FORMAL POLITICAL INSTITUTIONS

2.
Mothers and Electoral Politics

A Research Agenda

SIMONE BOHN

IT IS HARDLY A NOVELTY to state that women have historically been latecomers to the political realm in most of world's "polyarchies" (Dahl)—namely those countries whose political regimes follow (albeit in different degrees) the basic tenets of liberal representative democracies. Women were one of the last large groups of citizens to win the right to vote and to stand as candidates in elections.

Several decades after women's obtainment of full political citizenship in most Western countries, a myriad of studies of the most different facets of the relationship between gender and elections has been produced. A purported "gender gap in politics," in which women are portrayed as having less interest in electoral politics than men, has been the object of a heated debate (Campus; Morgan et al.). Similarly, scholars have attempted to gauge how womanhood affects voter turnout (Fullerton and Stern; Ondercin and Bernstein), party affiliation (Fridkin and Kenny), positioning vis-à-vis wedge issues (Kellstedt et al.), and of course, voting (Corder and Wolbrecht; Dolan; Giger; Norrander). Since the entrance of women into the world of electoral politics, studies have started to focus on what women do when they are in a legislature (Dodson, *The Impact*; Taylor-Robinson and Heath; Osborn and Mendez), especially what kind of bills they propose (Little et al.; Swers, "Connecting," *The Difference*), what types of committee assignments they get, and how they are treated by their male colleagues (Arnold and King; Norton; Rosenthal). Other studies have looked at what "women's issues" and "women's interests" are (Baldez; Molyneux; Reingold and Swers; Sapiro; Vickers; Young) and at whether having women in a legislature creates a conflation between "descriptive representation" (Pitkin)—more women bodies in parliaments, and other elected arenas—and "substantive representation," namely the defense of "women's interests" (Celis et al.; Mansbridge, "Should"). In the last three decades or so, a call for more female descriptive representation has generated an outpouring of scholarship on gender quotas, their successes, and shortcomings (Dahlerup; Krook; Jones; Mansbridge, "Quota").

Interestingly, not much empirical attention has been paid to the relationship between an important, and sizeable, group of women and electoral politics: mothers. In fact, this chapter argues that the links between motherhood and "politico-electoral ambition" have been underresearched. First of all, as discussed below, a dearth of official data exists on the theme, as "motherhood," or "parenthood," does not normally figure in the roster of candidate characteristics that governments make available to voters (and researchers). Similarly, supranational organizations devote zero attention to the mothers-and-elections issue. All of this results in a lack of reliable comparative, multilevel indicators, which would enable cross-country analyses as well as studies across various levels of government in a single polity.

Finally, not only are data scarce, but the literature on the political ambition of mothers is scant and has points of disagreement. At least two major distinct views can be detected. First is the view that motherhood works as a gatekeeper, keeping women with children from running for elected jobs. From this perspective, mothers either lack, or are momentarily unable to possess, interest in getting elected. Second are the studies that posit a strong, positive relationship between motherhood and elected jobs. Motherhood, from this viewpoint, makes women more aware of specific issues and hones their expertise regarding particular political domains. In addition, this side posits that motherhood imbues women with values that voters deem highly desirable in current politics.

The goal of this chapter is to navigate through this landscape of deficiencies and to propose a research agenda that aims at overcoming the mothers-in-electoral-politics oblivion. The next section surveys works that illustrate different perspectives regarding the electoral ambition of women with children. In the sequence, the data scarcity and its effects are examined. The chapter concludes with a tentative proposal to add a "matricentric" perspective (O'Reilly) to electoral studies.

MOTHERS AS DOMESTIC PATRIOTS

Although some societies' civic narratives do attribute a high value to women's motherly role (Isike and Uzodike; Plant, *Mom*; Ryang; Zagarri), that appreciation tends to emphasize where this role should be performed: the domestic sphere. As "domestic patriots" (Yaszek), mothers are praised for their important contribution to childrearing and (ultimately) society's reproduction. Interestingly, underneath this praise, one sees unequivocal evidence of the perceived or desired place of belonging of mothers: they belong to the private realm and not to the *res publica*.

This rather patriarchal *Weltanschauung*—which can be traced back to at least Aristotle's fourth-century-BCE *Politics*—evinces the degree to which societal perceptions about the implications of women's reproductive role contribute to curtailing mothers' "political ambition" (i.e., their interest in pursuing or their ability to seek elective office [Black]). In addition, this view lays bare the interconnectedness of the private and the public realms in the case of mothers (Carroll, "The Personal"). That is to say, sociocultural expectations regarding gender roles, family structure, and (perhaps, most important) the division of family labour affect decisively mothers' ability to launch an electoral candidacy (Conway et al.; Norris and Inglehart). For women with children, the motherhood-related tasks are perceived to be so encompassing that these women are deemed to lack the independence needed to participate in politics (Clavero and Galligan; Moretti; Plant, "Anti-Maternalism").

Tellingly, even in the so-called postindustrial societies (Bell)—which have different family structures and are marked by an increased presence of women in the labour market and politics (Norris)—the motherhood as an electoral gatekeeper narrative seems to ring true. Much literature (albeit on a very limited number

15

of empirical cases) indicates that elected female officeholders tend to predominantly be childless; and when they do have a family, they most likely have grown-up children (Carroll, "The Personal," *Women*; Dodson, "Change"; Fox and Lawless; Lee; Thomas).

In addition, for women in their childrearing years, the calculus to run for elected office is very complex, especially if they have small children. First, as discussed, if they are portrayed as "domestic patriots," then the perception is that they should refrain (at least temporarily) from entering electoral politics. Second, the so-called "double bind" (Jamieson)—the view that says women who excel in the public realm must excel at home first—also impedes the political ambition of mothers. When this perspective is prevalent, mothers experience intense guilt and emotional distress for having to make their childrearing tasks compatible with activities outside the home (Guendouzi). In fact, studies show that the compatibility of an electoral career with childrearing remains one of the key concerns for women legislators, but it does not rank nearly as high for male legislators, including those with small children (Carroll, "The Personal"; Lawless and Fox). Needless to say, once elected, female officeholders seem to enthusiastically support measures to transform parliaments into more family-friendly working environments (Knight et al.).

One additional factor, which is central for fostering political ambition, tends to be negative for mothers. Studies have demonstrated that patterns of early political socialization highly affect individuals' decision to seek elected office, particularly when one has received encouragement to run from parents (Almond and Verba). Remarkably, women—especially the ones who are mothers—have a much lower probability of being encouraged to run from their inner circle of family members and friends than other groups of individuals (Lawless and Fox). As a consequence, even though mothers, when interviewed, say that they always wanted to enter electoral politics as candidates, they opt to delay their political ambition until their children are grown (Carroll, "The Personal"; Dodson, "The Change"; Lawless and Fox).

When women with children finally decide to run, some of them assume that voters have a negative view of mothers competing for elected positions. Dianne Bystrom et al., for instance, show that mother candidates tend to display their children in campaign advertisements much less often than father candidates do (see also Adcock). Similarly, Brittany Stalsburg and Mona Kleinberg indicate that while mothers tend to downplay their families in the campaign trail, fathers tend to display their families prominently, particularly with the intent of humanizing their candidacies. Mothers, on the other hand, resort to these imageries much less often, due to the fear of being perceived as too "motherly" and, as such, unable to succeed in the world of politics. To what extent is that assumption correct? In other words, to what degree do voters value traditional family arrangements in which mothers solely take up the role of "domestic patriots" and use that against women-with-children candidates?

Using experimental research, Virginia Sapiro shows that (unspoken) prejudice against women candidates (not necessarily mothers) seems to be at play. Interestingly, in this experiment, participants read campaign letters that were identical in all aspects (but for the fact that some were signed by a male candidate, and others by a female candidate), and they were invited to assess the candidacies. Remarkably, the study highlights how in electoral contexts of limited information and in which the candidates' gender is the only cue, voters tend to discriminate against female candidates and to perceive male candidates as more competent regarding specific policy issues. Few academic studies have reproduced this type of analysis focusing on mothers. Among them, Stalsburg demonstrates that voters believe childless female candidates have much more time availability to tackle an elected position than mother candidates, regardless of whether the latter have small or grown children. In addition, this study reveals that voters differently evaluate the viability of the candidacy of parents of small children. Voters are much more inclined to believe that fathers with small children will win than they are to believe that mothers with small children will succeed in their electoral contest. In other words, the existing (scant) evidence suggests that some voters may indeed react negatively to the electoral ambition of mothers, especially those with small children.

Can motherhood be an electoral advantage? Studies that put forth this argument are examined next.

MOTHERHOOD AS AN ELECTORAL ADVANTAGE

Motherhood is depicted as an electoral asset, first, by those who deem that mothers inject positive values into the negative world of politics. These authors claim that elected female politicians play the role of "super-mothers" (Chaney). They bring to the *res publica* the values and behaviour that guide their action in the domestic realm. Through motherhood, these authors argue, women develop values—such as pacifism, tolerance, compassion and a spirit of self-sacrifice on behalf of a bigger cause (Greenlee; Ruddick)—that some voters believe could be important additions to politics. In this sense, Anand Swamy et al. contend that corruption, for instance, tends to be less intense in countries "where women hold a larger share of parliamentary seats and senior positions in the government bureaucracy, and comprise a larger share of the labor force" (25). They explain these findings through stating that "women, who are typically more involved in raising children, may find they have to practice honesty in order to teach their children the appropriate values." In other words, motherhood bestows upon women values (and related practices) that, from the perspective of some voters, modern-day politics lacks and badly needs.

A second perspective highlights that more than just values, motherhood provides women good common sense and valuable political expertise. Female politicians who are mothers are regarded as more knowledgeable and, as such, savvier decision-makers than other types of politicians, particularly when it comes to specific political domains, such as family affairs, education, and children's and women's health (Matland and King; Schwindt-Bayer; Stalsburg). In the 2008 American presidential race, for example, the Republic vice-presidential candidate Sarah Palin's self-portrayal as an average, commonsensical "hockey mom" of five kids did appeal to some voters, who believed that she could relate better to the problems of ordinary citizens, particularly parents (Woodwall et al.). In a similar vein, a mother politician running for governor in the state of Oklahoma in the United States in 2010 highlighted her motherhood in her (successful) campaign trail. She claimed that the experience of having and raising children gave her an important edge over her childless opponent, as she understood better the difficulties and obstacles that regular parents and families in her state faced (Stalsburg and Kleinberg).

Interestingly, this perspective may have broader implications than just the electoral arena. Joanna McKay, for instance, shows that the German public in 2002 bitterly criticized the appointment of a woman who was not married and did not have children for the position of "spokesperson of family affairs," as it was believed that because of her being single and childless, she lacked expertise to do this particular type of job (71).

From these two viewpoints, a strong interconnectedness exists between the private and the public realms, as the electoral-elected persona of women with children continues to be essentially dominated by their motherhood. However, the links between the private and the public arenas are different now. Previously seen as an electoral gatekeeper, motherhood is now portrayed as a feature that endows women with children with an important electoral advantage.

EMPIRICAL RESEARCH: MOTHERHOOD IN OBLIVION

How much empirical data are there for researchers interested in studying the electoral ambition of mothers? No supranational organizations systematically compile comparative, longitudinal information on the theme.

One of the key sources for comparative research on women and elections is the International Parliamentary Union (IPU), which, since 1997 has compiled comparative data on the issue. IPU gathers information on the magnitude of the presence of women in legislatures around the world, and ranks countries based on the percentage of women in the lower house—which in the case of some nations, is the only chamber. In its November 2016 report, for instance, the IPU surveyed 193 countries, and ranked Rwanda on top (with 63.8 percent of women in their lower house) and Haiti, Micronesia, Palau, Qatar, Tonga, Vanuatu, and Yemen at the bottom (with no women in the legislature).

Interestingly, IPU data form the basis of three important indicators. The first one is the so-called Global Gender Gap, which is produced by the World Economic Forum (WEF). The latter is a composite of four subindices: economic participation and opportunity, educational attainment, health and survival, and political empowerment. This last subindex of political empowerment is calculated using data on "the gap between men and women at the highest level of political decision-making through the ratio of women to men in minister-level positions and the ratio of women to men in parliamentary positions ... [and] the ratio of women to men in terms of years in executive office (prime minister or president) for the last 50 years" (WEF 5). Their key source of data is the information compiled by the IPU.

The IPU data also support a component of the Gender Inequality Index (GII), elaborated by the United Nations Development Programme. The IPU country-level information on the shares of seats held by female in national legislatures, along with data on the female population with at least secondary education, forms the basis of its "female empowerment" subindex. The GII's other subcomponents are female reproductive health index and female labour market index. Norway, Australia, and Switzerland are ranked on the top when it comes to their GII numbers; Chad, Niger, and Central African Republic appear on the bottom (UNDP).

The third cross-country index, which also uses IPU data, is the SIGI, or Social Institutions and Gender Index, from the OECD (the Organization for Economic Cooperation and Development). The IPU share of women in legislatures is used to create the variable "political participation," which along with an indicator on political quotas for women, forms the basis of the "women's political voice" subindex. The SIGI is a composite index that measures social discrimination against women in multiple realms, such as the family, the physical public space, and the political realm. Unlike the other indices, countries are not ranked but are classified from "very low" to "very high" when it comes to the level of discrimination that women face in each of the subcategories (SIGI).

Though important for scholarly research, the IPU data and the indices mentioned here do not enable comparative analysis of the links between motherhood and elected jobs. Do country-level electoral management bodies have pertinent information? The bulk of these boards do not have substantial information on the profile of the candidates. Elections Canada, for instance, only lists the candidate's first and last names, party affiliation, and district name and number. In the United States, on the other hand, subnational entities (e.g., states and cities) have considerable power when it comes to the organization of the details of the electoral process; as a consequence, the list with each candidate's personal features varies substantially. Other countries, such as Brazil, have considerable information on the candidates to the federal legislature—such as each's first and last name, party affiliation, date and place of birth, nationality, gender, self-described ethnicity, marital status, educational level, profession, occupation, wealth (financial assets are described in detail), whether the candidate is under investigation or has been found guilty of any electoral crime, his or her campaign spending limit, and whether the candidate has participated in previous elections. However, there is no information on the parental status of the candidate.

The scant availability of data makes clear that "matricentric" electoral studies are in their infancy and that more scholarly investment needs to be done in this particular area. What would be the important step towards addressing this gap?

A TENTATIVE RESEARCH AGENDA
FOR MATRICENTRIC ELECTORAL STUDIES

Different databases need to be built and diverse methodologies need to be deployed to advance the study of the electoral ambition of mothers.

One preliminary research question is whether it is empirically true that in a larger number of cases, most elected women for the national legislature are either childless or have grown-up children. In other words, how often does one find women with preschool children in elected positions in polyarchies? In order to address this question, national databases need to be created and compared. Cross-country analyses can compare groups of countries based upon their placement in the Human Development Index and their Freedom House scores. That way one can begin to gauge the impact of human development and democratic "development" on the presence of mothers in the parliament. Evidently, scholars interested in particular countries could expand the focus and analyze whether there are any variations, in any given polity, across different types of elected positions—such as, whether there are more or fewer elected mothers for political bodies at the local level (in part-time elected positions, such as school trustee, or fulltime ones, such as councillor), at the state or provincial level, or at the level of the central government. In addition, scholars may choose to expand their analytical scope and to verify whether there is an impact in other types of offices as well. Are most women elected as mayors, governors, premiers, presidents, prime ministers childless? Or do they have grown-up children or small ones? Are these offices essentially out of the reach of mothers of preschool children?

After that preliminary question is addressed, a second step would involve examining the pre-election moment to verify whether elections are in fact almost insurmountable glass ceilings for mothers. In other words, the analysis would focus on how many mother candidates actually present their candidacies in elections for the national legislatures and whether they fare well. What is the percentage of women candidates who are mothers? How do mother candidates fare in comparison to other women candidates, male candidates, and father candidates? Moreover, if the candidate's party, ethnicity (Welch), and previous electoral record are added to the picture, would one get similar results? Further sophistication of the analysis could include data on the campaign resources that mothers, in comparison to other types of candidates, can amass. Although cross-country analyses are possible, this type of investigation would be more easily conducted if a specific country or a very small number of cases were chosen.

Although steps one and two just described are essentially quantitative (longitudinal and cross-sectional, small-number, or single case) research, qualitative methods need to be used to understand the impact, among others, of socialization patterns, systems of informal support, and the "double bind" predicament on mothers' decision to run for elected office. In-depth semistructured interviews and life stories would need to be carried out to analyze this pre-election moment and to verify whether mothers (particularly those with small children) do not self-select out of electoral pools.

Using qualitative instruments, a fourth research stream could focus on donors, party recruiters and leaders, incumbents, and other elected officeholders, as well as the parties' cadre of professional militants or campaign organizers, in order to assess whether forms of veiled or open discrimination against mother candidates are at play.

A fifth research area pertains to the analysis of the voters' perception of mother candidates and their electoral potential. In this regard, Laurel Elder and Steven Greene, for instance, show that the political attitudes of voters with children are very different than those without children, and that male parents develop opinions about policy issues that differ from those of women parents. Surveys and experimental research could then be deployed to examine the extent to which the parental status of a candidate affects his or her perceived electoral potential from the perspective of different groups of voters. Similarly, one could study how parent candidates portray their children in the campaign trail and to test whether the findings based on the United States case (discussed previously) applies to other countries as well.

Finally, a sixth research inquiry could centre on the experiences of elected mothers. In this case, one could investigate the perceived impact of legislative work on the static or progressive electoral ambition of mothers. Does the way in which politics is structured (at the local, state level, or national level) negatively affect the ability of elected mothers to perform at an optimum level? Does it affect their overall chances of getting re-elected or elected for a higher office?

In sum, there are multiple research problems to be tackled and a lot of promising avenues to be pursued in order for one to add a matricentric perspective to electoral studies, and to start filling an important gap in the literature.

WORKS CITED

Adcock, Charlotte. "The Politician, the Wife, the Citizen, and Her Newspaper. Rethinking women, democracy, and media(ted) representation." *Feminist Media Studies*, vol. 10, no. 2, 2010, pp. 135-59.

Almond, Gabriel and Sidney Verba. *The Civic Culture. Political Attitudes and Democracy in Five Nations.* Princeton University Press. 1963.

Arnold, Laura W., and Barbara M. King. "Women, Committees, and Institutional Change in the Senate." *Women Transforming Congress,* edited by Cindy Simon Rosenthal, University of Oklahoma Press, 2002, pp. 284-315.

Baldez, Lisa. "The UN Convention to Eliminate All Forms of Discrimination Against Women (CEDAW): A New Way to Measure Women's Interests." *Politics & Gender,* vol. 7, no. 3 2010, pp. 419-23.

Bell, Daniel. *The Coming of Post-Industrial Society. A Venture in Social Forecasting.* Basic Books, 1973.

Black, Gordon S. "A Theory of Political Ambition: Career Choices and the Role of Structural Incentives." *American Political Science Review,* vol. 66, no. 1, 1972, pp. 144-59.

Bystrom, Dianne et al. *Gender and Candidate Communication: VideoStyle, WebStyle, and NewsStyle.* Routledge, 2004.

Campus, Donatella. "Political Discussion, Views of Political Expertise and Women's Representation in Italy." *The European Journal of Women's Studies* 17.3 (2010): 249-67. Print.

Carroll, Susan J. *Women as Candidates in American Politics.* Indiana University Press, 1994.

Carroll, Susan J. "The Personal is Political" *Women & Politics,* vol. 9, no. 2, 1989, pp. 51-67.

Celis, Karen et al. "Rethinking Women's Substantive Representation." *Representation,* vol. 44, no. 2, 2008, pp. 99-110.

Chaney, Elsa. *Supermadres: Women in Politics in Latin America.* University of Texas Press, 1979.

Clavero, Sara, and Yvonne Galligan. "'A Job in Politics Is Not for Women': Analysing Barriers to Women's Political Representation in CEE." *Czech Sociological Review,* vol. 41, no. 6, 2005, pp. 979-1004.

Corder, J. Kevin, and Christina Wolbrecht. *Counting Women's Ballots: Female Voters from Suffrage through the New Deal.* Cambridge University Press, 2016.

Conway, M. Margaret, et al. *Women and Political Participation.* Congressional Quarterly Press, 1997.

Dahl, Robert A. *Polyarchy: Participation and Opposition.* Yale University Press, 1971.

Dahlerup, Drude. "Electoral Gender Quotas: Between Equality of Opportunity and Equality of Result." *Representation,* vol. 43, no. 2, 2007, 73-92.

Dolan, Kathleen. "Is There a 'Gender Affinity Effect' in American Politics? Information, Affect, and Candidate Sex in US House Elections." *Political Research Quarterly,* vol. 61, no. 1, 2008, pp. 79-89.

Dodson, Debra. *The Impact of Women in Congress.* New York: Oxford University Press, 2006.

Dodson, Debra. "Change and Continuity in the Relationship between Private Responsibilities and Public Officeholding: The More Things Change, the More They Stay the Same." *Policy Studies Journal,* vol. 25, no. 4, 1997, pp. 569-84.

Elder, Laurel, and Steven Greene. *The Politics of Parenthood: Causes and Consequences of the Politicization and Polarization of the American Family.* State of New York University Press, 2012.

Fox, Richard, and Jennifer Lawless. "Family Structure, Sex-Role Socialization, and the Decision to Run for Office." *Women & Politics,* vol. 24, no. 4, 2003, pp. 19-47.

Fridkin, Kim L., and Patrick J. Kenney. "Examining the Gender Gap in Children's Attitudes Toward Politics." *Sex Roles: A Journal of Research,* vol. 56, no. 3-4, 2007, 133-40.

Fullerton, Andrew S., and Michael J. Stern. "Explaining the Persistence and Eventual Decline of the Gender Gap in Voter Registration and Turnout in the American South, 1956-1980." *Social Science History* 34.2 (2010): 129-69. Print.

Guendouzi, Jackie. "'The Guilt Thing': Balancing Domestic and Professional Roles." *Journal of Marriage and Family,* vol. 68, no. 4, 2006, pp. 901-09.

Giger, Nathalie. "Towards a Modern Gender Gap in Europe?" *The Social Science Journal,* vol. 46, no. 3, 2009, 474-92.

Greenlee, Jill. *The Politics of Motherhood.* University of Michigan Press, 2014.

Isike, Christopher, and Ufo Okeke Uzodike. "Marginalising Women in Politics: Recent Trends in KwaZulu-Natal." *Development Southern Africa,* vol. 28, no. 2, 2011, pp. 225-40.

International Parliamentary Union. "Women in National Parliaments," *International Parliamentary Union*, 1 Nov. 2016, www.ipu.org/wmn-e/arc/classif011116.htm. Accessed 6 June 2017.

Jamieson, Kathleen Hall. *Beyond the Double Bind*. Oxford University Press, 1995.

Jones, Mark P. "Increasing Women's Representation via Gender Quotas: The Argentine Ley de Cupos." *Women and Politics*, vol. 16, no. 4, 1996, pp. 75-98.

Kellstedt, Paul M., et al. "The Macro Politics of a Gender Gap." *Public Opinion Quarterly*, vol.74, no. 3, 2010, pp. 477-98.

Knight, Kathleen, et al. "Equalizing Opportunities for Women in Electoral Politics in Ireland." *Women & Politics*, vol. 26, no. 1, 2004, pp. 1-20.

Krook, Mona L. *Quotas for Women in Politics: Gender and Candidate Selection Reform Worldwide*. Oxford University Press, 2009.

Lawless, Jennifer L., and Richard L. Fox. *It Takes a Candidate: Why Women Don't Run for Office*. Cambridge University Press, 2005.

Lee, Marcia Manning. "Why So Few Women Hold Public Office: Democracy and Sexual Roles." *Political Science Quarterly*, vol. 91, no. 2, 1976, pp. 297-314.

Little, Thomas H. et al. "A View from the Top." *Women & Politics*, vol. 22, no. 4, 2001, pp. 29-50.

McKay, Joanna. "Women in German Politics: Still Jobs for the Boys?" *German Politics*, vol. 13, no. 1, 2004, pp. 56-80.

Mansbridge, Jane. "Should Blacks Represent Blacks and Women Represent Women? A Contingent 'Yes.'" *Journal of Politics*, vol. 61, no. 3, 1999, pp. 628-57.

Mansbridge, Jane. "Quota Problems: Combating the Dangers of Essentialism." *Politics and Gender*, vol. 1, no. 4, 2005, pp. 621-38.

Matland, Richard E., and David C. King. "Women as Candidates in Congressional Elections." *Women Transforming Congress*, edited by Cindy Simon Rosenthal, University of Oklahoma Press, 2002, pp. 119-45.

Molyneux, Maxine. "Mobilization without Emancipation? Women's Interests, the State, and Revolution in Nicaragua." *Feminist Studies*, vol. 11, 2, 1985, pp. 227-54.

Moretti, Erica. "Beyond Biological Ties: Sibilla Aleramo, Maria Montessori, and the Construction of Social Motherhood", *Italian*

Culture, vol. 32, no. 1, 2014, pp. 32-49.

Morgan, Jana, et al. "Gender Politics in the Dominican Republic: Advances for Women, Ambivalence from Men." *Politics & Gender*, vol. 4, no. 1, 2008, pp. 35-63.

Norrander, Barbara. "The History of the Gender Gaps." *Voting the Gender Gap*, edited by Lois Duke Whitaker, University of Illinois Press, 2008, pp. 9-32.

Norris, Pippa. "From Traditional Roles toward Gender Equality." *Rising Tide. Gender Equality and Cultural Change around the World*, edited by Ronald Inglehart and Pippa Norris, Cambridge University Press, 2003, pp. 29-48.

Norris, Pippa and Ronald Inglehart. "Cultural Obstacles to Equal Representation," *Journal of Democracy*, vol. 12, no. 3, 2001, pp. 126-40.

Norton, Noelle. "Transforming Policy from the Inside: Participation in Committee." *Women Transforming Congress*, edited by Cindy Simon Rosenthal, University of Oklahoma Press, 2002, pp. 316-40.

Ondercin, Heather L., and Jeffrey L. Bernstein. "Context Matters: The Influence of State and Campaign Factors on the Gender Gap in Senate Elections, 1988-2000." *Politics & Gender*, vol. 3, no. 1, 2007, pp. 33-53.

O'Reilly, Andrea. *Matricentric Feminism: Theory, Activism, and Practice*. Demeter Press, 2016.

Osborn, Tracy, and Jeanette Morehouse Mendez. "Speaking as Women: Women and Floor Speeches in the Senate." *Journal of Women, Politics & Policy*, vol. 31, no. 1, 2010), pp. 1-21.

Pitkin, Hanna. *The Concept of Representation*. University of California Press, 1967.

Plant, Rebecca Jo. "Anti-Maternalism: A New Perspective on the Transformation of Gender Ideology in the Twentieth-Century United States." *Social Politics: International Studies in Gender, State & Society*, vol. 22, no. 2, 2015, pp. 283-88.

Plant, Rebecca Jo. *Mom. The Transformation of Motherhood in Modern America*. Chicago University Press, 2010.

Reingold, Beth, and Michele Swers. "An Endogenous Approach to Women's Interests: When Interests Are Interesting in and of Themselves." *Politics & Gender*, vol. 7, no. 3. 2011, pp. 429-35.

Rosenthal, Cindy Simon. "A View of Their Own: Women's Committee Leadership Styles and State Legislatures." *Policy Studies Journal*, vol. 25, no. 4, 1997, pp. 585-600.

Ruddick, Sara. *Maternal thinking: Toward a politics of peace.* Boston: Beacon Press, 1989. Print.

Ryang, Sonya. "Gender in Oblivion: Women in the Democratic People's Republic of Korea (North Korea)." *Journal of Asian and African Studies*, vol. 35, no. 3, 2000, pp. 323-49.

Sapiro, Virginia. "Research Frontier Essay: When Are Interests Interesting? The Problem of Political Representation of Women." *The American Political Science Review*, vol. 75, no. 3, 1981, 701-16.

Schwindt-Bayer, Leslie. "Still Supermadres? Gender and the Policy Priorities of Latin American Legislators." *American Journal of Political Science*, vol. 50, no. 3, 2006, pp. 570-85.

Social Institutions and Gender Index. "SIGI Methodological Background," 2014, www.genderindex.org/. Accessed 6 June 2017.

Stalsburg, Brittany L. "Voting for Mom: The Political Consequences of Being a Parent for Male and Female Candidates." *Politics & Gender*, vol. 6, no. 3, 2010, pp. 373-404.

Stalsburg, Brittany, and Mona S. Kleinberg. "'A Mom First and a Candidate Second': Gender Differences in Candidates' Self-Presentation of Family." *Journal of Political Marketing*, vol. 15, no. 4, 2016, pp. 285-310.

Swamy, Anand, et al. "Gender and Corruption." *Journal of Development Economics*, vol. 64, no. 1, 2001, pp. 25-55.

Swers, Michele L. "Connecting Descriptive and Substantive Representation: An Analysis of Sex Differences in Cosponsorship Activity in the House of Representatives." *Legislative Studies Quarterly*, vol. 30, no. 3, 2005, pp. 407-33.

Swers, Michele L. *The Difference Women Make: The Policy Impact of Women in Congress.* The University of Chicago Press, 2002.

Taylor-Robinson, Michele M., and Roseanna Michelle Heath. "Do Women Legislators Have Different Policy Priorities than Their Male Colleagues? A Critical Case Test." *Women and Politics*, vol. 24, no. 4, 2003, pp. 77-101.

Thomas, Sue. "The Personal Is the Political: Antecedents of Gendered Choices of Elected Representatives." *Sex Roles*, vol. 47, no. 7-8, 2002, pp. 343-53.

United Nations Development Programme. "Human Development Report 2016. Human Development for Everyone," *United Nations Development Programme*, 2016, hdr.undp.org/sites/default/files/2016_human_development_report.pdf. Accessed 6 June 2017.

Vickers, Jill. "The Problem with Interests: Making Political Claims for 'Women.'" In *The Politics of Women's Interests: New Comparative Perspectives*, edited by Louise Chappell and Lisa Hill, Routledge, 2006, pp. 5-38.

Welch, Susan. "Commentary on "Recruitment of Women to Public Office: A Discriminant Analysis." *Political Research Quarterly*, vol. 61, no. 1, 2008, pp. 29-31.

Woodwall, Gina Serignese, et al. "Sarah Palin: 'Beauty is Beastly?' An Exploratory Content Analysis of Media Coverage." *Cracking the Highest Glass Ceiling. A Global Comparison of Women's Campaigns for Executive Office*, edited by Murray Rainbow, Praeger, 2010, pp. 91-112.

World Economic Forum. "The Global Gender Gap Report", 2016, http://www3.weforum.org/docs/GGGR16/WEF_Global_Gender_Gap_Report_2016.pdf. Accessed 3 Sept. 2016.

Yaszek, Lisa. "Stories 'That Only a Mother' Could Write: Midcentury Peace Activism, Maternalist Politics, and Judith Merril's Early Fiction." *NWSA Journal*, vol. 16, no. 2, 2004, pp. 70-97.

Young, Iris Marion. *Inclusion and Democracy.* Oxford, 2000. Print.

Zagarri, Rosemarie. "Politics and Civil Society: A Discussion of Mary Kelley's *Learning to Stand and Speak*." *Journal of the Early Republic*, vol. 28, no.1, 2008, pp. 61-73.

3.
Motherhood and Public Service

An Exploration of School Board Trustees

REBECCA E. DEEN AND BETH ANNE SHELTON

OVER THE LAST THIRTY YEARS, research into women standing for and winning public office has revealed much about the path women take to elected office (Darcy et al.), characteristics of successful women candidates, and how this has changed over time (Carroll, "Political Elites"), and political ambition (Lawless, *Becoming*; Lawless and Fox, *It Takes*, *Why*, *It Still*). However, less is known about the calculus to run for school board, the networks on which these candidates draw for support, and the ways in which one's private sphere of family and parenting intersect with running for public office.

Local politics, like school boards, can be a launching pad for women. For example, Senator Patty Murray's first substantial engagement with the political system was when she went to the Washington State Legislature to express her concern over funding cuts to a preschool program. She was told she was "just a mom in tennis shoes," which motivated her entry into politics (qtd. in Mikulski et al.). She went on to serve on the Shoreline School Board and then the Washington State Senate before being elected to the US Senate. Indeed, women have fared better in terms of their proportion on school boards than in other elected bodies. At the end of the last century, women were approximately 40 percent of all school boards (Hess) and now make up 44 percent (National School Boards Association), reflecting greater representation than in other levels of office ("Facts: Levels of Office").

To redress this lack of research, we examine school board officials' electoral campaigns, their motivations for running for office, and

30

the degree to which their roles as parents (both inside and outside the home) inform their public office. We explore the experience of women elected to school boards—while comparing it to those of men in terms of their motivation to run for office —their varied backgrounds, and the networks that support them. We test the following existing hypotheses about gender differences among elected officials: the eligibility pool hypothesis (Darcy et al.); gender differences in ambition (Lawless and Fox, *Why, It Still*; Lawless; Fox and Lawless, "Entering," "If Only," and "Gendered"); and the civic volunteerism model (Burns et al.).

LITERATURE REVIEW

Women in Elected Office: A Brief Overview

Why are there fewer women in elected office than men? This question has been the focus of much scholarship over the past thirty years. As the number of women in elected office has risen (though yet nowhere near their proportion of the electorate), scholars can better examine the patterns that have emerged.

We know women's experiences in society have informed their entry into the political world. Although women in the United States earned the right to vote in 1920, with the Nineteenth Amendment to the US Constitution, they did not immediately become active in politics. Through the mid-twentieth century, men voted at higher rates than women (Center for American Women and Politics, Facts: Voters), and public opinion surveys documented the widespread belief that men were fit for public service and women were not. Relevant to our work, this included fitness to head parent-teacher organizations. It was not until the 1980s that women's turnout matched that of men; since then, the gap has steadily widened such that now women consistently vote at rates higher than men. Also in the 1980s a persistent gender gap in vote choice emerged, which continues today: women in the United States tend to support Democratic Party candidates at higher rates than men, and a higher proportion of women elected officials are Democrats than are Republicans (Center for American Women and Politics, Facts: Voters).

Currently, women make up only about a fifth of members of Congress, a quarter of state legislators and statewide elected of-

ficials (e.g., governors, lieutenant governors), and 19 percent of
the one hundred largest US cities are headed by women. However,
women did not begin to hold office in significant numbers until the
1970s and 1980s ("Facts: Levels of Office"). During this first wave
of women being elected officials—when there were the smallest
percentages of women holding office (for example in 1971 only
4.5 percent of state legislators were women)—the successful female
politicians tended to be older and without young children. As more
women joined their ranks during the 1990s and into the twenty-first
century, the median age has dropped and the likelihood of these
women balancing childrearing and career increased (Darcy et al).

As women have become more fully integrated into electoral
politics, the possible explanations for their success have also
become more sophisticated. For many years, the "eligibility pool
hypothesis" (Darcy et al.) held purchase. The expectation was that
as more women enter career paths from which politicians have
been drawn (e.g., law, business), more women will run for office.
Research on members of Congress and state legislatures reveals
that these lawmakers are overwhelmingly attorneys and business
people (Stanley and Neim; Davidson and Oleszek; Niven, "Party
Elites"). The logic is that as women run and win lower office, they
will move up the political career ladder to state legislatures and
U.S. Congress. Labor trends, however, run counter to this potential
avenue for women. In addition to the fact that these professions are
segregated by sex (Bureau of Labor Statistics), women politicians
are more likely to come from backgrounds in education (Carroll,
Women). Among school board members, where one would expect
many people to be educational professionals, women are even more
likely than are men to have been teachers prior to being elected to
boards of education (Deckman, "Woman Running").

Early research also revealed that, for a time, those serving as
gatekeepers to successful electoral campaigns (largely the political
parties) discouraged women candidates (Niven, "Party Elites,"
"Throwing"; Lawless and Fox, *Why*; Constantini and Bell). Parties
have a vested interest in finding the candidate with the best chance
of winning. Early on, when elites did support female candidates, it
was often to serve as "sacrificial lambs"—that is to have a woman
from the party on the ballot but with every understanding that she

was going to lose the election (Flammang). Party leaders are also likely to choose people "like them," and as most officials were men, they saw men as more electable than women (Niven, "Party Elites"). These trends have largely dissipated, however, as party leaders see advantages to female candidates. Women are more likely to be seen as "change agents" and as more trustworthy than men (Huddy and Terkildsen), which can make them attractive candidates.

Political Ambition

Another possible explanation for the disparity in women elected officials is that women may have less political ambition than men do. Perhaps they are less likely to seek office for the express goal of gaining the experience necessary to be successful at higher offices (i.e., progressive political ambition [Schlesinger]). Early research found that women focused on advancement within the party structure apparatus rather than in elected office (Constantini and Craik; Rhode; Constantini; Sapiro and Farah) and that they rarely had ambition beyond the state legislative level (Carroll, "Political Elites"). Even when these women go on to higher office, they remain in lower level offices longer than their male counterparts (Burt-Way and Kelly). A study of city council members, for example, revealed much higher levels of progressive ambition among men; they saw being on the council as grooming for higher office (Bledsoe and Herring).

Most recently, our understanding of gender differences in political ambition has been expanded, primarily by the work of Richard Fox and Jennifer Lawless (Fox and Lawless, "Entering"; Lawless and Fox *Why, It Still*). Whereas early work on ambition suggested that women possessed less progressive ambition than did men, Lawless and Fox's research has uncovered a deeper gender difference: women have less latent ambition. They see themselves as less qualified to hold office at all, so when approached to stand for office, they decline. When they do consider running for office, women are more likely to choose a local or municipal office, whereas men are more likely to aspire to state legislature or U.S. Congress as their initial foray into politics.

Richard Fox and Jennifer Lawless' work also reveals the importance of a network of encouragers (Fox and Lawless, "Gendered,"

"If Only"). Women need to be asked several times before considering a possible run for office as a viable option. Men are more likely to be self-starters, needing less encouragement (see also Carroll, "Political Elites"; Kirkpatrick). Women also benefit from being mentored and having the process of running a campaign explained explicitly (Fox et al.). Some research suggests that they have less confidence in their abilities (Keyserling). The role of family in these networks is important; women are more likely to be encouraged by family than representatives of the political structure, and they cite family and spousal support as crucial to their decisions to run (National Women's Political Caucus).

Women are also more likely to be motivated by policy goals or to solve a particular problem than are men (Fox; Thomas et al.; Constantini 759; Flammang 140; Kirkpatrick; Mandel). They are less likely to cite personal ambition and more likely to point to issue-based motivations than are men (Darcy et al.; Fox; van Hightower; van Assendelft and O'Connor; Swers).

Interestingly, especially for our work, data gathered from the late 1990s found this trend reversed among school board candidates (Deckman, "Gender Differences"). In this national survey of school board members, men were more likely to have run to affect educational policy. They cited both issue specific and general morality concerns. This study also found that school board members were not likely to say they were using their time in public office to gain experience for a run at higher office.

Whereas early work found that women board members were likely to conceptualize school board service as part of a broader civic mindedness (Bers), Melissa Deckman ("School Board"; "Gender Differences") notes that research is scant in this area and finds no support for a gender difference in motivations based on community service, involvement, or parent-teacher organization membership. (None of these variables is significant in multivariate analyses.) Drawing on the same dataset, Deckman finds that women school board members are likely to be Republican conservatives (in contrast to broader patterns of women being more likely to identify with the Democratic Party) and to be moderates (Center for American Women and Politics, Facts: Voters). More in keeping with other trends, Deckman's study finds women board members to be moderate on social issues and to have views characterized as mainstream ("School Board").

Dekman's work also points to the school board as a launching pad for higher office ("Gender Differences"). She notes that, at the time of her writing, six current members of Congress began their public service on a school board. Of all current and former US Senators, three began their careers on a school board ("Facts: Levels of Office").

Civic Skills

Along with ambition, another precursor to political participation is acquiring and developing civic skills (Verba et al). Women have historically lagged behind men in their acquisition of these skills, and the domains in which the skills are enhanced are different. Women are more likely to become politically capable through volunteering in their communities, involvement in women's organizations, and in civic and nonprofit groups (Darcy et al.; Kirkpatrick; Merritt; van Hightower; Flammang).

In these local venues, women are socialized to see politics and policy issues as salient. These may be related to education (parent-teacher organization, protesting the lack of stoplights near schools) or neighbourhood issues (conservation, safe bike paths) (Flammang). Harriet Woods (former lieutenant governor of Missouri) recounts first becoming socialized to local politics when speeding cars caused a manhole cover to bang loudly, waking her napping children (Woods). US Senator Patty Murray (D-WA) as previously described was not taken seriously when she lobbied her state legislators to oppose proposed school funding cuts (qtd. in Mikulski et al; Knickerbocker). Barbara Roberts, who went on to serve as Oregon's governor from 1991 to 1995, first involved herself in politics by lobbying the state legislature on behalf of her special needs child (Woods 19).

In fact, parent-teacher organizations, as well as other school-related volunteer opportunities are often where these mothers become politically socialized (Brady et al.) and able to engage in civic life (Deen and Shelton, "Bake Sales"). This public motherhood allows them to develop civic skills of communication, organization, and leadership (Burns et al.; Deen and Shelton, "Bake Sales"). These experiences also allow them to create networks of support crucial to successful political campaigns. As Lawless and Fox (*It Still*) tell us, those networks of family and friends are especially determinative for women candidates. Without them, they are less likely to agree to run at all.

SETTING AND DATA

To assess the patterns of support networks, motivations for running for office, and political skills and ambition, we conducted in-depth interviews with current and former members of the school board in a midsize city in the Southwestern United States. The interviews were recorded and transcribed, with each conversation lasting approximately sixty to eighty minutes. In addition, we collected information about candidates from campaign materials, public forums, self-descriptions, and videos of school board meetings.

We began our sampling with recent candidates for school board and expanded it to include interviewing and collecting data on all current, including newly elected, school board members as well as those who lost reelection at the end of their terms in 2015. The school board has seven members; all members are elected at large (i.e., citywide voting for each position) with three year terms.

Although our respondents are public figures, our interviews covered topics some are hesitant to speak about publicly, so all respondents are referred to by pseudonyms to protect their identity. The average length of time our respondents have served on the school board is five and a half years, with a range from a few months to ten years. Of the nine individuals in our sample, seven are current school board members and two are former school board members. Four of the nine are men and two are members of racial and ethnic minority groups, representation that mirrors the current board membership as well as the national data on school board representation of women and racial and ethnic minority group members.

We analyzed our data using modified open coding, working from transcribed interviews and notes. In modified open coding, we use concepts identified in previous research (in our case, political ambition and political networks of support) as the framework for our analysis of the data. However, in conducting the analysis, we remain open to other themes that may emerge—for example, mentions of family, a faith tradition, or a civic duty as motivating factors for public service.

RESULTS

We began by exploring the initial process of considering a run for school board. What were the circumstances surrounding the decision to run? How did people make the decision? Were there any gender differences in this calculus? The early work on the eligibility pool thesis began with the observation that politicians generally come from similar occupations and then examined what impediments existed to getting more women into these pipeline occupations. In that way, the hypothesis assumes little gender difference in the paths to office. More recent studies of political ambition (Lawless and Fox, *It Still*) find that women are less likely than men, even in these so-called pipeline professions, to believe themselves capable of running for political office.

Through our in-depth interviews asking respondents to elaborate on their initial decision to run, we find two general paths to a position on the school board that are differentiated by gender. The first path to school board we identify develops from an individual's civic engagement, his or her interest in the community, and the extent to which he or she has become involved in groups or organizations. Those whose interest in being on the school board reflects their general interest in community service and civic life develop this interest in a variety of venues—including city advisory boards and voluntary groups, secondary school booster clubs, and their employment and/or business community. In our data, this is the route that is more common for men than for women.

It is interesting to note that there is a degree of heterogeneity in terms of the profiles of board members in this group. Some of their interests are born out of their direct involvement in the schools, as either volunteers or employees. Some people who identify a clear "heart for service" or "desire to serve my country and community" are motivated by civic mindedness more broadly as well as an interest in local politics.

A second path to school board interest develops from concern about a specific issue or set of issues. All of the women in our sample ran for school board to address a specific issue, although many of them had other broader interests as well. This group can be further differentiated into those whose interests reflect their jobs or involvement in other organizations and those whose interests arise from their involvement in their children's schools.

Although there is diversity among the candidates and members of the school board we interviewed, these two general paths describe the basic gender differences. We first describe the typically male path and then contrast this with the route more common among the women in our sample.

Community and Civic Involvement

Some school board candidates and members become interested in attaining a position on the school board through their paid or volunteer work related to the school district. For some, volunteering within the booster club structure (activity-specific groups that support a specific activity such as band, football, or choir) fosters these individuals' interest in broader issues within the school district. For this type of school volunteer, their work in these parent organizations serves as a springboard for their increased involvement in the school district more generally (Deen and Shelton, "It's For the Children").

Working in the schools can also sometimes foster an interest in running for school board. In our sample, one board member became interested in the school board because of his experience as a teacher. In the civic involvement group, a teacher develops a general interest in education and may believe that he or she possesses the skills to serve effectively on the school board. Indeed, among the board members with whom we talked, many pointed to particular seats on the school board as "the teacher seat" and needing to have a "teacher on the board."

Paul Bishop, an experienced teacher, reported that he "thought [he] could do a good job for the kids and the teachers, as a teacher for the kids and a teacher representative for the employees." When he was defeated when running for reelection, other board members expressed dismay stating that "people don't know what an advocate [for teachers] they lost." Paul, like almost all of the men we interviewed, made the decision to run quickly and did not require convincing (Fox and Lawless, "If Only"). In fact, when an incumbent did not seek reelection, thus creating an open space, he said, "I'll run for school board." In deciding to run, there was no specific issue about which he was concerned; rather, he sought to represent the interests of teachers and students generally. This is indicative of the types of male attitudes Fox and Lawless found in their sample of potential candidates.

Other civic involvement candidates develop an interest in school board through their work in school-related groups (Dads' clubs and booster clubs) but are interested in broader concerns of the school board rather than a set of specific issues. James Penn, for example, cites a "calling to serve" as his reason for running. (Interestingly, it was a third civic candidate, David Lamb, who claims to have encouraged James to run because David "knew James's heart for his community.") James became involved in education as a school parent volunteer in booster and support clubs. He was and remains active in other community venues: his church and other philanthropic boards in the city. He and his wife are well known in the community as civic leaders.

Jacob MacArthur also came to school board service through his involvement in the community. As a business owner, he became invested in neighborhood associations, professional organizations and ultimately in the Dad's club at his children's elementary school. It was his reputation for innovative thinking (creating explicit partnerships between the school district and the city leadership) that led to his recruitment onto the board.

David Lamb is, in some ways, the most typically male candidate. When he first ran, he was among the youngest to run (under thirty-five) and was unmarried and childless. The child of two teachers, David moved back to his hometown in his late twenties. He was "a political guy" in college (a member of the Young Republicans club), had volunteered on local and state legislative campaigns, and was president of a prominent male civic organization in the city. He was quickly appointed to an oversight committee (that regularly reports to the school board). The oversight committee is drawn from the entire school district rather than from any subset of schools. Membership on such a committee provides an opportunity to make contacts across the entire school district. It was while serving on the districtwide committee that a retiring board member encouraged him to run for his seat. Lamb clearly has both latent and progressive political ambition, whereas the other men in our community and civic involvement group have latent ambition but significantly less or no progressive ambition.

ISSUES ORIENTED

In contrast to this general interest pattern, all of the women we interviewed initially decided to run for school board because of a specific issue, although for one candidate the interest reflected her job as a teacher; for others, their concerns reflected their involvement in their children's schools.

Teachers

Wilma Pithy, also a longtime teacher, ran because of her concern about changes in personnel policies. Moreover, she did not report that she thought she was the best person for the job or that she "just decided to run" but that she ran because no others were doing so and she was concerned about changes in the school district. She identified her initial interest in running for the school board as a response to how school district employees "are being treated... [She reported that she said to herself] 'I've got to do something. I have got to do something.'"

The decision to indicate her interest officially in a school board position was sudden but is consistent with other findings (Fox and Lawless, "Entering"; "If Only"). A large group of potential supporters met with her and encouraged her to file as a candidate. In essence, she ran because she disagreed with the way teachers were being treated under a revised human resources system that sought to rationalize how the school district dealt with personnel. Wilma Pithy felt that the new system was mistreating teachers, who "are nurturers" and who should be treated as such.

Public Mothers

The second and largest group concerned with issues is what

we call "public mothers" (Deen and Shelton, "It's for the Children"). All but one woman in our sample fall into this group. These women became active in their children's schools as part of what they felt was their responsibility as good mothers. The public mothers started volunteering in their children's schools when the children entered kindergarten, most often through the Parent Teacher Association (PTA) or other volunteer positions available in the schools (e.g., room parent). As part of their involvement in their children's lives, these women volunteered not only at their children's schools but also in other organizations in the schools or in the district (local or regional parent-teacher organizations). Through their experiences, they eventually became interested in issues that could be addressed through the school board rather than only through the school-based organizations. Moreover, as Deen and Shelton ("Bake Sales") report, volunteering in schools gives women the opportunity to develop civic skills necessary for political participation more broadly (Burns et al.).

Among those who run for school board through the motherhood path, some decide to run because of their interest in or concern about one or more specific issues related directly to their children. These issues may include school district policies about classroom structure, recess, fine arts, or curriculum, but they all have a direct effect on the person's child or children. For example, one candidate for school board, Crystal Clarkson, became frustrated when she learned that some teachers held students from recess as a punishment, in violation of district policy. Crystal felt not only that the district policy should be followed but that children, including her child, should have recess each school day. She reported that "The recess [issue] was the door into seeing how things were going on in the [school] board…. The recess [issue] led me to the wellness policy."

Furthermore, she argued that her interest in running for the board reflected her status as "just a concerned mom." In fact, she reported that she hoped only to get her issues addressed and that she "didn't think [she] was going to win." Initially, she was trying to convince others in her "mom network" to run and it was only because she was not successful that she decided to become a candidate.

Many of the public mothers in our sample developed their civic skills through their involvement in parent-teacher organizations and their children's schools. Although initially they volunteered in their children's schools as part of what they thought of as their responsibilities as mothers, through their volunteer activities, they developed skills and contacts that eventually led them to run for school board. Still, they were motivated by specific issues but developed skills that helped them to understand the workings of the school district and to formulate campaigns. Janet Tate decided to run for school board after the influx of a large number of students into the district in general and into her child's school in particular, which "had tremendous diversity of academics and student achievement and diversity in their human experience." Janet reported that the challenges posed by the influx of students allowed her to understand better that some issues and problems "didn't fit the [parent-teacher organization] framework so well." As a result, she became more active in districtwide committees, created an educational foundation to support the schools, and, eventually, ran for and won a seat on the school board. Janet, like other women in this group, developed her civic skills in school parent-teacher organizations, as well as on districtwide committees.

Trisha Bonds and Jenny Solis also came to elected office through a combination of parent-teacher organizations and service on districtwide committees. Trisha and Jenny cited their work in their local parent-teacher organizations and then citywide district and state councils as preparing them for school board work. Trisha noted that it was through PTA that she gained public speaking, organizational, and "soft power" people skills that have benefitted her in her board work. Trisha and Jenny exemplify a pattern we saw in all but one of our public mothers. Specifically, after becoming active in the schools as part of their perceived responsibilities as mothers, these women develop broader interests in educational policy that transcend their interest in their child or children. This type of candidate may, for example, be interested in ensuring fiscal responsibility for the school district, enhancing diversity on the school board, or managing school district growth. Certainly, their knowledge of the issues that interest them stems from how they mother their children, but the issues are broader than those cited above. It was through the parent-teacher organizations that these women not only developed civic skills (e.g., organizational skills, knowledge about how the school district works) but also had access to a wider array of political actors who were important in helping them succeed when they did run for the school board (Verba et al.; Brady et al). Within these broader networks, the experiences of the women and men in our sample converge, although their access to these networks develops differently. All but one of the public mothers who eventually ran and won a place on the school board first became members of a districtwide committee dealing with the school district budget. Similarly, the majority of men in our sample sat on a districtwide financial affairs or bond committee before running for school board. So, in effect, we have at least two different paths to the school board, but those paths converge on financial affairs committees, which are districtwide and give members access to civic leaders from across the city and help them acquire knowledge (i.e., skills) (see Figure 1). Thus, the proximate eligibility pool is the same for most men and women in our sample (school districtwide financial affairs committees), but their route to the committees is quite different. This parallels the literature on gender differences in political participation in the electorate more broadly; men and women acquire skills, knowledge, and interest to engage in politics differently (Verba et al.; Brady et al.).

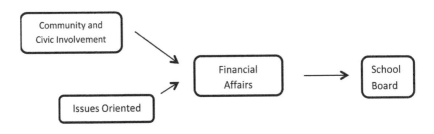

Figure 1: Routes to School Board

Although all but two of the school board candidates and members we interviewed served on a financial affairs committee, they discussed their candidacies in different terms. The men centre the discussions of their campaigns on why they are good candidates for the school board or on the nuts and bolts of running a successful campaign (i.e., determining sources of support), whereas the women discuss their interests or concerns, staying focused on the specific issues that got them involved is district politics in the first place. This trend is consistent with previous work showing women's candidacies as an extension of their concerns for specific issues or events (Darcy et al.).

CONCLUSION AND IMPLICATION FOR FUTURE RESEARCH

Through in-depth interviews with current and former school board members, our study has uncovered interesting gender differences in the paths taken to elected office, specifically school boards. The domains, venues and environments in which men and women develop civic skills and become politically engaged regarding education policy differ. Men are more likely to describe this process in terms of generalized civic engagement: "a heart for service," "how I can serve my country and community," and "servant leadership." Male board members are more likely to have been active in political, professional, and civic organizations that not only socialize them into local governance but also create and foster networks of support on which they will later draw in their campaigns. Men are also more likely to express progressive ambition; half of the men in our sample explicitly said they are considering runs for higher office.

By contrast, women board members describe their paths to the board and their work on the board in different ways. Each of them, in some way, contextualizes her initial involvement in schools as an extension of her role as mother and/or grandmother. For all but one woman, their experiences as school volunteers (parent-teacher organizations, volunteer room parent) socialized them to the challenges facing the schools, and it was from these networks of parents that they drew electoral support. These women, in contrast to the men, were also motivated to run for the board by particular issues or events that served as the catalyst.

We also add to our understanding of the gender differences in ambition and of the role of recruitment in these local elections.

Service on districtwide committees is the training ground for potential school board candidates. Not only did board members talk explicitly about grooming potential members from this committee, but also all but two in our sample of current and former members served on this committee. However, the pathway to the committee is different for men and women. Women come to the committee as an extension of their public motherhood, whereas men are recruited because of reputations they have built through civic, political, and professional experiences.

Our findings lay the groundwork for future study. What are the "training ground" opportunities in other local elections and do similar gendered patterns exist? To what degree do other financial affairs committee members possess latent political ambition? Are our findings bound by time and space? If we were to interview board members who served in decades past, or in other parts of the country, would we discover different dynamics? Our research clearly indicates the need to examine more fully the processes through which women enter politics and how these may differ from men's experiences. In addition, rather than conceptualizing motherhood as acted out in the private sphere, scholars need to explore how mothers participate in the public sphere (e.g., schools, politics) as part of their performance of motherhood.

ENDNOTES

[1]An exception to this is the work of Melissa Deckman, see "School Board"; "Gender Differences."

[2]For an interesting discussion of these data, see McGlen et al.

[3]School boards are the (usually elected) governing bodies for local school districts, which typically encompass a city, town, or rural area, but may be any relatively small geographic area.

[4]Parent-teacher organization (PTO) membership, however, is not as useful a measure of parental involvement as parent-teacher organization participation. Many schools have parent-teacher organization membership drives in an attempt to sign up as many "members" as possible (parents, grandparents, stepparents), as there are intercampus competitions for the ratio of student-to-adult involvement. Most parent-teacher organization

"members" do little more than attend bimonthly meetings, if they even do that.

[5]The two former members—one male and one female—lost their bids for reelection. This is unusual for this city's politics. Most people we spoke with attributed the losses to an anti-incumbent mood, a high profile mayoral race where the incumbent also lost, and higher turnout because of a referendum on a controversial red-light camera initiative.

[6]Even the female outlier cited her role as a parent in the schools and later as a grandparent.

[7]Some of these women also cite their professions as giving them skills, for example with public relations or with fiscal issues.

WORKS CITED

Bers, Trudy. H. "Local Political Elites: Men and Women on Boards of Education." *Western Political Quarterly*, vol. 31, no. 3, 1978, pp. 381-91.

Bledsoe, Timothy, and Mary Herring. "Victims of Circumstances: Women in Pursuit of Political Office." *American Political Science Review*, vol. 84, no. 1, 1990, pp. 213-23.

Brady, Henry E. et al. "Beyond SES: A resource Model of Political Participation." *American Political Science Review*, vol. 89, no. 2, 1995, pp. 271-94.

Bureau of Labor Statistics. "Labor Force Statistics from the Current Population Survey." *Bureau of Labor Statistics*, 2011, bls.gov/cps/cpsaat11.htm. Accessed 24 Sept. 2015.

Burns, Nancy, et al. *The Private Roots of Public Action: Gender, Equality, and Political Participation*. Harvard University Press. 2001.

Burt-Way, Barbara J., and Rita Mae Kelly. "Gender and Sustaining Political Ambition: A Study of Arizona Elected Officials." *Western Political Quarterly*, vol. 45, no.1, 1992, pp. 11-25.

Carroll, Susan J. "Political Elites and Sex Differences in Political Ambition: A Reconsideration." *Journal of Politics*, vol. 47, no. 4, 1985, pp. 1231-43.

Carroll, Susan J. *Women as Candidates in American Politics*. 2nd ed. Indiana University Press, 1994.

Constantini, Edmond. "Political Women and Political Ambition: Closing the Gender Gap." *American Journal of Political Science*, vol. 34, no. 3, 1990, pp. 741-70.

Constantini, Edmond, and Julie Davis Bell. "Women in Political Parties: Gender Differences in Motives among California Party Activists." *Political Women: Current Roles in State and Local Government*, edited by Janet Flammang, Sage, 1984, pp 114-48.

Constantini, Edmond, and Kenneth H. Craik. "Women as Politicians: The Social Background, Personality and Political Careers of Female Party Leaders." *Journal of Social Issues*, vol. 28, no. 2, 1972, pp. 217-36.

Darcy, Robert, et al. *Women, Elections and Representation*. Longman, 1994.

Davidson, Roger H., and Walter Oleszek. *Congress and Its Members*. Congressional Quarterly Press, 2012.

Deckman, Melissa. "Gender Differences in the Decision to Run for School Board." *American Politics Research*, vol. 35, no. 4, 2007, pp. 541-63

Deckman, Melissa. "School Board Candidates and Gender: Ideology, Party and Policy Concerns." *Journal of Women, Politics and Policy*, vol. 28, no. 1, 2006, pp. 87-117.

Deckman, Melissa. "Women Running Locally: How Gender Affects School Board Elections." *PS: Political Science & Politics*, vol. 36, no. 1, 2004, pp. 61-2.

Deen, Rebecca E., and Beth Anne Shelton "Bake Sales for a Better America: The Role of School Volunteers in Civic Life" *International Journal of Interdisciplinary Social Sciences*, vol. 6, no. 7, 2011, pp. 25-38.

Deen, Rebecca E., and Beth Anne Shelton "It's for the Children': Intensive Mothering and the School Volunteer." Hawaii International Conference on Social Sciences, 2010, Honolulu, Hawaii.

"Facts: Levels of Office." *Center for American Women and Politics*, www.cawp.rutgers.edu/levels_of_office.. Accessed 24 Sept. 2015.

"Facts: Voters." *Center for American Women and Politics*, www.cawp.rutgers.edu/voters. Accessed 24 Sept. 2015.

Flammang, Janet. *Women's Political Voice: How Women Are Transforming the Practice and Study of Politics*. Temple University Press, 1997.

Fox, Richard L. *Gender Dynamics in Congressional Elections*. Sage, 1997.

Fox, Richard L. and Jennifer L. Lawless. "Entering the Arena: Gender and the Decision to Run for Office." *American Journal of Political Science*, vol. 48, no. 2, 2004, pp. 264-80.

Fox, Richard L. and Jennifer L. Lawless. "Gendered Perceptions and Political Candidacies: A Central Barrier to Women's Equality in Electoral Politics." *American Journal of Political Science*, vol. 55, no. 1, 2011, pp. 59-73.

Fox, Richard L. and Jennifer L. Lawless. "If Only They'd Ask: Gender, Recruitment, and Political Ambition." *Journal of Politics*, vol. 72, no. 2, 2010, pp. 310-36.

Fox, Richard, et al. "Gender and the Decision to Run for Office." *Legislative Studies Quarterly*, vol. 6, no. 3, 2001, pp. 411-31.

Hess, F. *School Boards at the Dawn of the 21st Century*. American School Boards Association, 2002.

Huddy, Leonie, and Nayda Terkildsen. "Gender Stereotypes and the Perception of Male and Female Candidates." *American Journal of Political Science*, vol. 37, no. 1, 1993, pp. 119-47.

Keyserling, Harriet. *Against the Tide: One Woman's Political Struggle*. University of South Carolina Press, 1998.

Kirkpatrick, Jeane J. *Political Woman*. Basic Books, 1974.

Knickerbocker, Brad. "Democrats Rally behind Their 'Mom in Tennis Shoes,' Sen. Patty Murray." *Christian Science Monitor*, 29 Sept. 2010, www.csmonitor.com/USA/Elections/Senate/2010/0929/Democrats-rally-behind-their-mom-in-tennis-shoes-Sen.-Patty-Murray. Accessed 24 Sept. 2015.

Lawless, Jennifer L. *Becoming a Candidate: Political Ambition and the Decision to Run for Office*. Cambridge University Press, 2012.

Lawless, Jennifer L., and Richard L. Fox. *It Takes a Candidate: Why Women Don't Run for Office*. Cambridge University Press, 2005.

Lawless, Jennifer L., and Richard L. Fox. *It Still Takes a Candidate: Why Women Don't Run for Office*. Cambridge University Press, 2010.

Lawless, Jennifer L., and Richard L. Fox. *Why are Women Still not Running for Public Office?* Brookings Institution, 2008.

Mandel, Ruth B. *In the Running: The New Woman Candidate*. Beacon Press, 1983.

McGlen, Nancy E., et al. *Women, Politics, and American Society*. New York: Pearson Longman, 2005.

Merritt, Sharyne. "Winners and Losers: Sex Differences in Municipal Elections." *American Journal of Political Science*, vol. 21, no. 4, 1977, pp. 731-43.

National School Boards Association. www.nsba.org. Accessed 10 Sept. 2015.

National Women's Political Caucus. *"Why Don't More Women Run?"* Mellman, Lazarus, Lake, 1994.

Mikulski, Barbara, et al. *Nine and Counting: The Women of the Senate*. Perennial, 2001.

Niven, David. "Party Elites and Women Candidates: The Shape of Bias." *Women & Politics*, vol. 19, no. 2, 1998, pp. 57-80.

Niven, David. "Throwing Your Hat Out of the Ring: Negative Recruitment and the Gender Imbalance in State Legislative Candidacy." *Politics & Gender*, vol. 4, no. 4, 2006, pp. 473-89.

Rhode, David W. "Risk-Bearing and Progressive Ambition: The Case of Members of the United State House of Representatives." *American Journal of Political Science*, vol. 23, no. 1, 1979, pp. 1-26.

Sanbonmatsu, Kira. *Where Women Run: Gender and Party in the American States*. University of Michigan Press, 2006.

Sapiro, Virginia, and Barbara G. Farah. "New Pride and Old Prejudice: Political Ambition and Role Orientations among Female Partisan Elites." *Women & Politics*, vol. 1, no. 1, 1980, pp. 13-36.

Schlesinger, Joseph A. *Ambition and Politics: Political Careers in the United States*. Rand McNally, 1966.

Stanley, Harold W., and Richard G. Niemi. *Vital Statistics on American Politics*. Congressional Quarterly Press, 2011.

Swers, Michele L. 2002. *The Difference Women Make*. University of Chicago Press, 2002.

Thomas, Sue, et al. "Legislative Careers: The Personal and the Political." *Women Transforming Congress*, edited by Cindy Simon Rosenthal, University of Oklahoma Press, 2002, pp. 397-421.

van Assendelft, Laura, and Karen O'Connor. "Backgrounds, Motivations, and Interests: A Comparison of Male and Female Local Party Activists." *Women & Politics*, vol. 14, no. 3, 1994, pp. 77-93.

van Hightower, Nikki R. "The Recruitment of Women in Public Office." *American Politics Quarterly*, vol. 5, no. 3, 1977, pp. 301-14.

Verba, Sidney, et al. "Family Ties: Understanding the Intergenerational Transmission of Political Participation" *The Social Logic of Politics*, edited by Alan S. Zuckerman, Temple University Press, 2004, pp. 95-116.

Woods, Harriett. *Stepping Up to Power: the Political Journey of American Women*. Basic Books, 2001.

4.
The Marriage and Children Gap?

Marital Status, Parenthood,
and Social Welfare Attitudes

SHIRLEY ADELSTEIN

GENDER DIFFERENCES IN POLITICAL ATTITUDES are driving factors contributing to gender gaps in partisan identification and voting behaviour. Social welfare attitudes are a key area in which gender differences have been consistently documented, as women tend to register higher levels of support for government services and spending for social programs (Chaney et al.; Deitch; Howell and Day; Sapiro and Shames; Shapiro and Mahajan). Researchers have offered numerous explanations for these attitude differences, including the emergence of feminist consciousness (Conover; Cook and Wilcox), women's socioeconomic status as recipients and providers of welfare services (Deitch; Erie and Rein), and gender role socialization (Sapiro).

Related research has investigated the political relevance of marital status and parenthood, suggesting that the effects of these experiences on political attitudes also contribute to the gender gap by differentially affecting political attitudes among men and women. In the 1980s, researchers in the United States began to observe a "marriage gap," whereby married individuals tended to be more right-leaning than those who were unmarried. Recent research has also provided evidence of a "children gap," demonstrating that parenthood affects political attitudes, including support for social welfare policies. Yet despite variation in the experience of parenthood across marital status, little research has examined the intersection of these factors.

This study argues that marital status and parenthood should be understood as interactive rather than additive contributors to political gender gaps. In addition, it is important to disaggregate the "unmarried" category to understand the political implications of both marital status and parenthood. In many parts of the world, rates of nonmarital childbearing are increasing (Scott et al.). As of 2014, between one-third and one-half of children were born outside of marriage in much of Europe. At the same time, roughly 30 percent of children in Australia and Canada and roughly 40 percent of children in the United States were born out of wedlock. Meanwhile, women continue to bear the majority of custodial and caregiving responsibilities in both Europe and North America.

The result of this study suggests that these trends in family structure have the potential to substantially alter public support and demand for social welfare policies. The findings show that never-married mothers in the United States are more likely than other groups of parents and nonparents to support government action to promote social welfare and socioeconomic inclusion. Thus, the increasing prevalence of unmarried parenthood—particularly among women who have never married—may drive widening political gender gaps and higher levels of support over time for government programs. More broadly, changing family structures are not just a social issue; they are also shifting the political landscape.

PREVIOUS RESEARCH

Theoretical Perspectives on Marital Status and Parenthood

The expectation that marital status and parenthood will affect political attitudes draws partly on socialization theories, which suggests that experiences that occur in early childhood as well as in adulthood shape an individual's values and identity. For example, marriage and parenthood are important junctures for adult socialization because they trigger the fulfillment of traditional gender roles, such as caregiving for women and breadwinning for men (Sapiro). There is also evidence that within marriage, spouses undergo a mutual socialization process that increases their similarity on political attitudes and behaviour (Jennings and Stoker; Stoker and Jennings). Thus, some socialization processes may promote similarities among men and women while others promote differences.

Whereas socialization theories suggest that women may be more compassionate because they are socialized to perform certain roles, maternalist theories stress the impact of the actual experience of caregiving on values and ethics. Through the experience of caregiving, a more compassionate, relational "maternal thinking" is thought to emerge (Ruddick). Thus, it is possible that differences in attitudes could diminish to the extent that differences in responsibilities do. These responsibilities tend to vary by gender as well as by marital status. However, despite shifting gender norms, women of all marital statuses continue to bear disproportionate responsibility for caregiving (Casper and Bianchi).

Marital status and parenthood may also influence political attitudes by fundamentally altering material self-interests (Deitch; Edlund and Pande; Elder and Greene, "The Children Gap"; Plissner). For example, parents may have a more immediate interest in support for childcare or education, or unmarried people may feel less economically secure. This perspective suggests that the association between marital status, parenthood, and political attitudes is driven by variation in economic vulnerability and demand for government services. To the extent that marital status and parenthood change material self-interest, these experiences should affect attitudes on support for government spending and services.

All of these mechanisms may be heightened by the prevalence of political discourse using family-related frames. For example, research by Laurel Elder and Steven Greene ("The Children Gap," *The Politics of Parenthood*) documents the increasing "politicization of the family" by American media and political elites. For example, whereas Republicans have increasingly used a "family" frame to advocate for conservative policies (e.g., lower taxes benefit families), Democrats have increasingly used the "family" frame to advocate for supporting liberal social welfare policies (e.g., leave for family and medical needs). This, they argue, has primed people to think of politics in terms of family.

THE MARRIAGE AND CHILDREN GAPS

Existing research supports the political relevance of family roles. Since the 1980s, researchers have debated the importance of marital status in influencing political attitudes and voting behaviour (e.g., Kingston and Finkel; Plutzer and McBurnett). In the United States, marital status differences in voting behavior—commonly referred to as the "marriage gap"—appear to vary across elections. But a consistent finding has been that married people are generally more conservative than single people.

There is also evidence that political gender gaps are larger among the unmarried because of such factors as the mutual socialization and convergence of interests that occurs among married couples (Burrel; Frankovic; Stoker and Jennings). This suggests that increases in gender gaps over time may be related to growth in the prevalence of unmarried women. Research in this vein argues that the economic vulnerability associated with nonmarriage increases demand and support for redistributive policies (Box-Steffensmeier et al.; Edlund and Pande). Unmarried women tend to fare worse economically than their male counterparts, and transitions into and out of marriage tend to have larger negative economic impacts for women (Casper and Bianchi).

Research on the "children gap" is relatively more recent, although all of the existing research highlights the importance of gender. For example, Susan Howell and Christine Day find that the gender gap on social welfare attitudes is only significant among those with children. More extensive analysis of survey data has shown that motherhood is associated with more liberal social welfare attitudes, but fatherhood has the opposite or no effect (Elder and Greene "The Children Gap," "The Myth," "Parenthood," *The Politics of Parenthood*; Greenlee, *The Political Consequences*). In addition, the effects of parenthood are lifelong and persist beyond the presence of children in the home. And for women, the degree of parental involvement is positively associated with support for social welfare policies (Elder and Greene, "Parenthood").

It is possible that political differences associated with marriage and parenthood result from people with different characteristics selecting into and out of these statuses. However, longitudinal studies have supported the conclusion that differences in political attitudes cannot be attributed to selection bias alone for either marriage (Edlund and Pande; Edlund et al.) or parenthood (Greenlee, "Soccer Moms," *The Political Consequences*).

Intersecting Marital Status and Parenthood

Additive models of marital status and parenthood have shown that both attributes predict variation in political attitudes. However, little research has examined these experiences as an interactive dynamic. In addition, when interactive relationships have been considered, it has been largely without regard to differences across types of nonmarriage.

In one of the few analyses to interact marital status and parenthood, Elder and Greene (*The Politics of Parenthood*) find no significant interactions between parenthood and marital status when predicting social welfare attitudes. This analysis, however, is limited by the use of a binary indicator for marital status (married versus unmarried) and data from only a single year (2008). In an analysis of survey data spanning multiple U.S. presidential election years, Jill Greenlee (*The Political Consequences*) finds that single mothers do have more liberal social welfare attitudes on some issues than married mothers. But this comparison is also limited to a combined indicator for nonmarriage.

Demographic research provides ample evidence that the experience of parenthood varies considerably across marital status, which suggests that political effects are unlikely to be additive in nature or consistent across types of nonmarriage. For example, with respect to indicators of socioeconomic disadvantage—such as income, employment, and education—unmarried parents are considerably worse off relative to their married counterparts. This is most pronounced for single mothers, who are much more likely than men to be primary custodians and who are most likely to be impoverished (Edlund et al; McLanahan and Percheski).

There are also important differences among unmarried parents. For men and women alike, different types of nonmarriage are associated with different levels of socioeconomic status and economic wellbeing. Within gender, comparing women to women and men to men, there exists a hierarchy of disadvantage. Never-married parents are the most disadvantaged, followed by separated and divorced parents, and finally by married parents. Although this hierarchy is evident for mothers and fathers alike, in every category of nonmarriage, mothers tend to be more disadvantaged than their male counterparts (Casper and Bianchi).

Combinations of marital status and parenthood also affect responsibilities associated with childcare. Mothers in all categories bear disproportionate responsibility for childcare, but differences are greater for women who are solely responsible for the care of their children, as is commonly the case for single mothers. In addition to being generally more disadvantaged than their male counterparts, mothers are overwhelmingly more likely to have sole custody of their children, though joint custody is becoming more common (Kelly). Thus, to the degree that the experience of parenthood—including childcare responsibilities, economic well-being, and real or perceived economic vulnerability—differs across marital status, we should see variation in the effects of parenthood on support for social welfare spending and services.

RESEARCH QUESTIONS AND THEORETICAL FRAMEWORK

Previous research suggests that marital status and parenthood influence attitudes about social welfare and that these effects are more pronounced among women. This study builds on these findings to examine two research questions. First, are there interactive effects of marital status, parenthood, and gender on social welfare attitudes? Second, do different types of unmarried parenthood have different effects on social welfare attitudes?

From a theoretical standpoint, this study draws on the previous research discussed above to foreground the importance of two related mechanisms linking marital status, parenthood, and social welfare attitudes. First, the *economic* mechanism pertains to variation in material self-interest, socioeconomic wellbeing, and real or perceived economic vulnerability. Second, the *parenting* mechanism pertains to variation in the personal responsibilities and experiences associated with parenting, including the emergence of a more relational ethic and the fulfillment of socialization into adult gender roles.

These mechanisms suggest that higher levels of parental engagement or economic vulnerability should be associated with increasingly liberal social welfare attitudes. These mechanisms could operate independently but in practice are likely to operate in combination. Thus, on average, parents should be more liberal than nonparents. Similarly never-married parents should be more liberal than divorced/separated parents and married parents. Finally, parenthood effects should be larger for women than men.

DATA AND METHODOLOGY

Data for this analysis come from thirteen waves of the General Social Survey (GSS) spanning between 1988 and 2008. The GSS is conducted by the National Opinion Research Center, and its purpose is to track American public opinion and social change over time (National Opinion Research Center). Each survey is cross-sectional and consists of a national probability sample of approximately fifteen hundred observations. Although the data span the period of 1988 and 2008, there are gaps in the time series because surveys were not conducted each year. The selection of this time period was dictated by the availability of relevant survey items.[1] An additional advantage of using data beginning in 1988 is that question wordings for relevant variables were largely unchanged between 1988 and 2008. However, although interviews were conducted in person until 2000, beginning in 2002, the GSS was conducted by computer-assisted personal interviewing.

The key dependent variable is a social welfare attitudes index that includes self-placement on four three-point scales measuring support for spending on welfare, social security, improving the nation's education system, and improving and protecting the nation's health. In addition, it includes self-placement on two five-point scales measuring support for the government improving living standards for the poor and support for the government helping people pay for doctors and hospital bills. The index was created by averaging individual scores for each item, and the resulting variable was subsequently standardized to have a mean equal to zero and a standard deviation equal to one (alpha=0.61).

An advantage of using an index composed of several questions is that multi-item measures can help reduce the effects of measurement error, making them more reliable (Nunnally and Bernstein). The selection of survey items for the index was guided by previous research, the consistent availability of survey items in the GSS over time, and an effort to maximize index reliability. However, given the moderate reliability coefficient and concerns that individual items may drive the results, sensitivity tests were conducted to assess the sensitivity of the findings to the construction of the index.

To ascertain the effects of marital status and parenthood among men and women, the analysis examines differences in social welfare index values between parents and nonparents and looks separately at men and women in three marital status categories: married, divorced/separated, and never married. Widows and widowers are excluded from all analyses in recognition of important differences that distinguish them from other unmarried respondents.[2] Parents include any respondent who reported ever having had at least one child, consistent with evidence that the effects of parenthood are lifelong and are not limited to periods of custodial care (Elder and Greene, "Parenthood").

The analysis begins with a descriptive comparison of mean social welfare attitudes across gender, marital status, and parenthood groupings. Next, ordinary least squares (OLS) regressions predicting social welfare attitudes are presented separately by both gender and marital status, controlling for survey year and additional demographic and attitudinal variables. Finally, to address the possibility that observed differences are attributable to large differences in the characteristics of mothers in different marital status categories, propensity score analysis is used to minimize the potential impact of these differences on estimates.

RESULTS

Descriptive Results

Table 1 presents mean values for the social welfare index by gender, marital status, and parenthood. The third column also provides the difference in mean social welfare attitudes between men and women in each combined marital status and parenthood category. Higher values for the social welfare attitudes index indicate more liberal attitudes (greater support for government spending and services), and positive values for the differences between men and women indicate that women are more liberal than men.

These descriptive results provide some support for the expectations outlined above. In terms of gender, in every category of marital status and parenthood women are significantly more liberal than their male counterparts, which confirms the well-established gender gap in social welfare attitudes for every group.

Social welfare attitudes within gender generally appear to be more liberal among the unmarried than the married and with the exception of married women, more liberal among parents than nonparents. As expected, never-married parents have the most liberal social welfare attitudes, followed in order by divorced/separated and married parents. However, within-gender differences (comparing women to women and men to men) in the social welfare attitudes of parents and nonparents are only significant for never-married men and women. Meanwhile, within-gender differences in attitudes across marital status categories are almost all significant only among parents. These preliminary results strongly suggest that the relationship between marital status, parenthood, and social welfare attitudes is interactive.

Table 1 provides limited support for the expectation that parenthood is more impactful for women. Considering the never-married subsample, for whom the only significant parent and nonparent differences are observed, the difference between parents and nonparents is almost identical in magnitude for men and women. For the married subsample, the difference between mothers and nonmothers is slightly larger than the difference between fathers and nonfathers, but it does not move in the expected direction. The expectation that parenthood has a larger effect on women is supported for the divorced/separated subsample, but parent/nonparent differences are not significant for this group.

Regression Results

The descriptive results in Table 1 only provide preliminary evidence because they do not control for other potentially confounding factors. To address this possibility, multivariate analyses are necessary. Table 2 presents regression results predicting social welfare attitudes separately by gender and marital status. The results are striking. They show that the effect of unmarried parenthood among men and women alike is driven by never-married parents and not by divorced/separated parents. For men, never-married parenthood is associated with an increase of 0.222 standard deviations in social welfare support compared to nonparenthood (p<0.01), whereas for women never-married parenthood is associated with an increase of 0.310 standard deviations (p<0.01), all else equal. These results seem to indicate that the effect of parenthood is larger for women than for men, but these coefficients are not statistically distinguishable.

The parenthood effect is nonsignificant for the married and divorced/separated subsamples. However, it is interesting to note that the magnitudes of the coefficients move precisely along the lines of the hierarchy observed in Table 1. The effect of parenthood becomes larger and increasingly positive moving from married to divorced/separated to never-married results.

Given that the outcome variable in these analyses is an index that combines multiple responses to questions about social welfare policy, it is reasonable to wonder whether the results are being driven by individual items. Table 3 addresses this possibility. It presents the parenthood coefficients from ordinal logistic regressions and predicts each of the constituent variables in the social welfare index. What stands out is that only two results are statistically significant at conventional levels. For never married men, parenthood is associated with increased support for social security spending (p<0.01), whereas for never-married women, parenthood is associated with increased support for government help to the poor (p<0.01).

Although the results in Table 3 seem to suggest that individual items may underlie the parenthood effects observed in other analyses, replicating the regression analyses with a revised social welfare attitudes index that excludes social security spending and government aid to the poor shows that this is not the case (results not shown). When these two items are removed from the index, the parenthood effect becomes nonsignificant for never-married men, but it remains highly significant for never-married women (b=0.206; p<0.01).

Key findings are also robust to the exclusion of support for welfare spending, which is notable because previous research shows that the way people respond to questions about social issues is sensitive to the language that is used. For example, in the United States, negative racial stereotypes have been associated with terms such as "welfare" because of racialized political discourse associating dependence on government support with marginalized minority groups (Gilens). Observing a robust effect even when more sensitive survey items are excluded further supports the argument that parenthood is in fact associated with an overall pattern of liberalized social welfare attitudes—a finding that appears to be concentrated among never-married women.

Propensity Score Matching

One objection to this conclusion may be that the significant, liberalizing effect of parenthood for never-married mothers compared to never-married nonmothers is attributable to differences in their characteristics. That is, differences in the characteristics of never-married mothers and nonmothers are larger than the differences between mothers and nonmothers in other marital status categories.

In order to address the possibility that these differences account for the observed parenthood effect among never-married women, a propensity score matching analysis was used to generate a matched sample of never-married mothers and nonmothers who have comparable characteristics. In propensity score matching, members of treatment and comparison groups are matched based on similarity of propensity scores, which capture the likelihood of being in the treatment group but is conditional on a wide range of measured characteristics. To the extent that selection into treatment is a function of observed characteristics, this method can effectively reduce selection bias by comparing the outcomes of treatment and control groups that are as similar as possible (Dehejia and Wahba, "Casual Effects," "Propensity Score-Matching"; Rosenbaum and Rubin, "The Central Role," "Constructing"). Applying this method identified a comparison group of never-married nonmothers and a "treatment" group of never-married mothers with very similar in observable characteristics.[3]

Following matching with parametric analysis helps account for inexact matching and reduces model dependency (Ho et al.). Table 4 shows the results of an OLS regression predicting the original social welfare index for the matched sample of never-married women. Remarkably, even after matching and the associated reduction in sample size, the parenthood effect remains substantial in magnitude and highly significant. For never-married women, being a mother is associated with a 0.369 standard deviation increase in social welfare support (p<0.01). As in the previous analyses, this result is robust to the use of the revised social welfare index (b=0.325; p<0.01). Matching can only account for unmeasured characteristics to the extent that they are associated with measured characteristics. Nevertheless, differences in key observable variables do not appear to account for the liberalizing effect of parenthood among never-married mothers.

DISCUSSION AND CONCLUSIONS

Changing patterns in family formation can have important political implications by shaping public support for government policies. This study examined one salient dimension of the relationship between marital status, parenthood, and political attitudes: support for social welfare services and spending. The findings suggest that understanding the importance of marital status and parenthood for political attitudes requires attention to their interactive relationship, and this relationship has a gendered component.

The results presented here using data from the United States show that marital status and parenthood have interactive political impacts. Parenthood does influence social welfare attitudes, but the effect is concentrated among unmarried parents. In addition, there are distinctions among different types of nonmarriage. The liberalizing effect of unmarried parenthood reflects never-married parents, particularly never-married mothers. This is consistent with the idea that the parenthood effect is driven by factors such as economic interests and caregiving responsibilities. In the absence of longitudinal data, causal inferences cannot be made with certainty. However, the results underscore the point that in politics, as elsewhere, parenthood does not operate in isolation.

More broadly, the findings of this study underscore the relevance of demographic trends for the political landscape. The increasing prevalence of unmarried parenthood—particularly for mothers—is not merely a social issue. This parenthood experience differs from experiences associated with other marital statuses in ways that may drive widening gender gaps and heightened support for government action to promote social welfare and socioeconomic inclusion. Consequently, these demographic trends have significant political implications.

ENDNOTES

[1]Surveys used for this study include the following years: 1988, 1989, 1990, 1991 1993, 1994, 1996, 1998, 2000, 2002, 2004, 2006, and 2008. Each survey since 1988 has used a split-ballot design in order to maximize the inclusion of rotating survey items. Thus, each year is divided into three subsamples, each of which received a different series of questions. All respondents were asked a series of "core" questions, including respondent background characteristics. As a result of this design, this analysis includes the sample from each survey year that was administered the ballot containing all questions of interest.

[2]Widows and widowers constitute the smallest subsample, and they are disproportionately over sixty years old and female, which make comparisons more difficult.

[3]By one fairly stringent standard, standardized differences should be below 10 percent to constitute balance. Only three variables had standardized differences greater than this: income (13.6 percent), intact childhood family (10.2 percent), and redistributive occupation (33.3 percent). The first two are very close to 10 percent, and both constitute about 77 percent reductions in bias. For the larger difference remaining for redistributive occupation (25 percent of nonmothers and 12 percent of mothers), the direction of the bias would be expected to lead to understated rather than overstated parenthood effects.

WORKS CITED

Box-Steffensmeier, Janet M., at al. "The Dynamics of the Partisan Gender Gap." *The American Political Science Review*, vol. 98, no. 3, 2004, pp. 515-28.

Casper, Lynne M., and Suzanne M. Bianchi. *Continuity & Change in the American Family*. Sage Publications, 2002.

Chaney, Carole Kennedy, et al. "Exploring the Gender Gap in U.S. Presidential Elections, 1980-1992." *Political Research Quarterly*, vol. 51, no. 2, 1998, pp. 311-39.

Conover, Pamela Johnston. "Feminists and the Gender Gap." *Journal of Politics*, vol. 50, no. 4, 1988, pp. 985-1010.

Cook, Elizabeth Adell, and Clyde Wilcox. "Feminism and the Gender Gap—A Second Look." *The Journal of Politics*, vol. 53, no. 4, 1991, pp. 1111-22.

Dehejia, Rajeev H. and Sadek Wahba. "Causal Effects in Non-experimental Studies: Reevaluating the Evaluation of Training Programs." *Journal of the American Statistical Association*, vol. 94, no. 448, 1999, pp. 1053-62.

Dehejia, Rajeev H. and Sadek Wahba. "Propensity Score-Matching Methods for Nonexperimental Causal Studies." *Review of Economics and Statistics*, vol. 84, no. 1, 2002, pp. 151-61.

Deitch, Cynthia. "Sex Differences in Support for Government Spending." *The Politics of the Gender Gap*, edited by Carol M. Mueller, Sage Publications, 1988, pp. 192-216,

Edlund, Lena, and Rohini Pande. "Why Have Women Become Left-Wing? The Political Gender Gap and the Decline in Marriage." *The Quarterly Journal of Economics*, vol. 117, no. 3, 2002, pp. 917-61.

Edlund, Lena, et al. "Unmarried Parenthood and Redistributive Politics." *Journal of the European Economic Association*, vol. 3, no. 1, 2005, pp. 95-119.

Elder, Laurel, and Steven Greene. "Parenthood and the Gender Gap." *Voting the Gender Gap*, edited by Loris Duke Whitaker, University of Illinois Press, 2008, pp 119-140.

Elder, Laurel, and Steven Greene. "The Children Gap on Social Welfare and the Politicization of American Parents, 1984-2000." *Politics & Gender*, vol. 2, no. 4, 2006, pp. 451-72.

Elder, Laurel, and Steven Greene. "The Myth of 'Security Moms' and 'NASCAR Dads': Parenthood, Political Stereotypes, and the 2004 Election." *Social Science Quarterly*, vol. 88, no. 1, 2007, pp. 1-19.

Elder, Laurel, and Steven Greene. *The Politics of Parenthood.* SUNY Press, 2012.

Erie, Steven P., and Martin Rein. "Women and the Welfare State."

The Politics of the Gender Gap, edited by Carol M. Mueller, Sage Publications, 1988, pp. 173-191.

Frankovic, Kathleen A. "Sex and Politics—New Alignments, Old Issues." *PS: Political Science & Politics*, vol. 15, no. 3, 1982, pp. 439-48.

Gilens, Martin. *Why Americans Hate Welfare: Race, Media, and the Politics of Antipoverty Policy.* University of Chicago Press, 1999.

Greenlee, Jill S. "Soccer Moms, Hockey Moms, and the Question of 'Transformative' Motherhood." *Politics & Gender*, vol. 6, no. 3, 2010, pp. 405-31.

Greenlee, Jill S. *The Political Consequences of Motherhood.* University of Michigan Press, 2014.

Ho, Daniel E., et al. "Matching as Nonparametric Preprocessing for Reducing Model Dependence in Parametric Causal Inference." *Political Analysis*, vol. 15, no. 3, 2007, pp. 199-236.

Howell, Susan E., and Christine L. Day. "Complexities of the Gender Gap." *Journal of Politics*, vol. 62, no. 3, 2000, pp. 858-74.

Jennings, M. Kent, and Laura Stoker. "Political Similarity and Influence between Husbands and Wives." American Political Science Association Annual Meeting, 2000, Washington D.C.

Kelly, Joan B. "Children's Living Arrangements Following Separation and Divorce: Insights from Empirical and Clinical Research." *Family Process*, vol. 46, no. 1, 2007, pp. 35-52.

Kingston, Paul William and Steven E. Finkel. "Is There a Marriage Gap in Politics?" *Journal of Marriage and the Family*, vol. 49, no. 1, 1987, pp. 57-64.

McLanahan, Sara, and Christine Percheski. "Family Structure and the Reproduction of Inequalities." *Annual Review of Sociology* vol. 34, no. 1, 2008, pp. 257-76.

Nunnally, Jum C., and Ira H. Bernstein. *Psychometric Theory.* McGraw Hill, 1994.

Plissner, Martin. "The Marriage Gap." *Public Opinion*, vol. 5, no. 4, 1983, pp. 53.

Plutzer, Eric, and Michael McBurnett. "The 'Marriage Gap' Reconsidered." *The Public Opinion Quarterly*, vol. 55, no. 1, 1991, pp. 113-27.

Rosenbaum, Paul R., and Donald B. Rubin. "Constructing a Control Group Using Multivariate Matched Sampling Methods that Incorporate the Propensity Score." *American Statistician*, vol. 39, no. 1, 1985, pp. 33-38.

Rosenbaum, Paul R., and Donald B. Rubin. "The Central Role of the Propensity Score in Observational Studies for Causal Effects." *Biometrika*, vol.70, no. 1, 1983, pp. 41-55.

Ruddick, Sara. "Maternal Thinking." *Feminist Studies*, vol. 6, no. 2, 1980, pp. 342-67.

Sapiro, Virginia. *The Political Integration of Women: Roles, Socialization, and Politics*. University of Illinois Press, 1984.

Sapiro, Virginia, and Shauna L. Shames. "The Gender Basis of Public Opinion." *Understanding Public Opinion*, edited by Barbara Norrander and Clyde Wilcox, CQ Press, 2009, pp. 5-24.

Scott, Mindy E., et al. *World Family Map 2015: Mapping Family Change and Child Well-being Outcomes*. Child Trends, 2015.

Shapiro, Robert Y., and Harpreet Mahajan. "Gender Differences in Policy Preferences: A Summary of Trends from the 1960s to the 1980s." *The Public Opinion Quarterly*, vol. 50, no. 1, 1986, pp. 42-61.

Stoker, Laura, and M. Kent Jennings. "Life Cycle Transitions and Political Participation: The Case of Marriage." *The American Political Science Review*, vol. 89, no. 2, 1995, pp. 421-33.

Weisberg, Herbert F. "The Demographics of a New Voting Gap: Marital Differences in American Voting." *The Public Opinion Quarterly*, vol. 51, no. 3, 1987, pp. 335-43.

Table 1. Mean Social Welfare Attitudes by Gender, Marital Status, and Parenthood

	Men	Women	Difference (W-M)
Married			
Parent	-0.167 a b	0.002 a b	0.169 d
Non-parent	-0.212 bb	0.068	0.280 d
Divorced/ separated			
Parent	0.003 c	0.332 c	0.329 d
Non-parent	-0.043	0.185	0.228 ddd
Never married			
Parent	0.355*	0.552*	0.197 dd
Non-parent	-0.043	0.153	0.196 d

Source: General Social Survey 1988-2008.

Within gender and marital status, parent/non-parent difference: * $p<0.01$.

Within gender and parenthood status, married/divorced difference: a $p<0.01$.

Within gender and parenthood status, married/never married difference: b $p<0.01$; bb $p<0.05$.

Within gender and parenthood status, divorced/never married difference: c $p<0.01$.

Within marital and parenthood status, women/men difference: d $p<0.01$; dd $p<0.05$; ddd $p<0.10$.

Table 2. Predicting Social Welfare Attitudes by Gender and Marital Status, 1988-2008.

	Men			Women		
	Married	Divorced/ Separated	Never Married	Married	Divorced/ Separated	Never Married
Age	-0.005**	-0.009**	0.000	-0.007***	-0.007***	-0.004
	(0.002)	(0.004)	(0.003)	(0.002)	(0.003)	(0.002)
Black	0.463***	0.032	0.146	0.338***	0.174**	-0.079
	(0.088)	(0.121)	(0.097)	(0.075)	(0.081)	(0.088)
Other race	0.133	0.278*	-0.051	-0.117	0.134	-0.096
	(0.099)	(0.148)	(0.104)	(0.084)	(0.103)	(0.121)
Income (log)	-0.100***	-0.079	-0.074**	-0.119***	-0.106***	-0.063*
	(0.033)	(0.050)	(0.033)	(0.029)	(0.040)	(0.034)
Income missing	-0.994***	-0.811	-0.742**	-1.248***	-0.887**	-0.619*
	(0.356)	(0.539)	(0.347)	(0.311)	(0.392)	(0.341)
Less than high school	0.181**	0.186	0.135	0.203***	-0.193*	-0.144
	(0.074)	(0.121)	(0.110)	(0.070)	(0.114)	(0.108)
Some college	0.015	0.061	0.047	-0.071	0.030	0.146
	(0.087)	(0.146)	(0.106)	(0.073)	(0.103)	(0.110)
College degree	-0.245***	-0.219**	-0.176**	-0.123**	0.061	0.069
	(0.087)	(0.146)	(0.106)	(0.073)	(0.103)	(0.069)

	Men			Women		
	Married	Divorced/Separated	Never Married	Married	Divorced/Separated	Never Married
South (U.S. region)	-0.007 (0.053)	0.049 (0.105)	-0.041 (0.075)	0.024 (0.052)	-0.048 (0.087)	0.137** (0.076)
Employed	-0.033 (0.046)	-0.123 (0.080)	0.109 (0.065)	-0.046 (0.042)	-0.057 (0.066)	0.006 (0.068)
Redistributive occupation	0.178** (0.086)	0.211 (0.138)	0.087 (0.113)	-0.022 (0.048)	0.031 (0.075)	0.052 (0.075)
Ideology	0.193*** (0.019)	0.172*** (0.032)	0.157*** (0.023)	0.200*** (0.017)	0.106*** (0.024)	0.121*** (0.025)
Ideology missing	0.645*** (0.210)	0.661* (0.351)	0.845*** (0.240)	0.758*** (0.144)	0.600*** (0.214)	0.633*** (0.227)
Help blacks scale	0.240*** (0.020)	0.255*** (0.034)	0.275*** (0.027)	0.233*** (0.018)	0.230*** (0.026)	0.250*** (0.030)
Church attendance	-0.018** (0.008)	0.002 (0.016)	0.004 (0.014)	-0.005 (0.008)	-0.006 (0.013)	-0.006 (0.030)
Intact childhood family	-0.069	-0.096	-0.060	0.047	-0.121*	-0.134**

	Men			Women		
	Married	Divorced/ Separated	Never Married	Married	Divorced/ Separated	Never Married
	(0.053)	(0.085)	(0.066)	(0.046)	(0.070)	(0.065)
Parent	-0.032	0.008	0.222***	0.020	0.055	0.310***
	(0.061)	(0.103)	(0.086)	(0.053)	(0.090)	(0.077)
Constant	-0.025	0.108	-0.960**	0.170	0.631	-0.328
	(0.375)	(0.624)	(0.412)	(0.327)	(0.435)	(0.366)
Observations	1,790	533	784	1,803	770	714
R-squared	0.28	0.27	0.33	0.27	0.24	0.27

Source: General Social Survey 1988-2008.

Note. Model includes dummy variables for individual years, though results are not shown. Robust standard errors are in parentheses.

*

Table 3. Effect of Parenthood on Support for Components of Social Welfare Index by Gender and Marital Status, 1988-2008.

	Men			Women		
	Married	Divorced/ Separated	Never Married	Married	Divorced/ Separated	Never Married
Outcome variable						
Education spending	-0.078	0.442*	0.466*	-0.009	0.234	0.048

	Men			Women		
	Married	Divorced/ Separated	Never Married	Married	Divorced/ Separated	Never Married
	(0.146)	(0.249)	(0.242)	(0.156)	(0.225)	(0.216)
Health spending	0.057	0.169	-0.123	0.004	0.298	-0.013
	(0.141)	(0.236)	(0.246)	(0.150)	(0.243)	(0.230)
Social security spending	-0.008	0.183	0.610***	0.173*	0.153	0.177
	(0.097)	(0.157)	(0.168)	(0.097)	(0.151)	(0.133)
Welfare spending	0.091	-0.139	-0.035	-0.138	-0.033	0.299*
	(0.125)	(0.211)	(0.197)	(0.121)	(0.187)	(0.177)
Government help to poor	0.116	-0.065	0.144	0.121	0.061	0.637***
	(0.087)	(0.129)	(0.153)	(0.083)	(0.119)	(0.133)
Government help to sick	-0.034	-0.050	-0.129	-0.016	0.120	0.236*
	(0.085)	(0.142)	(0.150)	(0.080)	(0.125)	(0.126)

Source: General Social Survey 1988-2008.
Note. Results are from ordinal logistic regressions controlling for age, race, income, income missing, education, region, employment status, redistributive occupation, ideology, ideology missing, support for government help to blacks, church attendance, intact childhood family, and year. For all variables, higher values indicate higher levels of support. Robust standard errors are in parentheses.

* p<0.10; ** p<0.05; *** p<0.01.

Table 4. Predicting Social Welfare Attitudes for Matched Sample, 1988-2008.

	Never Married Women
Age	0.010
	(0.006)
Black	-0.469***
	(0.172)
Other race	-0.096
	(0.180)
Income (log)	-0.114*
	(0.060)
Income missing	-0.768
	(0.579)
Less than high school	-0.444**
	(0.199)
Some college	-0.420
	(0.290)
College degree	-0.188
	(0.169)
South (U.S. region)	0.268*
	(0.157)
Employed	-0.118
	(0.163)
Redistributive occupation	0.369**
	(0.161)
Ideology	0.106**
	(0.047)
Ideology missing	0.123
	(0.405)

	Never Married Women
Help blacks scale	0.291***
	(0.054)
Church attendance	0.025
	(0.024)
Intact childhood family	-0.302**
	(0.123)
Parent	0.369***
	(0.119)
Observations	210
R-squared	0.37

Source: General Social Survey 1988-2008.

Note. Results based on sample matched using nearest-neighbor one-to-one matching with replacement and a caliper of 0.001. Observations are weighted to account for matching with replacement. Robust standard errors were adjusted to account for clustering by observation. Model includes dummy variables for individual years, though results are not shown.

* p<0.10; ** p<0.05; *** p<0.01.

Appendix
Question Wordings for Variables Used in Analysis

Social Welfare Attitudes Index

We are faced with many problems in this country, none of which can be solved easily or inexpensively. I'm going to name some of these problems, and for each one I'd like you to tell me whether you think we're spending too much money on it, too little money or about the right amount...Are we spending too much, too little, or just the right amount on

Improving and protecting the nation's health?
Improving the nation's education system?
Welfare?
Social Security?

Some people think that the government in Washington should do everything possible to improve the standard of living of all poor Americans; they are Point 1 on this card. Other people think it is not the government's responsibility, and that each person should take care of himself; they are at point 5. Where would you place yourself on this scale, or haven't you made up your mind on this?

In general, some people think that it is the responsibility of the government in Washington to see to it that people have help in paying for doctors and hospital bills. Others think that these matters are not the responsibility of the federal government and that people should take care of these things themselves. Where would you place yourself on this scale, or haven't you made up your mind on this? [Scale ranges from I strongly agree it is the responsibility of government to help (1) to I strongly agree people should take care of themselves (5).]

Scale is coded so higher values indicate more liberal responses.

Ideology

We hear a lot of talk these days about liberals and conservatives. I'm going to show you a seven-point scale on which the political views that people might hold are arranged from extremely liberal—point 1—to extremely conservative—point 7. Where would you place yourself on this scale? [Scale ranges Extremely liberal (1), Liberal, Slightly liberal, Moderate middle of the road, Slightly conservative, Conservative, Extremely Conservative (7).]

Racial Attitudes Scale

Some people think that (Blacks/Negroes/African-Americans) have been discriminated against for so long that the government has a special obligation to improve their living standards. Others believe the government should not be giving special treatment to (Blacks/Negroes/African-Americans). Where would you place yourself on this scale, or haven't you made up your mind on this? [Scale ranges from I strongly agree the government is obligated to help blacks (1) to I strongly agree that government shouldn't give special treatment (5).]

Religiosity

How often do you attend religious services? [Scale ranges Never (1), Less than once a year, About once or twice a year, About once a month, 2-3 times a month, Nearly every week, Every week, Several times a week (8).]

NARRATIVES ON MOTHERHOOD
AND POLITICS

5.
Shared Advice for Political Marriages

The Epistolary Dialogues
Between Mothers and Daughters

MARY T. DUARTE

BORN THREE GENERATIONS APART but direct descendants of the Empress of Habsburg Maria Theresa, the Queen of the Two Sicilies Maria Caroline (1752-1814) and the Queen of the Belgians Louise-Marie (1812-1850) both went into politically arranged marriages. The goal of Empress Maria Therese and the rulers that succeeded her was to gain a diplomatic edge through the placement of their daughters in key marriages and locations. Maria Caroline married the son of the King of Spain, establishing a link between the Habsburg dynasty and the Spanish Bourbon House. With Habsburg holdings throughout Europe including the Netherlands and Italy, this marriage provided an informal alliance between two great powers. Louise-Marie married the king of the newly created Belgium. As the young nation was not recognized by its former ruler, King William of the Netherlands, an alliance with the French provided a counterweight and eventually the necessary troops needed to retain its hegemony, whereas the French benefited from a strong friendship to its north. Both women realized what was expected of them, yet they went into these marriages woefully unprepared. Bound by the desire to have their daughters pure of mind and body, as dictated by the Catholic Church and customs of the time, the mothers of these two women did not prepare their daughters for the demands of matrimony. Not only were Maria Caroline and Louise-Marie both totally naïve of the carnal side of their marital union, but they had also not been trained for the political roles that would be required of them. Yet once married, these women needed to be educated in the new realities of their situation. Separated from their mothers, the difficult advice that the daughters needed was conveyed in letters. Begun by Empress Maria Theresa and transmitted through the maternal line of the Habsburg dynasty, this correspondence played an essential role for instructing these newly wedded women. Although the mother-daughter dynamics of this exchange slowly evolved, the advice and desired outcomes for these political arranged marriages remained unchanged: to create a daughter who was the perfect woman—modest, faithful and, dutiful both to her husband as well as to the wishes of her mother as the representative of their families' interests.

The correspondence between these women goes beyond the personal into the political. Only recently has there been recognition that epistolary studies, and more specifically letters between women, not only explore female views of society and culture but also have a political significance. Previously read only for social and cultural insights, the political value of letters has led to a concerted effort to revisit the unexplored wealth of information in letters written by and between women. In 2004, *Gender and Politics in the Age of Letter Writing, 1750-2000* claimed to be the "first attempt to use letters as a source of gendered political history" by breaking through the assumption that women's letters should be "pigeonholed as feminine." Recognizing the larger value of these letters, other edited epistolary works have attempted to "read these correspondences as texts and as concrete historical artifacts strongly rooted in particular contexts" (Bland and Cross 5). The letters shared between the women covered here are clearly more than personal, as the very nature of a politically arranged marriage demands political success; an unsuccessful marriage could have diplomatic and local ramifications. Yet defining the political nature of letters written between a mother and her daughter can be a difficult task because what appears to be personal advice could have political overtones. Questions of fashion, for example, could be advice on modesty, which had political significance as the queen sought to retain her reputation within the royal court and, thus, her influence over her spouse. In the case of the letters explored here, the political blends with the personal in the epistolary dialogue: a mother must give her newly wedded daughter advice to assure her both political as well as private success. Her daughter must exemplify publically accepted gender norms, but she was also required in certain cases to quietly bend those same rules in order to achieve political success. As in the case of Marie Caroline, she was advised to remain publically submissive, while, privately, she gained political control from having a weaker spouse.

Within this correspondence, the mother took a dominant role and expected her daughter to follow her instructions passively. Unfamiliar with her new role, the daughter did not have a choice as she was completely dependent on her mother for guidance. According to Katharine Jensen, this mother-daughter reflectivity guaranteed a "replication of feminine identity and behavior from one generation to the next [that] was intended to ensure that women stayed virgins until marriage and submitted to authority throughout their lives whether that authority was maternal, paternal, conjugal, or religious" (Jensen 23). Daughters were expected to fulfill their mothers' wishes as if they were their very own. The mother sought to create a daughter in her own image with distinct gender-specific behaviour (23). Mothers assumed their daughters would accept the advice given to them without questioning that their mothers' wishes might not be their own. Empress Maria Theresa expected that her daughters would carry out her instructions and had spies within their respective courts to report back any failure to do so. Three generations later, the nature of the mother-daughter relationship had changed, and instructions had become motherly advice. But the ultimate goal of total obedience remained. Without the power of the empress, Louise-Marie's mother, the Queen of the French Marie Amélie, used a new vocabulary to achieve her aims. "Duty" became a key word in their correspondence and ultimately meant obedience to the wishes of her mother, her family, and the dynastic role that had been given to her. Like the empress generations before her, she too was not above using visitors to the Belgian court to spy on her daughter. Though in this case, the daughter gently pushed back, letting her mother know she was aware of her actions. In one letter, she provides detailed account of her clothes and hairstyle, noting that the French ambassador told her that her mother quizzed those who attended her court about her appearance (d'Orléans).[1] Generations earlier, Maria Theresa's daughters would have never been so bold.

This evolution in the mother-daughter relationship also reflects a changing view of marriage. The arranged aristocratic marriage, with its medieval foundations, focused on kinship and the youth of the bride in order to guarantee fertility (Duby 192). Key was the notion of hierarchy, whether in vassalic bonds or the husband's full control over his wife (Davis ix). Empress Maria Theresa expected that her daughters would adhere to this model. But by the time Louise-Marie had married, the notion of marriage was transitioning to the bourgeois perception of marriage life that involved a partnership and fidelity.

The process of shared guidance began with Empress Maria Theresa. As the only surviving heir to the throne of the Habsburg Empire, her father Charles VI had fought to have has his daughter's succession to the throne guaranteed by the Pragmatic Sanction of 1713. Ironically, the emperor did not focus his energy on preparing her for the responsibilities that this would entail. Her formal education ended on her eighteenth birthday. In 1740, at the age of twenty-three year, her father died, which left Maria Theresa empress. As she did not have a close relationship with her own mother, the Empress Elisabeth-Christina who had become increasing aloof as she grew older, the young empress was unable to turn to her for assistance (Pick 38).

Quickly realizing her own faults and unpreparedness for this new life of leadership, Maria Theresa found the direction she needed from a Portuguese noble, Don Manoel Telles de Menezes e Castro, Count Taroucca, later the Duke of Silva, who had served her father. She gave him the task of observing her, finding her weaknesses and then giving her a written plan to correct them. This was an unenviable assignment but one that Taroucca took very seriously. In his reports to her, Tarouca emphasized to Maria Theresa the value of self-discipline and time management; he designated set times during the day for both governmental and personal responsibilities. She was to be pious and above public reproach by attending mass daily after her morning prayers and by spending time on her personal grooming as to properly present herself to her royal court. She also had to spend time with her husband and allow him to help her, which helped her to balance of roles of wife and ruler and maintain the appearance of female subservience, at least within her marriage (Pick 74-5).

It was this counsel that she received in her early years that she would pass on to her own children. Yet Maria Theresa was exceptional as she was the primary ruler of the Habsburg Empire, and although she had to placate her husband as directed by her advisor, the power ultimately laid with her. From her own position of authority, she attempted to control the fate of her daughters whom she sent throughout Europe to form dynastically beneficial marriages. Her correspondence allowed the empress to create a "fiction of self" (Earle 2) or an idealized version of the perfect female ruling partner. For her, that meant applying Taroucca's outline, which successfully realized the ideals of noble womanhood: purity, modesty, and submissiveness. She believed the success of a marriage was determined by the wife—although her daughters did not enjoy the advantaged position of their mother, as they were given away in political marriages in which it was expected that they play a supporting role.

When her children left her household, Maria Theresa gave each instruction on religious observance, personal discipline, and the duties of his or her new position. If it was a loveless marriage, she also provided advice on winning a spouse's affection or, at least, his respect, counsel that was only necessary for her daughters. Depending on her concern over her children's perceived deficiencies in their new roles, they were directed to reread these instructions once every six months, as was the case for her son Maximilian, or monthly, as was the case for her youngest daughter, and perhaps least disciplined child, the future Queen of France Marie Antoinette. The empress followed up these instructions through a series of letters, in which she attempted to meld her children to her ideals.

The empress had arranged for one of her daughters to marry Ferdinand IV, the son of King Charles III of Spain, thus strengthening the goodwill between the two ruling houses. Ferdinand was the King of the Two Sicilies (a position his father had given up upon ascension to the Spanish throne). Descriptions of Ferdinand's intelligence were unfavourable, as his education had been purposefully neglected because of the fear that if he was overtaxed, it could trigger an ongoing family condition of insanity. It was also said that he favoured "low company" (Dyson 20-2). Yet this was a political match that would solidify the friendship between the Habsburg dynasty and the Spanish Bourbon House. The first choice for his wife was the empress's fifth daughter Josepha, but she died of smallpox on the day she was scheduled to leave for Sicily. Chosen to replace her was Maria Caroline Charlotte, the thirteenth of the sixteen children born to Maria Theresa and her husband Francis.

Maria Caroline was married by proxy in Vienna 17 April 1768 and at Caserta 13 May 1768. When she finally met her husband Ferdinand, she found him unattractive and lazy. Weeks after her marriage, she wrote her former governess of her desire to kill herself, noting that only her faith prevented from acting. Her married life was that of "a martyrdom, all the worse because one has to appear pleased" (qtd. in Dyson 23). These words were written to her former governess and not her mother from whom she could not expect any sympathy. Instead her mother was telling her that at fifteen, she would no longer consider her daughter a child, which clearly placed the success of the marriage on her. It was her inadequacies, not her husband's, that jeopardized the success of this union. Her mother would say the following: "you say your prayers carelessly and without reverence. Do not be surprised if after such a beginning of the day nothing goes well" (qtd. in Dyson 22). Personal discipline and piety played a key role in Marie Theresa's view of success and were fundamental ideals of womanhood.

Letters giving Maria Caroline specific instructions on all levels of her life followed. They focused on self-discipline, maintaining her reputation and the husband-wife relationship. There is no pretense of an epistolary dialogue; these instructions were expected to be followed without question. At fifteen, Maria Caroline was still a young girl who had been raised in a very sheltered environment and was unprepared for her new life as the wife of Ferdinand IV. The first task of the empress was to teach her daughter about the responsibilities and expectations of adulthood by counselling her to learn to control her childish impulses. Warning her that people judged an innocent maiden differently than a married woman, her mother advised her to be mindful of what she wore and said.

Vanity was something to guard against, so she should avoid friv-
olous purchases, which gave the "appearance of coquetry." Firm
control over what she said, whether in anger or as gossip, was
essential as harsh words or idle chatter could drive people away
from her. Discipline was essential as "nothing makes even worthy
people more insufferable than careless ways" (Habsburg, *Letters*
100). To succeed, her daughter must find acceptance in her new
society and to do so she had to start acting like an adult. Childlike innocence was a required trait as she entered into marriage,
but once married, childlike behaviour would not serve her or the
Habsburg reputation.

For the young Maria Caroline, these letters of advice were a very
long list of what not to do, and they had to be followed faithfully.
Even though her daughter was still a child, the empress did not
view her instructions as motherly advice but guidelines to guarantee personal and political success. They were impartially given,
much as Taroucca had done for her. It was a priority to appear
publically as a good wife so as not to embarrass the Habsburgs
reputation with deviant behaviour. Conduct that might have been
acceptable for most women—vanity, gossiping, and overextrava-
gance—was not permitted. In the mother-daughter dynamic, her
daughter's success would clearly be her mother's, who not only
arranged the marriage but attempted to form her daughter into
the perfect political wife.

Most importantly, the empress told Maria Caroline, as well as her
other sisters, that if they did not love their husbands, they should
not let their spouses become aware of this. It was through their
ability to win the devotion of their husbands that they would gain
influence. As Maria Theresa wrote to one daughter, "Passionate
love vanishes quickly. Each must respect the other, and each must
be useful to the other, each must feel true friendship for the other
in order to be content in marriage" (Habsburg, *Letters* 100-2).
The empress noted that the husband must enjoy his time with his
wife and never be burdened with complaints; he must find only
happiness in her presence. When with her spouse, a wife should
always give the appearance of cheerfulness and friendliness. Maria
Theresa insisted that even if this was forced with consistent repetition, these pleasant moods would become habit, and the husband

would enjoy his partner's company more for it. By following this strategy the empress was convinced that her daughters would win the affection of their spouses and even their trust. But once achieved it should never be taken for granted, boasted about or abused (Hapsburg, *Letters* 100).

The empress also counselled her daughters to ignore their husbands' extramarital affairs. They should never be referred to even as a joke among friends, as it would be disrespectful and could lead to anger, harsh words, and eventually dislike between the partners. Marital passivity was essential for success. On this subject, the empress struggled to follow the advice she gave her daughters. She had warned her daughters that whether they married for love or political expediency, they should not appear jealous. Maria Theresa was unable to control her own husband's infidelities, she bore them without overt public displays of jealousy even when her husband brought his mistresses to family events. Yet privately, she was a jealous woman but aware of the problems that this could cause.

Early in Maria Caroline's marriage, the empress advised her to give no special attention to her husband's mistresses, thereby treating them as everyone else. In this way, her views would not appear too divergent from or critical of her husband: "To be silent and to give the impression of noticing nothing, therein lies the only means to us in this case" (Habsburg, *Letters* 100). Although her husband was not faithful to her, it appears that Maria Caroline and Ferdinand developed some affection for each other as she followed her mother's counsel and made herself his confidante and partner, and not his critic. Ferdinand came to rely on his wife's intellect and governing abilities. He would respond to questions on government matters by saying, "Ask my wife, she knows everything" (qtd. in Dyson 26). Through her daughter, the empress secured a strong diplomatic relationship on the Italian peninsula.

Marie Caroline's third child, a son, was born in 1775, and with him, her political power increased. Recognizing the need for a political as well as personal role for her daughter, the Empress Maria Theresa had stipulated in the marriage contract that with the birth of a son, Marie Caroline gained the right to participate in the state council. Queen Maria Caroline used this opportunity to eventually remove all opponents to her increasing power. Knowing the kingdom would fall into chaos without strong leadership, she took that role while her husband continued to ignore his daily duties. Upon his return from a day of sports, she would meet with him to settle the political matters of the day and get his signature when needed (Acton 134, 202).

Ferdinand and Maria Caroline would have eighteen children. Her fourth was a daughter, Maria Amélie, who was born in 1782, two years after the death of her grandmother Maria Theresa. Yet despite Maria Caroline's own ability to make the best of a politically arranged marriage, she knew the hardships that she had overcome and lamented the arranged marriage between her younger sister Marie Antoinette and the future Louis XVI in 1770. She seemed, however, to forget these concerns when it came to her own children, as she followed her mother's tradition of arranging politically expedient marriages that benefited both the mother and the dynasty. Maria Caroline's close relationship with her younger sister Marie Antoinette, who became Queen of France in 1774, guaranteed that a marriage would be arranged between their children. So it was planned that the heir to the French throne would marry his cousin Marie Amélie, who was two years his junior. However, he was a sickly child and died when he was only eight years old. The events that followed in France prevented any other marriage to be arranged between the two families.

Despite these initial hurdles, Marie Amélie was destined to be the ruler of the French. In 1808, Louis Philippe, the Duc d'Orleans and a cousin to the former dauphin, arrived for a visit. Having fled the French armies and Napoleon, the family was then living in Sicily. During his visit, Louis Philippe had to work hard to win the affections of the displaced royal family, as his father had voted for the death of Marie Antoinette's husband. The young man knew the value of an alliance with this family in securing his own position with the displaced Bourbon monarchy.

Though not a beauty, Marie Amélie was tall, thin, had a long neck, light hair, and blue eyes. Her teeth were irregular, but she carried herself with distinction and grace that won praise from those who saw her (Boigne 187-88). She also had a distinguished pedigree among the royal families of Europe. She descended from Louis XIV through the Spanish branch on her father's side and, of course, through Maria Theresa and the Habsburgs on her mother's side. Louis Philippe was aware of the advantage that such a marriage would be for him. In a letter to a friend, he admits that such an arrangement would never been possible if her family had not been driven from Naples by Napoleon's armies and found themselves under the protection of the British. Writing about his pending marriage with Marie Amélie, he recognized that "it would be difficult for me to make a marriage in any respect more advantageous to me. What a benefit it will be to me! What a slap at prejudice! What a means of reconciliation with the elder branch of my family, and of entering into close relations with the royal family of Austria! What an advantage for me to marry a Bourbon" (qtd. in Dyson 106). He believed his marriage would help temper the breach between the two branches of the French Bourbon family, which was created by his father's regicidal vote. It was the medieval notion of kinship rather than youth and fertility that motivated this marriage.

Louis Philippe was well aware of not only the dynastic advantages possessed by his wife but also the social and political ones as well: "for she had been trained by a mother who, whatever defects of character she may have had, was certainly a devoted and affectionate wife to an unfaithful husband, her inferior in mind and manners" (qtd. in Dyson 107). Marie Amélie also had other advantages that her mother did not. She was not an inexperienced child of fifteen when she first met her husband, but was twenty-six years old. He was thirty-five. She also had a say in bringing about this union. Unlike her mother, she had met her future spouse prior to the wedding, and she encouraged the courtship. She even threatened to become a Capuchin nun if her marriage to Louis Philippe had been denied by her parents. She believed that God had intervened in her life to help fulfill her destiny and that with the Duc d'Orleans she would find happiness (70).

With the restoration of the Bourbon government following the fall of Napoleon, the Duc d'Orleans returned to Paris to be received by King Louis XVIII. With her lineage, Marie Amélie was well received by the French royal court, more so than her husband, as the king never fully forgave him for his father's actions (Dyson 126). With Napoleon's return, the family fled to England where they lived for two years. Upon returning to France, the enlarging family, seven children by 1828, divided their time between their home in Paris and their estates at Neuilly. Marie Amélie was a devoted mother who wrote her children whenever they were apart—keeping Maria Theresa's tradition of providing detailed advice on fulfilling their duties and maintaining their religious obligations.

She also followed the counsel given to her mother by the Empress Maria Theresa. She was a religious woman, and she tried to live a virtuous life. She supported her husband in his every desire. She believed that every decision he made was the "Wisest, discreetest [sic], best" (qtd. in Boigne 191). So despite her numerous misgivings and extreme reluctance, when her husband accepted the French crown after the fall and exile of Louis XVIII's heir and brother Charles X, she accepted this change to their lives.

The wave of revolutions in 1830 that brought Louis Philippe to the throne of France also brought about the independence of Belgium from the Netherlands. A conference of the great powers, which met in London, offered the throne of the new country to Leopold of Saxe-Colburg-Gotha, who had strong ties from a previous marriage with Great Britain and the royal family. He needed a counterbalance to British support and turned to France. He married the oldest daughter of Marie Amélie and King Louis Philippe on 9 August 1832, and potentially gained a strong ally.

Louise-Marie and her mother wrote each other daily and often received multiple posts in a single day, given the closeness of their capitals. Although her mother's letters have been lost to posterity, they were full of instructions to her daughter regarding many of the issues established by Maria Theresa. Entering the marriage ignorant of all she needed to know, Louise-Marie thanked her mother constantly for her words of wisdom and guidance that were designed to help her succeed in her new role. Marie Amélie's advice clearly included descriptions of her own life experiences and obligations so that her daughter was aware of the shared responsibilities the two had as royal consorts. Their obligations as political spouses were clear.

Maria Theresa had advised her own daughter to not neglect her religious duties and to live a life above reproach. That counsel is echoed two generations later. Louise-Marie's piety is important for both herself and her mother, and she is reminded by her mother to find a chaplain and attend mass daily. This proved to be an issue between Leopold, who was a Lutheran, and his Catholic wife as Louise-Marie pointed out to her mother that her husband was a late sleeper, so the morning routine was often too late for early attendance at mass. When she revealed her mother's instructions to her husband in order to gain his awareness of her dilemma, Leopold burst out in laughter (d'Orléans). Torn between promises to her mother, her own piety, and her husband's lack of support, Louise-Marie followed her mother's, and by reflection her own, priorities; she found time to attend mass when her husband was working.

A week after her marriage, Marie-Louise wrote to her mother: "I cannot believe that I am a wife, the property of a man, that he loves me ... that I am finally married and all of my existence has changed" (d'Orléans). The notion of marriage had evolved since that of Maria Caroline, and although it was still a political union in which the wife entered into a publically submissive role, the expectation of love had entered into the dialogue between mothers and daughters and between daughters and their husbands. Empress Maria Theresa had counselled her daughters to use love or at least devotion as a tool to bind their husbands to them in order to strengthen their own position. By witnessing her own parents' devoted relationship, Louise-Marie viewed love not as a method of achieving power or control but as a normal part of a wedded life. Her expectations included love along with companionship and trust. She believed that with this intimate relationship, she would gain the essential political influence that was the fundamental reason for the union. She anticipated that she would soon love Leopold as greatly as he claimed to love her (d'Orléans). Though affectionate and attentive to her in the early months of her marriage, her husband did not include her in his confidence and often laughed at the suggestions that she made at the behest of her mother. He was not looking for the loving confidante envisioned by his wife; instead, he adhered to the more traditional aristocratic view. He recognized the political but less personal significance of this union, as he wrote to his niece, the future Queen Victoria, that that "she is a very great prize, which I highly value and cherish" (Victoria).

The difficulty of achieving this personal relationship, so desired by the queen, came to fruition almost a week later when Louise-Marie confessed that she felt no love for her husband and that the carnal side of the relationship was repulsive to her. Like her grandmother Maria Caroline, she acknowledged that these feelings were made worse, since she had to pretend that they did not exist. When her husband questioned her love, she was obligated to reassure him and submit to him completely as it was, in her words, his sacred right (d'Orléans). Yet unlike Maria Caroline, who revealed her feelings to a former governess and not to her parent from whom she would have received no sympathy, Louise-Marie shared her feelings with her mother. It is her one true heartfelt confession regarding her unhappiness and her abhorrence toward sexual relations and the more intimate side of marriage. Yet despite the generational difference between the mothers, Marie Amélie responded as the empress would have. These daughters did not have the luxury of finding aspects of their marriage distasteful as that union, for they had a clearly defined political purpose. The continuity of proven successful gender roles, especially in a political marriage, was essential. Instead of receiving the expected sympathy, Louise-Marie was reprimanded by her mother. The young queen's next letter begged for forgiveness for what she had previously shared and asked that the letter be burned (d'Orléans).

Louise-Marie reverted back to the advice given generations earlier: she must bind herself to her husband and subjugate her true feelings and pretense. She did the same with her mother as she spent the next few letters focusing on the growing closeness of her marital relationship, a deception intended to pacify her parent. For this sheltered woman, who had probably never actively deceived her mother, this was a small step toward developing her own separate identity and challenging the continuity of mother-daughter reflectivity. Yet she continued to rely on her mother's advice. It is after her confession of not loving her husband that Louise-Marie started to refer to the notion of duty, an idea that appeared to come from her mother: "all that is duty, and I consider it as such; all that can be agreeable to my husband costs me nothing and it will never cost me. I always thank you, dear Maman, for your good advice and do not hesitate using them to my profit" (d'Orléans). She must give the appearance of happiness and enjoying her spouse's good company.

Maria Theresa had instructed her daughter to never forget that she was a German. She must be a good representative of her people, demonstrating the characteristics for which Germans were known—kindness and honesty. She must also protect the people of her motherland and forever remember their interests (Habsburg, *Letters* 1766). Generations later, this was easy advice for Louise-Marie to follow as she never forgot that she was French and her loyalties and heart clearly remained with her own homeland as she adjusted to her new role. After months of living in Belgium, Louise-Marie made a personally revealing observation while commenting on an encounter with French troops. After they failed to recognize the splendor of a nearby Belgian chateau, she observed that the French never find anything beautiful that is not in their own country (d'Orléans). Initially, the young queen shared those feelings, finding it difficult to find anything in Belgium that met her approval. Her loyalty to France was clear as Louise-Marie kept her parents informed of key events. She shared information that she knew that Leopold did not intend to be given to her family or the French government (d'Orléans).

Louise-Marie's view of marriage and the growth of nationalism in the nineteenth century, however, ultimately challenged the accepted norms of a political marriage established by the empress. During her first few months of marriage, Belgium moved closer to war with Holland over the evacuation of the Dutch-held fort at Antwerp. After a visit to that city, Louise-Marie's sympathies started to shift to those of her husband and the Belgian people. Slowly as she started to manifest opinions that differed from her parents, she rebelled against the passive role that had been assigned to her. As an obedient daughter who had never challenged her parents' political ideas, this caused her some discomfort as she stated in one of her letters, "concerning politics of which I have abstained from speaking to you in detail these days, dear Mama. I'll say to you that in spite of my totally French ideas, it is impossible for me to have the same opinion that you and that my father have" (d'Orléans). She admitted this was difficult for her, and she had to put it off. But once admitted, she returned to the subject again.

She began to share her pro-Belgian sympathies privately with her mother but not to her father. Passages were clearly marked with the caveats that it was for her mother's eyes only or "just between us" (d'Orléans). Louise-Marie had started to see events from the Belgian viewpoint, although she would not relinquish the "Frenchness" of her ideas. As she asserted her own or, perhaps more accurately, her husband's point of view, the dynamics of the mother–daughter reflectively and the ideal marriage instructions were broken. Asserting her individuality, Louise-Marie wanted her mother's advice, which she may or may not take. Louise-Marie even started to give her mother advice, especially with regards to the marriage of her younger sister. The mother-daughter dialogue slowly became one between equals rather than one of reflectivity.

Louise-Marie fulfilled her obligations by providing an heir and maintaining the public façade of happy wife. Her presence guaranteed goodwill between France and Belgium. Through it all, her relationship with her mother remained her lifeline, and she died in the arms of her mother on 11 October 1850.

She was survived by three children. Her only daughter, Charlotte, was born in 1840 and was only ten years old when her mother died. She would never receive the advice she needed from her mother. Charlotte married her second cousin, Archduke Maximillian of Austria, who would later become the ill-fated Emperor of Mexico. Yet the tradition of letter writing and advice continued, but in this case, it was from a grandmother, Marie Amelie, who was living in Claremont, England, who gave Charlotte advice on being the wife of the ruler of Mexico. Following the young empress's life in the newspaper and from their correspondence, the former queen of the French offered gentle reproaches on behaviour that she thought conflicted with the duties of the wife of a ruler. She reminded her granddaughter not to upstage her husband and warned her of dangerous displays of vanity. After a failed tenure as ruler, Maximilian was executed on 19 June 1867. Charlotte would die in Belgium in 1927, still mourning her husband's death and suffering from mental distress.

Although these women's fate to marry for political exigency was determined at birth, it appears that their training was ignored while under their mothers' direct care. Whether motivated to keep their daughters pure in thought or, perhaps an unwillingness to come to terms with their children's destiny, these mothers waited until after the wedding to properly prepare their daughters for their new life. Removed from their mothers' household, the daughters could only write them. There is an evolution in the letter writing, as the correspondence from Maria Theresa to her offspring is more authoritative, providing instructions to be followed. The letters written two generations later are more personal in nature and provide more guidance. For the Empress Maria Theresa, marriage was political; her daughter had forward her mother's (and the empire's) interests. But by the nineteenth century, the interest of state was tempered by the interest of her new husband and a new personal ideal of marriage. The advice from her mother softened to one of advisor, mentor, or kindred spirit, although the political function of the marriage was still recognized by both the mother and daughter. Still, the core values as established generations earlier remained the same: the dynamics of the politically arranged marriage had not changed.

The women examined in this study had their fate determined to them almost at birth. Their marriages would solidify dynastic and political alliances. The young participant played no role in determining who her partner would be. The advice from mother to daughter attempted not to question the existing political and patriarchal system but to instead find a way to achieve comfort if not success within the marriage and at the royal court. Empowerment for these women, the daughters, came from their relationship with their new spouse and acceptance by the nobility around them. An examination of their letters shows that these young women did not passively shift from their mother's to their spouse's home but sought to find ways gain as much personal power and satisfaction as possible.

Epistolary studies have always existed especially in relationship to women. Yet recently, correspondence between women has begun to be examined as more than a social intercourse. Traditionally, letters have been scrutinized to gain access to behind the scenes cultural and societal relations, but an examination of these works can also provide a gendered view of politics. This chapter has reviewed the letters written between mothers and daughters, queens to daughters. And although the advice remained fairly unchanged, as the focus was the daughter's political and not emotional success, the method did change over the decades, softening from authoritative to motherly.

ENDNOTE

[1] All translations from the d'Orléans, Louise-Marie d'Orléans were provided by Dr. John W. Rooney.

WORKS CITED

Primary Sources

d'Orléans, Louise-Marie. *Letters to her Mother*. August-December 1832, Fonds Leopold I. Archives Royales, Bruxelles, Belgium. Manuscript.

Published Memoirs and Correspondence:

Habsburg, Maria Theresa. *Letters of an Empress; A Collection of Intimate letters from Maria Theresa to Her Children and Friends*. Edited by G. Pusch. Translated by Eileen R. Taylor, Massie Publishing Company, 1939.
Victoria, Queen. *The Project Gutenberg EBook of the Letters of Queen Victoria. (1837-1843)*, www.gutenberg.org/ebooks/20023?msg=welcome_stranger#pagei. Accessed 28 May 2016.

Secondary Sources

Bland, Caroline, and Máire Cross. "Gender Politics: Breathing New Life into Old Letters." *Gender and Politics in the Age of Letter-Writing, 1750-2000*, edited by Caroline Bland and Máire Cross, Ashgate Publishing Limited, 2004, pp. 3-14.
Davis, Natalie Zemon. Introduction. Duby, Georges. *The Knight, the Lady and the Priest; the Making of Modern Marriage in Medieval France*, by Georges Duby. Translated by Barbara Bray.

Pantheon Books, 1983, pp. vii-xiii.

Duby, Georges. *The Knight, the Lady and the Priest; the Making of Modern Marriage in Medieval France.* Translated by Barbara Bray, Pantheon Books, 1983. Print.

Dyson, C. C. *The Life of Marie Amélie, Last Queen of the French, 1782-1866.* D. Appleton and Company, 1910.

Earle, Rebecca. "Introduction: Letters, Writers and the Historian." *Epistolary Selves: Letters and Letter-Writers, 1600-1945,* edited by Rebecca Earle, Ashgate Publishing, 1999, pp. 2-14.

Jensen, Katharine Ann. *Uneasy Possessions: The Mother-Daughter Dilemma in French Writings, 1671-1928.* University of Delaware Press, 2011.

Pick, Robert. *Empress Maria Theresa: The Earlier Years, 1717-1757.* Harper and Row, 1966.

6.
Motherliness and Women's Emancipation in the Published Articles of Ika Freudenberg

A Discursive Approach

MIRJAM HÖFNER

"THE MOTHER HAS TO CARE for her children, she has to bring them up, and in the evening she's glad if she can relax. But years later there will be leisure hours, and then there will come an uneasy feeling of having been restricted, of being untaught, of never having participated in something big and meaningful" (Freudenberg, "Was Heißt" 15).[1] This quotation is hardly a moderate statement in a context in which binary gender norms valorize maternity as the chief task for women. It devalues the ideal type of bourgeois woman at the turn of the twentieth century—her motherhood. By soberly reducing the merit of maternity into a few years of hard work without satisfying benefit, Ika Freudenberg (1858-1912) got to the core of one of the most controversial topics of the first-wave women's movement in Wilhelmine Germany (Allen 1-2). Instead of emotionally propagating motherhood as it was custom of the so-called moderate feminists, she branded the bourgeois ideal of women as worthless in contrast to "something big and meaningful." For childless Freudenberg, who pioneered the Bavarian women's movement during the peak of the German feminist movement previous to the Great War (Schmittner 149), motherhood and domestic care were not enough for a good life. Women needed to be freed from the constrictions of both home and an illiterate mind. But how did the intellectual "leader of the Bavarian women's movement" (Bäumer, *Gestalt und Wandel* 405) propagate her position within the moderate bourgeois feminist community? How did she try to convince her female contemporaries, who had grown up with the patriarchal discourse of motherhood as the only desirable achievement for women, to participate in feminist concerns?

This chapter is about the published articles of Ika Freudenberg, and it highlights the discursive links she drew between the social and political function of women—or rather mothers—care work, and women's emancipation. I argue that Freudenberg prominently used the concept of "motherliness" as a discursive strategy in order to reach her main objective of women's emancipation. This feminist concept, rooted in the "intellectual and social origins of 19th century feminism" (Allen 17), differentiates between motherhood, the biological fact of having children, and motherliness. By turning traditional maternal values such as nurture and compassion into a feminist "model of empowerment," the concept of motherliness presents an idea of "public motherhood," which is not linked to the biological motherhood (Allen 1-2). For Freudenberg, the notion of motherliness lent itself well to link feminist questions to broader political and social discourses. She thus deployed it in a pragmatic, emotionalized, and pedagogical manner, as my exemplary discursive analysis, following the literary method of close reading, will show below (Richards; Empson; Wenzel). Although this reading method has been developed in order to analyze poetics, it is a useful practice of interpretation to reveal subtexts (Volkmann 196). Additionally, this qualitative analysis is based on the three-level-scheme of the public sphere by Elisabeth Klaus (*Kommunikationswissenschaftliche* 2nd.), which is described later.

My chapter begins with a short biographical sketch of Ika Freudenberg, emphasizing her impact on the Bavarian women's movement against the background of the Munich social climate. Second, I offer some introductory words on the theoretical framing of this chapter— the concept of motherliness, the terminology used, and the employed method. In this little case study, I focus on the concept of motherliness merely in the context of the bourgeois first wave of the German women's movement. The third and last section provides the discourse analysis of Freudenberg's writings.

Given the impact of Ika Freudenberg on the Bavarian women's movement of her time, it is surprising to note that there has not been any academic research on her person or on her life's work yet. Apart from a dissertation by Monika Schmittner, which dedicates one chapter to Freudenberg's contribution to the Bavarian women's movement, she is hardly mentioned in the historiography (Bäumer, *Gestalt und Wandel*; Bäumer, *Lebens wie der Liebe*; Heuss; Kinnebrock; Panzer and Plößl; Schaser). Although this chapter does not aim to reconstruct Freudenberg's life—which is part of my ongoing research[2]—it offers, I hope, a little step on the way out of oblivion for this formerly famous feminist.

Ika Freudenberg (1858-1912) played a significant propagandistic role for the question of women's rights ("Frauenfrage" 38-42) in the Bavarian Kingdom. She was born in 1858 as Friederike Freudenberg in Raubach (Koblenz) as the fifth of seven children of Caroline Freudenberg, née Bernhardt (1817-1893), and Johann Philipp Freudenberg (1803-1890), who made his fortune in iron manufacturing (Renkhoff 206). She thus grew up in an upper-middle-class family and was nurtured within contemporary bourgeois values. Furthermore, she was an interested autodidact in literature and philosophy and studied classical piano at several conservatories (Schmittner 149). Over a few years Freudenberg cared for an incurably ill friend until she died, which might be interpreted as the beginning of her feminist awareness in matters of care and female professions (Bäumer, *Gestalt und Wandel* 402, 405).

The actual beginning of Ika Freudenberg's bourgeois feminist career was her move to Munich, where she got acquainted with Anita Augspurg (1857-1943), one of the so-called radical feminists, and her life partner Sophia Goudstikker (1865-1924), photographer and co-owner of the photographic studio "Elvira" (Dünnebier and Scheu 23-24). Augspurg and Goudstikker were the opalescent couple of Bohemian Munich, and their photographic work was applauded even in aristocratic society (Henke 28). Together with these two well-networked feminists and a few interested intellectual women and men Freudenberg co-founded in 1894 the "Society for the Advancement of Moral Interests of Women" ("*Gesellschaft zur Förderung der geistigen Interessen der Frau*"), which was renamed into the "Association for Women's Interest" ("*Verein für Fraueninteressen*," hereafter VfF) in 1899 (Volland 38).

Without any family obligations—Freudenberg was not married, and her parents died in the early 1890s—she acquired her prominent leading role by being the co-founder and long-standing chairwoman of both the fast growing and still existing association of moderate feminists in Munich, the aforementioned VfF, and the regional Bavarian association of women's movement, the "Main Federation of Bavarian Women's Association" ("*Hauptverband Bayerischer Frauenvereine*," established in 1909) (Schmittner 158). Furthermore, in 1899, Freudenberg implemented the well-attended annual "Bavarian Women's Day." As a member of its executive board since 1898, she was in regular and close contact with the "Federation of German Women's Associations" ("*Bund deutscher Frauenvereine*," hereafter BDF), the German feminist umbrella organization (Schmittner 159). She held all of her offices until she died of cancer in 1912 at the age of fifty-eight (Freund). With impressive commitment Ika Freudenberg launched the organized women's movement in the predominantly Catholic, conservative, and rural Bavarian Kingdom.

At the turn of the century, Munich was characterized by contradictions. On the one hand, the capital of the Bavarian Kingdom was said to be "the leading German City of Art" (Kinnebrock 112). The various concepts of modern literature, summarized under the term "fin de siècle," testify to a society "on the move" (Günther 23)—especially the predominantly male Munich naturalists, who initiated a programmatic literary renewal on the basis of bourgeois critical themes (Fähnders 17). Interestingly, contemporary well-educated writing women had great success adopting these new writing styles, as for example Helene Böhlau (1856-1940). Böhlau as well as other famous authors such Gabriele Reuter (1859-1941) were members of the 1894 founded "Society," headed by Freudenberg (Kinnebrock 112-14). Their widely circulated prose put the misogynist social circumstances of the time up for public discussion (Tebben 10-11): Helene Böhlau, for example, drafts the protagonist's mother in her novel "Halbtier" (1899) as "mysterious animal" and a half-human being (Böhlau 36). However, these artistic circles of "free spirits" had a lively exchange with the Munich women's movement (Kinnebrock 112, 115).

On the other hand, the majority of the Munich's bourgeois society and Bavaria's legislation were predominantly conservative (Kinnebrock 112; Schmittner 62). For this reason, it was not easy to establish feminist associations. As early as in 1891, three years before the foundation of Freudenberg's "Society," the Weimar "Association for Women's Education Reform" ("*Verein Frauenbildungsreform*"), which promoted "gainful employment for young women of the educated class" (Kinnebrock 121-22), opened a Munich local branch directed by the radical feminist Anita Augspurg. In 1893, Augspurg's local group came into conflict with the Bavarian royal police department, which was enforcing the law strictly: since 1850, Article 15 of the Bavarian Law on Associations excluded women from participating in political activities (Kinnebrock 122). In 1898, the law was amended for the benefit of women of full legal age, but it still took ten years before this misogynist Article 15 was finally abandoned in 1908, when the new Association Act, the "*Reichsvereinsgesetz*", took effect across the Reich and women were accepted into political associations (Schmittner 64-65). In this context, and considering the conflict between Augspurg's feminist local group and the Bavarian royal police, a feminist project with a moderate face appeared opportune. In 1894, the seemingly apolitical, harmlessly labelled "Society" started to promulgate its "ideas of the women's movement to a widest possible public" (Schmittner 142).

The contemporary bourgeois society was imbued with patriarchal gender ideals which were rooted in intellectual discourses from the eighteenth and nineteenth century (Rousseau; Schopenhauer). In times of upheaval, unsettled by the rapid technical progress since the beginning of the Industrial Revolution, leading intellectuals answered the aforementioned early feminist writings and sought to prove the validity of the patriarchal ideal of womanhood through psychological, scientific, and medical writings (Ferrero and Lombroso; Moebius; Weininger). These writings drew the picture of a passive, caring, apolitical woman, whose human qualities rested upon maternity, the presupposed female "biological and natural profession" in that time (Zahn 593). In contrast, every cultural progress was attributed exclusively to men, who were supposed to be equipped with a rational and intelligent character. This dichotomous gender relation concept determined the contemporary bourgeois as well as proletarian lifestyle (Budde; Schraut), which could be summed up as follows:

whereas decisive men made politics in public, women had to manage all the reproductive work at home, and abandon any claim for an individual lifestyle.

At the latest since the second half of the nineteenth century, a crucial feminist idea in Germany—as well as in other Western countries—was to modify the patriarchal concept of gender difference in order to expand women's participation in national politics and public life (Stoehr). The moderate feminists under the leadership of Helene Lange (1848-1930) postulated a modified conception of femininity: all women were motherly beings furnished with love, morality, and an internalized duty for care, even if they were not biological mothers. In keeping with their more remote objective of equal rights, the moderates worked at redefining the patriarchal gender difference by detaching typical female values from physical maternity (Schaser 99). In this way, they turned the patriarchal difference into the prime feminist version of gender difference (Meyer 121). Affirming the dichotomy of male and female qualities, they insisted on society's urgent need of a female influence to complete the "organic nation," which required to be nurtured by an equivalent male and female impact. The important word here was "motherliness" (Stoehr).

The concept of motherliness can be interpreted as a specific female policy that aims at changing the patriarchal order while holding on to the traditional assumption of gender difference (Stoehr 227; Schröder 15-16). Historicizing female living conditions, motherliness allowed public discussion on initially private issues. As such, the notion of motherliness enabled feminists to politicize the traditional female sphere: on the one hand, they could emphasize the previous significant cultural influence women had already had, and on the other hand, they could assert the social necessity for women to now also gain public, or rather political influence (Stoehr 226). For the moderate feminists who shaped the term of motherliness, women's emancipation was closely linked to a specific code of behavior that complied with what they called the "real female being" (Hege 12). Accordingly, they propagated strictly defined female tasks in the public fields of girls' education, common welfare, or even peace work (Freudenberg, "Moderne Sittlichkeitsprobleme," *Frauenbewegung*) in order to realize the aspired "organic cultural state" (Freudenberg, "Moderne Sittlich-keitsprobleme," *Die Frau* 72).

Yet many radical bourgeois or socialist feminists of the time, as well as of today, considered the strategy of motherliness as conservative, reactionary, and unsuitable to obtain real emancipation (Stoehr 225). For some of the opposing radical feminists it was important to underline that men and women were equal social beings without special male or female attributes. They rejected the concept as too closely linked with patriarchal traditions and defended women's rights as justified by natural law (Dohm, *Was die Pastoren*; *Wissenschaftliche Emancipation*).

As a matter of fact, the strategy of motherliness used by the bourgeois feminists proved to be sustainable. The feminists launched countless women's social associations, social women's schools, and teaching institutes of social work in order to prepare girls and women for their specific female social obligations. During the organized peak of the German women's movement in the years between 1890 and 1914, the bourgeois feminists and their rationale of motherliness paved the way for later female professions in the social sectors as well as female political participation in municipal welfare (Braches-Chyrek; Kuhlmann; Sachße). So did Ika Freudenberg. Under her leadership, in keeping with the concept of motherliness, the self-proclaimed "pioneer of professional care work," the VfF, created departments that took over tasks in the various fields of social care (Elferich 27). These were the precursors of the Munich Social Women's School (Hege 42).

As shown, Freudenberg dedicated her life to the question of women's rights. This "women's question" asked for "the positioning of women in the social organism" ("Frauenfrage" 38), so it was, from a feminist perspective, "the most important question" at the time (Klaus and Wischermann 111). Demanding equal status, the bourgeois feminists—the moderates as well as the radicals—saw their chance in solving the question by petitioning for educational reforms, by bundling interests and networking, and by establishing a variety of women's associations at the turn of the century ("Frauenfrage," Meyers 38-42).

Indeed, the original term "bourgeois feminism" was a polemical term used by former socialist feminists. It did not strictly describe the social background of the activists who were part of it. But in accordance with Kristina Schulz, I adhere to the expression "bourgeois" in terms of a "cognitive orientation" having effect on contemporary feminist group membership (Schulz 656). Thus, mainly women of the lower and upper middle class but also a few feminists of proletarian as well as of noble birth fought for the bourgeois feminist ideal of women's emancipation, which was represented in the concept of motherliness at the turn of the century.

Similar considerations apply to the distinction of "moderate" versus "radical" bourgeois feminism. In historical reality, the opposition between radical and moderate feminists was not as strong as purported by historiography (Greven-Aschoff; Gerhard; Schaser 15; Schröder; Wolff). Nevertheless, the contemporary labels were not merely constructed by the disputing intellectual leaders of the particular feminist branches (Freudenberg, *Visier auf!* 89). For instance, the moderates as well as the radicals sought full gender equality, but the radicals focused more on changing the political and juridical status quo, whereas the moderates spoke of an overarching cultural change without emphasizing women's vote. Furthermore, the relationship to the socialist women's movement separated the bourgeois feminist: whereas the radicals sought an alliance with the socialist feminists, the moderates refused any kind of cooperation (Kinnebrock 144-45). And even if moderate Freudenberg sympathized with radical thoughts, the simplified distinction helps understand the different tendencies of sociopolitical activism within the women's movement—ranging from the radical claim of instantaneously implementing full gender equality to the moderate way of step-by-step emancipation as it was pursued in the concept of motherliness (Stoehr 238-39).

As mentioned above, my analysis of the women's movement articles of Freudenberg is based on the three-level-scheme of the public sphere by Elisabeth Klaus, supplemented by the method of close reading. With reference to Jürgen Habermas, Nancy Fraser, and John Gastil, Klaus defines the public sphere as "a process by which society negotiates its values and rules" (Klaus and Wischermann 103, 105-06). Briefly summarized, she distinguishes three levels of public discourse: the "simple level" of everyday communication between individuals, the "medium level" of social movement communication, and finally the "complex communication" within parliaments or even mass media (Klaus, *Kommunikationswissenschaftliche*, 1st ed., 71-72). Following this three-level-scheme, my analysis focuses on those writings that Freudenberg published in the "medium public sphere" (*"mittlere* Öffentlichkeit"), those within the women's movement community.

In several articles, Freudenberg covered a broad range of issues concerning "general women's interests" ("Zum Sechsten" 55). Mainly speaking of the development and constitution of the women's movement, she made (liberal) politics, women's work, as well as art a subject of discussion, but never losing sight of her main topic: the evaluation of the relationship between women and culture. The special feature of this "medium level" is the mutual effect of association communication (Klaus, *Kommunikationswissenschaftliche*, 1st ed., 71). Serving, on the one hand, for information exchange and consensus building within the movement community, the discourse of the medium sphere can, on the other hand, be brought up and used by the "complex communication level" (Klaus and Wischermann 111). Thus, it has a significant influence on both public opinion and policymakers. But according to the guiding questions regarding her discourse strategy for convincing her female contemporaries of participating in feminist concerns, I choose to concentrate on revealing Freudenberg's argumentation lines, which she used within the movement community. The following questions are of major interest (cf. Bruns 191): how did Ika Freudenberg introduce and link the selected topics published in women's emancipation journals? What does this reveal about her discourse strategy to push her feminist agenda into political and public life?

The selected articles are taken from various periodicals of the feminist public sphere. Ika Freudenberg published in *Die Frau. Monatsschrift für das gesamte Frauenleben unserer Zeit* (1893-1943), edited by Helene Lange (1848-1930)—at that time, the supraregional referee of the German bourgeois women's movement press, mainly addressing educated and wealthy women (Stange-Fayos 12, 28) —and in the *Centralblatt des Bundes deutscher Frauenvereine* (1899-1913), renamed *Die Frauenfrage* (1913-1921), the nationwide organ of the moderate bourgeois BDF. Furthermore, the analysis includes her writings in *Frauenstreben* (1908-1918), the journal of the "Main Federation of Bavarian Women's Association" as well as printed versions of her lectures, which Freudenberg held within the movement community.

The main themes I discovered in Freudenberg's writings are the following: first, the historicization of cultural progress; second, the necessity to raise women's sense of social responsibility and community support; third, the importance of informing women about female rights and obligations in order to improve society, the nation, and even mankind; and fourth, the need as well as the benefit of women's intellectual education in conjunction with a professionalization of care work to counteract "private dilettantism." I address these themes looking in detail at her wordings concerning motherhood, motherliness, and mothers in political and public life.

The crucial basis as well as common theme of her writings was the historicization of female spheres. Freudenberg used every opportunity to link contemporary female experiences with a postulated teleological cultural evolution. In "How the Women's Movement Occurred" ("*Frauenbewegung Entstanden*"), she evoked the past when public social life was determined by "physical violence," as it was consistently regulated by strong men while women had been "naturally" assigned to the private sphere ("Frauenbewegung Entstanden" 5). With reference to the book *Women's Rights in the German Reich* (1876) by German pioneer feminist Louise Otto-Peters (1819-1895), Freudenberg constructed a living women's past: she spoke about earlier forms of housekeeping, which had been rich of fulfilling activities ("Frauenbewegung Entstanden" 10-12). In the next step, she compared this lively past with the prevailing emptiness in female life at the turn of the century. She described the progressive reduction of domestic work, which stemmed from the technological innovations of the Industrial Revolution ("Frauenbewegung Entstanden" 13).

Similarly, Freudenberg emphasized the "immense" but "invisible contribution" to cultural evolution of mothers by being "housekeeper, caregiver and teacher of mankind" ("Weshalb Wendet" 582). Against this backdrop, Freudenberg asked herself why the mother as "respected person beloved by all" was still politically immature ("Weshalb Wendet" 582). One possible explanation for her was that the hard work of running the household did not leave any historical traces because every mother's life work in the private family context disappeared with her, whereas men's visible, historical achievements remained after their disappearance ("Weshalb Wendet" 582).

Furthermore, Freudenberg referred to cultural history in order to condemn female dependence, which led to the undesirable situation that the man needed to be constantly concerned about his "unsteady wife with the unprotected children" ("Moderne Sittlichkeitsprobleme," *Die Frau*, 77). Contrary to this, she suggested that marriage be based on an equal relationship as a logical consequence of the achievements of civilization ("Moderne Sittlichkeitsprobleme," *Die Frau*, 77).

This kind of simplified narrative allows for various lines of interpretation. First of all, Ika Freudenberg made female spheres visible, thus revalorizing the female impact on cultural progress so far neglected by other historians and, moreover, raising consciousness concerning their own improvable position in society at that time. Thereby, the Bavarian women's movement leader construed women as both victims and agents of historical circumstances. Using plain language, Freudenberg provided a basis for women's solidarity within the "medium sphere" of the women's movement.

Secondly, Freudenberg's writings underline the necessity to raise women's public spirit. For her, solidarity amongst women as well as consciousness of the needs of common welfare was the preconditions to social change. In "The Woman as Employer" (*"Frau als Arbeitgeberin"*), she problematized the harshness of female employers toward their same-sex employees, which resulted from the missing sense of female community ("Frau als Arbeitgeberin" 148). In doing so, she rendered women into active beings and characterized the political and social emancipation of women as an active struggle for getting back former rights that had been taken away in the process of cultural progress ("Frau als Arbeitgeberin" 148).

One of these was the right to motherhood. Indeed, Ika Freudenberg often mentioned the joy of maternity, but she rejected maternity at all costs. Quoting the "maternal song of songs" from Helene Böhlau's novel "Halbtier" ("Moderne Sittlichkeitsprobleme," *Die Frau*, 76), Freudenberg advised caution when propagating "a child and employment" as the only key to women's happiness: Taking the artistic statement literally, as the radical feminist group around Helene Stöcker (1869-1943) did at the time, would not be the adequate way of female being. Mothers "would work themselves to death" (Freudenberg, "Moderne Sittlichkeitsprobleme," *Die Frau*, 76). Without a doubt, Freudenberg was in line with the bourgeois women's movement that propagated heterosexual marriage as a prerequisite for having children. But it was important to her that this marriage benefitted from two equivalent—but never equal ("Weshalb Wendet" 8)—male and female beings. For her, motherly care was "the only possible response" to counteract the "unifying tendencies of the masses" at the time ("Moderne Sittlichkeitsprobleme," *Die Frau*, 77). As such, she emphasized women's obligation to participate in national concerns in order to contribute to the social betterment of mankind ("Goethe-Bund" 18). Insisting on active verbal protest, Freudenberg requested consciousness concerning both women's solidarity as a precondition for feminist agency as well as "the bigger social women's tasks" ("Erste Kellnerinnenverein" 3; "Goethe-Bund" 17; "Moderne Sittlichkeitsprobleme" [*Frauenbewegung*] 4; Freudenberg and Stritt 8).

Third, Freudenberg emphasized the importance of informing women about their rights and obligations to strive for a better national society by using the topic of care—one of the constitutional factors in the ideal of womanhood justified by the female capacity of childbearing. The discourse of care provided several points of contact between the discourse of the contemporary social and national question as well as the discourse of femininity within the patriarchal difference concept: the perfect discursive link between two so apparently dichotomous discursive fields. First of all, Freudenberg addressed society's needs and demonstrated possibilities for women to become an active part in the public sphere. For example, she emotionally described the obligation of motherly love, which was thought as the purest emotion of mankind, to help every child in society, not only one's own ("Was Heißt" 15). Second, she declared this behavior resulting from the discursively fixed emotional caring female being, on the one hand, as the moral and social obligation of every woman, and, on the other hand, in a combative manner, as a means of getting women's civil rights ("Frauenbewegung Entstanden" 16). As such, Freudenberg called the female legal guardian "the most motherly public post" ("Der Anfang" 102), which could be held by women. The local poor relief would prove to be the key to extend the traditionally female domestic scope, which would be predestinated for the mother—notably the motherliness in every woman—at least, if she was taught to recognize it as well as to practice it professionally.

Last but not least, Freudenberg sought to counteract "private dilettantism." Unfortunately, in Freudenberg's view, women were merely taught by the family and often still followed their instinctive urge to care. For her, who was aspiring for a mankind consisting of equal, sophisticated—and considering her focus on "national greatness," white, Western, and Christian ("Goethe-Bund" 17-18)—people, this was a disastrous situation. She propagated the "fully intellectual equality of men and women" in a quite radical manner ("Goethe-Bund" 18; "Frauenbewegung Entstanden" 22). The intellectual leader of the Bavarian women's movement prepared the discursive ground for girls' and women's educational establishments, explaining compellingly that "everything must be learned, even social care work" (Freudenberg, "Frauenbewegung Entstanden" 15).

Appealing to the feminist youth in particular, Freudenberg tried to reassess the patriarchal ideal of motherhood in a more realistic manner. Mentioning the "boring" everyday life and the "pettiness" of the traditional women's fortune ("Frauenbewegung Entstanden" 30), she promised the "intellectual and mental women's grow- ing" as the "most beautiful outcome" of female social care work ("Frauenbewegung Entstanden" 23). In a quite maternal manner, she admonished the female youth of "wasting" their precious time in order to prevent a later "bitter feeling" of merely having moved within "narrow bounds" ("Was Heißt" 15). Yet she did not want to be "misunderstood": the compliance of the motherly obliga- tions was beyond all question to "avoid contracting moral debts" (Freudenberg, *Ein Wort* 21). For her, motherhood and caring merely inside of one's own family meant rather a "temporary renunciation" than a life fulfillment (Freudenberg, *Ein Wort* 21). Thus, she revealed where women's power lies, and the necessary impact of female love and care on the—teleological interpreted—"ongoing path of future mankind" ("Frau als Arbeitgeberin" 156).

The question of how Ika Freudenberg linked the discourse topics of motherhood, care work and women's emancipation, is not limited to the level of content. Therefore, I wish to provide some insight on her narrative style as well, which was one of a well-educated, rational, emotional, and motivating speaker. Initially, Freudenberg liked the use of great metaphors. For example, she compared the development of the women's movement with the genesis of a big river, which developed from a tiny source, nurtured by "thousands of visible and invisible trickles" into a "real stream of running water" ("Frauenbewegung Entstanden" 3). Or she described the women's movement in military words: the women's associations could be interpreted as a number of regiments of the same arm, and all municipal and rural associations together would build an army, which consisted of different corps, unified by manoeuvring within the same battlespace ("Gruppenbildung" 58). These big pictures addressed her audience on an emotional level and conveyed the feeling of participating in "something big and meaningful" ("Was Heißt" 15). Freudenberg's technique of using rhetorical questions served as a reassuring complement by anticipating a possible precariousness, which could be triggered by unknown consequences of the women's movement efforts. She picked it up in her question-and-answer game, integrating it in bigger contexts and providing a guideline of possible activities in the women's agenda, as in, for example: "Now you will ask me, what shall we do to fulfill the hopes that are pinned on us? Well, let me tell you: Get capable workers! For our movement is based on the belief in the capability of a woman" ("Weshalb Wendet" 8).

Furthermore, Freudenberg regulated her audience in a maternal and an educational manner. She spoke in an exhorting as well as in a motivating manner, always oscillating between the emotional and rational level. Thus, she used various adverbs and adjectives, which sometimes appeared almost a little bit elevated, claiming, for example, the "women's fight as much more important for our national prosperity" than that of men ("Goethe-Bund" 18). Using an inclusive "we" underlined her desire for raising female public spirit on the linguistic level. For example, she emphasized that "verbal and written propaganda" was "the only accepted way of direct means in order to enforce our efforts and to realize our principles for now" (Freudenberg and Stritt 18). In contrast, she used the opposing "them," creating two linguistically entities of "us" versus "them" or "the others," which supported the audience regulation in a more or less subtle way.

Finally, I want to return to the first question in the introductory part of this chapter: how did Ika Freudenberg convince the public community to pursue the feminist agency? Thorough scrutinizing her articles, it becomes apparent that the sophisticated Bavarian women's movement leader propagated her feminist objective on two different levels: on the content level by realizing the discursive concept of motherliness, and on the linguistic level, where she established herself as a sophisticated speaker with a great awareness for human and, in particular, female interests. For my analysis, the three-level-scheme of Elisabeth Klaus, supplemented by the method of close reading, revealed itself as an appropriate means. The concept of the "medium sphere" provided the scrutinizing of the theoretical communication structures, and finally, offered to disclose the two-level discourse strategy of motherliness, realized by Freudenberg within the movement's public. Covering the consensus-building communication in an emotional as well as in a pragmatic manner, and integrating female emancipation in the discourse of a society's needs, pioneered on a discursive level professional social care work, which will be proved in later research.

As shown, Freudenberg's idea of women's emancipation kept in line with the propagated ideals of the German moderate women's movement. Adhering to the dichotomous gender ideal in the modified version, she emphasized the necessity of female national impact. Regarding her view on the mother's role, Freudenberg challenged the superhuman ideal and tried to draft a more realistic picture of motherhood. Indeed, she did not propose a detailed social program with concrete political measures in order to realize gender equality. But by turning the motherly role from passive to active, she emphasized the crucial impact of mothers on mankind as caregivers and teachers. Paired with her sophisticated manner and considering the fast-growing women's associations under her leadership, Freudenberg's strategy of propagating the women's question proved successful even in conservative Bavaria.

Based on methods of literary and communication science, this first discursive historical approach on Freudenberg's articles provided insights into the bourgeois women's emancipatory means to reach their goal of widening the female participation in the political and public sphere. For me, in the end, Ika Freudenberg represents—at least within the women's movement community—the propagated ideal of motherliness, so I am tempted to call her "the maternal voice" of the Bavarian movement.

ENDNOTES

[1] I would like to thank Marie Muschalek, PhD, for her help in translating the quotations in this chapter and editing it linguistically.
[2] My project "Mothers for Nation" focuses on the discursive link between care work and women's social and political participation at the beginning of the twentieth century (1890-1918) and in the aftermath of the Second World War (1945-1960).

WORKS CITED

Allen, Ann Taylor. *Feminism and Motherhood in Germany, 1800-1914*. New Brunswick: Rutgers University Press, 1991.

Bäumer, Gertrud. *Gestalt und Wandel: Frauenbildnisse*. Herbig, 1939.

Bäumer, Gertrud. *Des Lebens wie der Liebe Band: Briefe*, edited by Emmy Beckmann. Wunderlich, 1956.

Böhlau, Helene. *Halbtier!*. F. Fontane & C., 1899.

Braches-Chyrek, Rita. *Jane Addams, Mary Richmond und Alice Salomon: Professionalisierung und Disziplinbildung Sozialer Arbeit*. Budrich, 2013.

Bruns, Claudia. "Wissen—Macht—Subjekt(e): Dimensionen historischer Diskursanalyse am Beispiel des Männerbunddiskurses im Wilhelminischen Kaiserreich." *Historische Diskursanalysen: Genealogie, Theorie, Anwendungen*, edited by Franz Eder, VS

Verlag für Sozialwissenschaften, 2006, pp. 189-203.

Budde, Gunilla. *Blütezeit des Bürgertums:* Bürgerlichkeit im 19. *Jahrhundert.* WBG, 2009.

Dohm, Hedwig. *Die wissenschaftliche Emancipation der Frau.* Wedekind and Schwieger, 1874.

Dohm, Hedwig. *Was die Pastoren von den Frauen denken.* Verlag Reinhold Schlingmann, 1872.

Dünnebier, Anne, and Ursula Scheu. *Die Rebellion ist eine Frau: Anita Augspurg und Lida G. Heymann, das schillerndste Paar der Frauenbewegung.* Hugendubel, 2002.

Elferich, Christa. "Aus dem Vereinsarchiv: Frauenpolitisches und soziales Engagement im Verein für Fraueninteressen 1894-1909." *Jahresbericht Verein für Fraueninteressen,* Compotext, 2009, pp. 27-28.

Empson, William. *Seven Types of Ambiguity.* Chatto and Windus, 3rd ed. 1956.

Fähnders, Walter. *Avantgarde und Moderne 1890–933: Lehrbuch Germanistik.* J.B. Metzler, 2010.

Ferrero, Guglielmo, and Cesare Lombroso. *Das Weib als Verbrecherin und Prostituirte: Anthoropologische Studien, gegründet auf eine Darstellung der Biologie und Psychologie des normalen Weibes.* Verlagsanstalt und Druckerei A.G., 1894. *Internet Archive,* 19 July 2009, archive.org/details/dasweibalsverbr00kure-goog. Accessed 9 Oct. 2015.

Fraser, Nancy. *Die halbierte Gerechtigkeit: Schlüsselbegriffe des postindustriellen Sozialstaats.* Suhrkamp, 2001.

"Frauenfrage." *Meyers Großes Konversationslexikon: Ein Nachschlagewerk des allgemeinen Wissens.* 6th ed., vol. 7, Bibliographisches Institut, 1908, pp. 38-42.

Freudenberg, Ika. "Der Anfang einer sozialen Frauenschule in München." *Frauenstreben. Veröffentlichungsorgan des Hauptverbandes bayerischer Frauenvereine,* vol. 7, 1910, pp. 102-03.

Freudenberg, Ika. "Der erste Kellnerinnenverein." *Centralblatt des Bundes deutscher Frauenvereine,* vol. 2, 1900, pp. 2-3.

Freudenberg, Ika. "Die Frau als Arbeitgeberin." *Centralblatt des Bundes deutscher Frauenvereine,* vol. 2, 1900, pp. 146-48; 154-56.

Freudenberg, Ika. *Ein Wort an die weibliche Jugend.* Verlag der Frauen-Rundschau, 1903.

Freudenberg, Ika. "Gruppenbildung innerhalb des Bundes." *Centralblatt des Bundes deutscher Frauenvereine*, vol. 1, 1899, pp. 58-59.

Freudenberg, Ika. "Moderne Sittlichkeitsprobleme." *Die Frau: Monatsschrift für das gesamte Frauenleben unserer Zeit*, vol. 11, 1903, pp. 65-79.

Freudenberg, Ika. "Moderne Sittlichkeitsprobleme." *Frauenbewegung und Sexualethik: Beiträge zur modernen Ehekritik*, edited by Gertrud Bäumer et al., Verlag von Eugen Salzer, 1909.

Freudenberg, Ika. "Visier auf!." *Centralblatt des Bundes deutscher Frauenvereine*, vol. 6, 1904, pp. 89-90.

Freudenberg, Ika. "Was der Goethe-Bund für die Frauen bedeutet." *Centralblatt des Bundes deutscher Frauenvereine*, vol. 2, 1900, pp. 17-18.

Freudenberg, Ika. "Was heißt, eine Persönlichkeit werden?" *Die Frau: Monatsschrift für das gesamte Frauenleben unserer Zeit*, vol. 14, 1906/07, pp. 13-19.

Freudenberg, Ika. "Weshalb wendet sich die Frauenbewegung an die Jugend?" *Neue Lebensziele: Ansprachen an junge Mädchen*, edited by Gertrud Bäumer, Voigtländer, 1905.

Freudenberg, Ika. "Wie die Frauenbewegung entstanden ist." *Vortrag gehalten im Verein Frauenheil, Würzburg*. Würzburg: Verlagsdrucken, 1899. *Bayerische Staatsbibliothek Digital*. www.mdz-nbn-resolving.de/urn/resolver.pl?urn=urn:nbn:de:b-vb:12-bsb11127154-6. Accessed 8 June 2017.

Freudenberg, Ika. "Zum sechsten bayerischen Frauentag." *Frauenstreben: Veröffentlichungsorgan des Hauptverbandes bayerischer Frauenvereine*, vol. 6, 1909, pp. 53-55.

Freudenberg, Ika, and Marie Stritt. *Der Bund Deutscher Frauenvereine: Eine Darlegung seiner Aufgaben und Ziele und seiner bisherigen Entwickelung, nebst einer kurzgefassten Übersicht über die Thätigkeit seiner Arbeits-Kommissionen*. L. Reisel, 1900.

Freund, Anna. "Gedächtnisrede: Gehalten bei der Trauerfeier für Ika Freudenberg im großen Saale des Künstlerhauses zu München am 31. Januar 1912." *Frauenstreben: Veröffentlichungsorgan des Hauptverbandes bayerischer Frauenvereine*, vol. 11, 1912, pp. 19-23.

Gastil, John. "Communication as Deliberation." *Communication as ...: Perspectives on Theory*, edited by Gregory J. Shepherd et al., Sage, 2006, pp. 164-173.

Gerhard, Ute. *Unerhört: Die Geschichte der deutschen Frauenbewegung*. Rowohlt, 1990.

Greven-Aschoff, Barbara. *Die bürgerliche Frauenbewegung in Deutschland 1894-1933*. Vandenhoeck and Ruprecht, 1981.

Günther, Stephanie. *Weiblichkeitsentwürfe des Fin de Siècle: Berliner Autorinnen. Alice Berend, Margarete Böhme, Clara Viebig*. Bouvier, 2007.

Habermas, Jürgen. *Faktizität und Geltung: Beiträge zur Diskurstheorie des Rechts und des demokratischen Rechtsstaats*. Suhrkamp, 1994.

Hege, Marianne. *Die soziale Frauenschule der Stadt München 1919-1945. Zur Geschichte der Professionalisierung geistiger und praktischer Mütterlichkeit*. Sandmann, 1999.

Henke, Christiane. *Anita Augspurg*. Rowohlt, 2000.

Heuss, Theodor. *Vorspiele des Lebens: Jugenderinnerungen*. Wunderlich, 1953.

Kinnebrock, Susanne. *Anita Augspurg (1857-1943): Feministin und Pazifistin zwischen Journalismus und Politik. Eine kommunikationshistorische Biographie*. Centaurus-Verlag, 2005.

Klaus, Elisabeth. *Kommunikationswissenschaftliche Geschlechterforschung: Zur Bedeutung der Frauen in den Massenmedien und im Journalismus*. Westdeutscher Verlag, 1998.

Klaus, Elisabeth. *Kommunikationswissenschaftliche Geschlechterforschung: Zur Bedeutung der Frauen in den Massenmedien und im Journalismus*. 2nd ed. LIT-Verlag, 2005.

Klaus, Elisabeth, and Ulla Wischermann. "Öffentlichkeit als Mehr-Ebenen-Prozess: Theoretische Überlegungen und empirische Befunde am Beispiel der Frauenbewegung um 1900." *Zeitschrift für Frauenforschung und Geschlechterstudien*, vol. 26, 2009, pp. 103-16.

Kuhlmann, Carola. *Geschichte Sozialer Arbeit*. Wochenschau-Verlag, 2008.

Meyer, Ursula I. *Einführung in die feministische Philosophie*. Einfachverlag, 2004.

Moebius, Paul Julius. *Über den physiologischen Schwachsinn des Weibes*. Verlag von Carl Marhold, 1907.

Panzer, Marita A., and Elisabeth Plößl. *Bavarias Töchter: Frauen-portraits aus fünf Jahrhunderten*. Pustet ,1997.

Renkhoff, Otto. *Nassauische Biographie: Kurzbiographien aus 13 Jahrhunderten*. Historische Komm. für Nassau, 1992.

Richards, Ivor A.: *Practical Criticism: A study of Literary Judgment*. Routledge and Kegan Paul, 1929.

Rousseau, Jean-Jaques. *Emil oder Ueber die Erziehung*. 1762. Ferdinand Schöningh, 1993.

Sachße, Christoph. *Mütterlichkeit als Beruf: Sozialarbeit, Sozialreform und Frauenbewegung 1871-1929*. BeltzVotum, 2003.

Schaser, Angelika. *Helene Lange und Gertrud Bäumer: Eine politische Lebensgemeinschaft*. Böhlau, 2010.

Schmittner, Monika. *Aschaffenburg, ein Schauplatz der Bayerischen Frauenbewegung: Frauenemanzipation in der "Provinz" vor dem Ersten Weltkrieg*. Lang GmbH, 1995.

Schopenhauer, Arthur. "Ueber die Weiber." *Parerga et Paralipomena: Kleine philosophische Schriften II*. 1851. Edited by Arthur Schopenhauer, WBG, 1976, pp. 719-35.

Schraut, Sylvia. *Bürgerinnen im Kaiserreich: Biografie eines Lebensstils*. Kohlhammer, 2013.

Schröder, Iris. *Arbeiten für eine bessere Welt. Frauenbewegung und Sozialreform, 1890-1914*. Campus-Verl., 2001.

Schulz, Kristina. "Sozialistische Frauenorganisationen, bürgerliche Frauenbewegung und der Erste Weltkrieg. Nationale und internationale Perspektiven." *Historische Zeitschrift*, vol. 298, no. 3, 2014, pp. 653-85.

Stange-Fayos, Christina. *Publizistik und Politisierung der Frauenbewegung in der wilhelminischen Epoche: Die Zeitschrift* Die Frau *(1893-1914). Diskurs und Rhetorik*. Peter Lang GmbH, 2014.

Stoehr, Irene. "'Organisierte Mütterlichkeit': Zur Politik der deutschen Frauenbewegung um 1900." *Frauen suchen ihre Geschichte: Historische Studien zum 19. und 20. Jahrhundert*, edited by Karin Hausen, C.H. Beck, 1987, 225-53.

Tebben, Karin. "Der weibliche Blick auf das Fin de Siècle. Schriftstellerinnen zwischen Naturalismus und Expressionismus: Zur Einleitung." *Deutschsprachige Schriftstellerinnen des Fin de siècle*, edited by Karin Tebben, WBG, 1999, pp. 266-89.

Volkmann, Laurenz. "New Historicism." *Grundbegriffe der Lit-*

eraturtheorie, edited by Ansgar Nünning, J.B. Metzler, 2004, 195-98.

Volland, Eva Maria. München—*Stadt der Frauen: Kampf für Frieden und Gleichberechtigung 1800-1945. Ein Lesebuch.* R. Piper GmbH and Co. KG, 1991.

Weininger, Otto. *Geschlecht und Charakter: Eine prinzipielle Untersuchung.* 1903. Wilhelm Braumüller, 1920.

Wenzel, Peter. "New Criticism." *Grundbegriffe der Literaturtheorie*, edited by Ansgar Nünning, J.B. Metzler, 2004, pp. 191-95.

Wischermann, Ulla. *Frauenbewegungen und Öffentlichkeiten um 1900: Netzwerke, Gegenöffentlichkeiten, Protestinszenierungen.* Helmer, 2003.

Wolff, Kerstin. *Stadtmütter: Bürgerliche Frauen und ihr Einfluss auf die Kommunalpolitik im 19. Jahrhundert (1860-1900).* Helmer, 2003.

Zahn, Friedrich. "Die Frau im bayerischen Erwerbsleben." *Die Frau: Monatsschrift für das gesamte Frauenleben unserer Zeit*, vol. 26, 1909, pp. 592-608.

7.
Women and the Paternal State

A Maternalist Frame for Gender Equality

PINAR MELIS YELSALI PARMAKSIZ

O N 27 MAY 2013 THE LARGEST civic political protest ever seen in Turkey sparked in the heart of İstanbul. It started as an ecological protest against the cutting down of trees as part of renovation plans by the government at Gezi Park in the Taksim area, and upon controversial statements made by the prime minister, mass civic unrest soon burst in İstanbul and spread all over the country. On that day, a group of protesters came to the park to stop the bulldozers and stayed overnight in the park; it was the start of days long "occupy" movement, which finally ended by harsh police intervention on 15 June. During those days, the park hosted hundreds of thousands of people, who came to the park to protest not only the removal of the green area but also the contemptuous attitude by the prime minister and the violent police intervention. Considering these motivations, Turkish academic and columnist Ahmet İnsel defines Gezi protests as "an honour uprising,"[1] which gathers those who feel that their civic honour and democratic values are negated.

Among the hundreds of thousands of people at Gezi Park and in nearby Taksim Square were mothers who came to Taksim on the seventeenth day of the protests. The day before, the governor of Istanbul and also Prime Minister Erdogan advised the mothers of the protesters to come to Gezi Park and take their children away. Thus, a group of mothers arrived at the park, not to take their children away, however, but to show their feelings of protection for the protesters against police brutality.

The mothers' appearance at the Gezi protests is unique in many ways, but women's presence as mothers in public protests has been perceived in particular occasions in Turkish politics. The earliest example is found in the late 1970s as related to activities of the Progressive Women's Association (İlerici *Kadınlar Derneği, İKD*), which was founded by the Turkish Communist Party (*Türkiye Komünist Partisi, TKP*) to mobilize women in and around the left political movement in 1975 (Arıkan et al.11-15). The women who founded and controlled İKD did not define themselves as feminist; however, they succeeded in addressing women's problems, especially those surrounding unequal working conditions and poverty. The association also campaigned for the creation of kindergarten classes and the extension of maternal leave for working mothers. More specifically, İKD campaigned against political murders, which had become common during the armed struggle among different political groups and the state on the eve of the 1980 military coup. The women in İKD demanded peace on behalf of mothers by advocating for punishment of the perpetrators end the grief of mothers whose children were politically murdered (Arıkan et al. 209). There were also mothers at that time whose children were political prisoners, and they had to struggle for the safety and the well-being of their beloved ones.[2] Starting from the early 1970s, mothers' activism in different areas has complemented one another, and together, they have laid the foundation for mothers' activism for peace.

A more recent and well-known example of mothers' activism is the "Saturday Mothers" (*Cumartesi Anneleri*). Holding the photographs of their lost beloved ones who are victims of political murders or forced disappearances, they have gathered every Saturday at 12 p.m. at Galatasaray Square in İstanbul since 1995. The Saturday Mothers can be seen as the byproduct of the conflict between the PKK (Kurdistan Workers Party) and the state. Founded in 1970s, the PKK has been in guerilla warfare with the state since 1980s. After several strategical ceasefires and a failed peace process, which started since 2013 but ended in 2016, the armed conflict continues, especially in the eastern and the southeastern regions in Turkey. The thirty years of warfare have cost the lives of more than thirty thousands of people—including soldiers, civilians, state officials, and Kurdish guerrillas—and have caused almost four hundred thousand people to leave their hometowns because of the ongoing conflict or other political reasons ("30 yılın"). The Kurdish insurgency in the region and the state's measures for suppression characterize the circumstances in which the people whom the Saturday Mothers have sought disappear.

Inspired by the "Mothers of the Plaza de Mayo," the foundation, organization, and objectives of the Saturday Mothers exemplify the characteristics of civil disobedience (Coşar qtd. in Genç Yılmaz 58). In the context of the "Mothers of the Plaza de Mayo," the mothers opened up a space for advocating political demands by means of performing their culturally appropriate role as good mothers. Similarly, the Saturday Mothers maintain their maternal suffering and distance themselves from institutionalized politics (Genç Yılmaz 58). However, what is considered as appropriate motherhood in the Turkish context differentiates the Saturday Mothers from the Mothers of the Plaza de Mayo. Whereas the latter originates from mostly urban and middle class sections of the population in Argentina, the former has an ethnic Kurdish identity with rural origins, which are associated with what is seen as backward and traditional as compared to the official middle-class, Republican Turkey identity. Thus, as far as they transgress appropriate motherhood, the Saturday Mothers could build an alternative public space for themselves (Genç Yılmaz 65).

As far as today is concerned, the permanence of the Saturday Mothers' movement proves that they have gained almost an institutional entity, which not only struggles for their loss but also intervenes in many social and political instances as part of the struggle for democracy (Genç Yılmaz 71). Notwithstanding, their presence in the public sphere contradicts with the mothers of Martyrs of Duty, those who lost their lives while serving in the Turkish army. The contradiction stems from the fact that motherhood has been used as a nationalist strategy within the official discourse both to bolster the moral strength and to stand against the address of the Kurdish question on the basis of national security (Gedik 24). Since falling as martyr, meaning "dying for the sake of nation," is the most valuable attribute for a person and his family, the martyr's family receives a respected position in society (Gedik 42) and is additionally official privileges granted by the state.

If women feel concerned as mothers because of ongoing social and political conflicts, they gather in the public sphere in order to stimulate a public awareness, which is highly common when political opposition was deepened and democratic dialogue was discouraged. At other times, women are addressed and invited to the political sphere as mothers as part of the populist and nationalist political discourse. In the latter case, women still have the chance to reclaim their voices even without necessarily addressing feminism. In the wake of this understanding, this chapter focuses on the activism of the mothers during the Gezi Park protests in June 2013 in order to examine both the role of mothers and motherhood in the public protest and the significance of acting as mothers in the public sphere.

GEZI PARK UPRISING:
CLAIMING A PLACE, ACTUAL OR SYMBOLIC

The Gezi Park protests started in a public square to protect a park and spread to minor streets and small neighbouhoods, not only in İstanbul but in eighty-one cities in Turkey. Actions ranging from occupying streets to banging pans and pots signified novel forms of civic protest and broadened the definition of democracy. Among the protesters were feminists, LGBT and human rights groups, environmentalists and trade unions, Alevis (a large group of heterodox Muslim Shias), anti-capitalist Muslims, soccer club fans, and left-wing revolutionaries (Patton 30). The high number of females among the protesters was noteworthy.[3] The protesters were young people (an average age of twenty-eight) with university degrees (42.8 percent were college graduates). More than half of them were employed (51.8 percent) and almost half of them were students (36.6 percent). White collar employees (15 percent) and private sector employees (17 percent) were the majority among the employed protesters. As for political affiliation, a very high ratio of the protestors (78.9 percent) was not affiliated with an institutional political body, a political party, or a nongovernmental organization, which is reflected in the fact that most of the protesters had come to the park as ordinary citizens (93.6 percent) rather representing a certain group (6.4 percent) ("Konda" 8-16).

The reasons why they participated in the protests varied. The strongest reason for the protesters to come to the park was the brutality of the police (49.1 percent). The second strongest reason was seeing that the trees were being uprooted (19 percent). Anger over the prime minister's uncompromising statements was the third reason (14.2 percent) ("Konda" 20). As it could be expected from the responses above, the strongest reason for the protesters was freedom (34.1 percent). Protesting human rights violations and demanding their rights were the second strongest motivation for the protestors (18.4 percent). Being against dictatorship and oppression was the third strongest motivation (9.7 percent).

Sociologist Nilüfer Göle explains that the destruction of the park in order to build up a shopping mall represented commercial greed and consumerism in the eyes of the protesters (9). Uprooting the trees and replacing the park with a shopping mall was regarded as the confiscation of a public space by private capital, which demonstrated that environmental sensitivity and criticism of capitalism became intertwined in the Gezi Uprising. In that sense, the neoliberal economic policies of the AKP government became an obvious target of popular discontent. In addition to that, the park represented a public sphere that was being suffocated because of tightening control of the mainstream media. Moreover, the government's moralist intrusions into the lives of its citizens were regarded by the protesters a threat to their lifestyle (Göle 10). As Antimo L. Farro and Deniz Günce Demirhisar clarify, the protestors' involvement reveals their critical choice against the authoritarian government, which they saw as a symbol of domination and control (192). Therefore, there were actual and symbolic references of claiming the park as a place. First of all, claiming the park as one of the last green areas in the city and protesting the transformation of urban landscape according to commercial aims presented actual references to claim the place as a park. Furthermore, claiming the park as one of the last resorts to protect against neoliberal reforms gave symbolic attributes to the place. The symbolism becomes even stronger if the role of the rigid statements of the prime minister is considered. Claiming the park as a symbolic place is also incorporated in the demands for freedom of both expression and choice. Considering the high ratio of women's participation in the protests, it would not be wrong to assert that the debates on motherhood and abortion had a strong share in the discontent reflected in the Gezi Park protests.

BETWEEN MOTHERHOOD AND ABORTION: WHOSE TERRITORY IS A WOMAN'S BODY?

Since it came to power in 2002, the AKP government has made unconvincing attempts to pursue gender equality in Turkey. At first, the government made several amendments in the legislation in order to harmonize the Turkish law with EU legislation, according to the principles of eliminating discrimination based on gender. Nevertheless, an overall feminist reading of the AKP's discourse and policy preferences on women proves that it lacks a gender equality perspective (Yelsalı Parmaksız, "Paternalism" 53-54). This is well reflected in the statements of Prime Minister Erdoğan, who has occasionally declared that he does not believe in gender equality. As he put it, women could not be equal to men because of their differences in nature (*fıtrat*) (Yelsalı Parmaksız, "Paternalism" 54).

The government's policy preferences in combatting violence against women are illustrative of its deficient gender equality perspective. Violence against women is one of the most urgent issues in Turkey. According to the results of nationwide research conducted in 2009, 34 percent of all women said that they had been subject to physical violence by their husbands at least once (Altınay and Arat 39). Moreover, femicide, meaning killing of women by their husbands or ex-husbands, is at a high rate. Although surprisingly there are no official statistics reporting male violence (beating, sexual harassment, rape and killing), academic and media institutions strive to fill the gap. According to independent media network Bianet's monitoring of male violence in Turkey, in the first seven months of 2016, men killed 153 women, raped 52 others, harassed 80, inflicted violence on 196 women, and sexually abused 297 girls (Tahaoğlu). In the years between 2010 and 2015, at least 1,134 women were murdered by men. 53.6 percent of all perpetrators were husbands or ex-husbands; 14.2 percent were boyfriends or ex-boyfriends; 18.8 percent were male relatives; and only 13.4 percent were in another category not related to the family. Moreover, 59.6 percent of victims were murdered in their family houses (Ulukaya). In this context, between 2009 and 2011, the Turkish government worked to adopt the Council of Europe Convention on Preventing and Combating Violence against Women and Domestic Violence (Istanbul Convention) and ratified it in 2012, being the first member state of the Council of Europe. After the ratification of the convention, it was expected from the government to amend the existing "Law on the Protection of the Family" (1998). The legislation titled "Law on the Protection of the Family and Prevention of Violence against Women" (2012), which offers protection for women within the family, was, however, behind expectations (Acar and Altunok 18-19). Throughout the process, the exclusion of the feminist organizations from the body of experts (GREVIO) monitoring the implementation of the convention raised questions about government's sincerity.

The disappointment related to the new law comes from its conceptualization of violence against women and the measures it takes to prevent violence. The convention defines violence against women as gender-based violence and emphasizes the strong connection between preventing gender based violence and promoting gender equality; however, the law offers protection to women, the victims of domestic violence within the family, seemingly under the auspice of the perpetrators. Therefore, family is defined as of top priority, and women are addressed within the family and, thus, are regarded above all as wives and mothers.

The speech of the prime minister at the International Parliamentarians Conference on the Action Plan for Population and Development in Istanbul on 25 May 2012 exemplifies the case. During his speech, he pointed out the importance of raising the birth rate for the country's population to grow further, which he regarded as good for the development of the country. He also asserted the sensitivity his government had about children, and then added his affection for children and, as he does at many occasions, advised women to have at least three children (Radikal qtd. in Ünal and Cindoğlu 22). He continued his speech as follows: "I am a prime minister who is against Caesarean section at birth. I see abortion as a murder. No one should have a right to allow this. You either kill the child in the womb or after the birth; there is no difference.

We ought to be very sensitive to this. We have to cooperate against this" (Seçkinelgin 273). Erdoğan believes that Caesarean sections are similar to abortion because they risk subsequent births, thus decreasing the number of children a woman may give birth to. He believes that these practices are done on purpose to prevent the population from growing (Ünal and Cindoğlu 22). One day later, during the AKP Women's Branch Meeting on 26 May 2012, the prime minister upheld his position as he stated that "each abortion is Uludere," which refers to the mass killings of Kurdish smugglers by the Turkish air forces in Uludere village in December 2011 (Ünal and Cindoğlu 22). He also asserted that there were preparations to amend the law in order to ban both abortion and Caesarean sections (*Hürriyet Daily News* qtd. in Eslen-Ziya and Erhart 5). The statements of the prime minister resulted in a strong reaction from women's rights defenders. Feminist groups and organizations made public statements defending women's right for an abortion. Activists for women's rights also organized a nationwide campaign through the media. The first outcome of the campaign was the start of a webpage and a petition both titled "Abortion Can't Be Banned" (Eslen-Ziya 866). Another stream of activism against antiabortion law was initiated by Bianet as an online campaign, which was titled "My Body My Choice" (*"Benim Bedenim Benim Kararım"*). It was a call for women to declare their rights and for men to stand in solidarity with women. Bianet called for women and men to send in pictures of themselves either holding signs or writing on their bodies with the following expressions: "My Body, My Decision"; "This Is My Issue" for women or "Woman's Body, Woman's Decision"; "My Wife's Body, My Wife's Decision"; "My Daughter's Body, My Daughter's Decision"; "My Girlfriend's Body, My Girlfriend's Decision"; "This is Women's Issue"; "My Sister's Decision"; "My Mother's Decision"; and for men, "Right to Abortion." The campaign broke out in social media and spread to conventional media. The columnists of the leading newspapers noted the campaign, and some of them announced their support. International media also showed attention and interest in the campaign. The campaign was started on 31 May 2012, and the Turkish government dropped the amendment of the anti-abortion law on 14 September 2012 (Eslen-Ziya 862). In this case, the use of social media proved its potential to create rapid and effective outcomes. The easy receipt and dissemination of information on social media strengthened the lobbying efforts of the activists by means of connecting them with broad sections of the community (Eltantawy and Wiest qtd. in Eslen-Ziya 868).

As a matter of fact, restrictive abortion legislation was in effect in Turkey in the first decades of the Republic. The first Penal Code of the Republic, adopted in 1926, introduced the first regulations about abortion. Later in 1930, pronatal policies, which prohibited both abortion and contraception, were adopted. The legislation was rigid until 1965 when a new law was adopted legalizing contraception for population planning. A limited relaxation of the legislation also included a regulation that allowed abortion if serious medical risks existed (Ünal and Cindoğlu 24). The latest legislation concerning abortion is the Population Planning Law (No: 2827), which was adopted in 1983 and is still in effect. The law allows for abortion up to ten weeks on the condition of husband's consent, and after ten weeks, if there is a serious medical risk either for mother or baby (Acar and Altunok 16).[4]

The statistics related to legal abortion indicate that the rate of the pregnancies that ended in abortion in Turkey was 10 percent in 2008, which is higher than for example Greece (7 percent in 2005) and Montenegro (8 percent in 2008), and is lower than for example France (18 percent in 2008), Sweden (22 percent in 2008), and New Zealand (20 percent in 2008) (Sedgh et al. 87-88). The statistics also demonstrate that there is no causality between the legal status of abortion and the abortion rates. Instead, evidence shows that the legal status of the abortion is linked with ending unintended pregnancies in a safe manner rather than its reported number (Sedgh et al. 92).

On the other hand, the rate of Caesarean births in Turkey in 2008 was 40.7 percent in all health institutions, public or private, which is higher than the World Health Organization suggested rate of 15 percent (Acar and Altunok 17). Such a difference can be interpreted as the result of increased medicalization (Cindoğlu and Sayan-Cengiz) and marketization of birth.

The above mentioned results demonstrate that independent from its legal status, abortion rate is always at a certain level because, whether legal or illegal, couples seek to end unintended pregnancies. Moreover, the issue of limiting the practice of Caesarean birth is related to the need to provide better service to support the reproductive health of mothers rather than controlling women's reproductive capacity for the state's pronatal policy targets. Neither of these explanations is sufficient, however, to tackle the statements of the prime minister. Instead, since his eventual goal seems to be to raise the fertility rate, thus the number of children, it is good to ask whether there is such a connection between the two.

It is suggested that there is actually a connection between the high level of fertility and the wealth of the country. The indicators in the last fifteen years show that among the OECD (Organization for Economic Cooperation and Development) members, the countries that have highest fertility rate also have the lowest poverty rates. Yet these are the countries in which women's participation rate in paid work is high (OECD qtd. in Thévenon 57). The increase in female labour could be achieved in these countries through policies that aim to reconcile work and family life, especially for women (Esping-Andersen and OECD qtd. in Thévenon 60). In this framework, policies have been implemented to promote equal share of both paid work and unpaid work between partners, including childcare (Lewis et al. qtd. in Thévenon 60). Pronatal policies could improve the wealth of the country only if parents, especially the mothers, can benefit from real equality both at work and at home. This requires the making and the implementation of policies that prioritize gender equality and not simply the protection of the family. In conservative contexts, however, including the AKP's religious-based neoliberal conservatism, the aim of strengthening the traditional family undermines the goal of achieving gender equality. For example, in continental Europe, Christian democratic parties have blocked measures to support employment of mothers. Whereas in secular contexts such as Scandinavia, the secularization of political life is a precondition for gender-sensitive public policies, hence policies that aim at gender equality at the expense of the demise of the traditional family model (Morgan 289). The discussion reveals that pronatal and nationalist political preferences may stake a claim to women's bodies, yet the only way to achieve such policy goals is to bolster gender equality in all areas of life.

SYMBOLIC ACTION FOR CLAIMING THE WOMB: MOTHERS AT GEZI PARK PROTESTS

As indicated above, the average age of the Gezi Park protesters was twenty-eight. To put it in detail, 30.8 percent of the protesters were between the ages of twenty-one and twenty-five, and 20.3 percent were between the ages of twenty-six and thirty. Only 22 percent of the Gezi Park protesters were twenty years old or younger ("Konda" 9). Yet the Gezi protest was labelled as a youth movement. The way they organized and the characteristics of the protests make it possible to identify generational features of the movement and thus to label it as a youth movement. However, it does not mean that there were only these young people in the protests and that they were also in conflict with the older generation. Yet this was not the case, as younger and older generations came together to protest (Göle 8), which was particularly evident in the discussion of maternal issues during the protests.

From the very beginning, mothers with small children were in the park to express their solidarity with the protesters. Motherhood was among the most popular issues related to the discursive repertoire of the protests. For example, at the entrance of the park, feminist socialists hung a giant banner saying "we don't owe children to men or to the state" (Erhart 302). During the protests, women displayed posters addressing the debates about motherhood and abortion. The posters they carried targeted the interfering attitude of the prime minister with the following messages: "I make love but I don't marry, I get pregnant but don't have a baby"; "Tayyip hands off my body"; "Abortion is a right"; and "We don't want an antiwomen PM'" (Seçkinelgin 271). One of the most popular slogans read "Tayyip, do you want three more kids like us?" (Seçkinelgin 271; Erhart 302). Yet on the seventeenth day of resistance at Gezi Park, mothers got the most visibility. The mothers who came to the park upon the call of the governor of İstanbul formed a mother's chain hand in hand and showed their support for the protesters by chanting the slogans: "Mothers are here" and "Resist, my dear, your mother is here." The protesters replied by chanting and applause, saying: "Resist Mother!" Simultaneously, #direnanne (#resistmother) became a trending topic on Twitter. By joining the protests, the mothers reacted against both the conceptualization of motherhood as a domestic duty and as the ultimate possible social role for women in society (Yelsalı Parmaksız, "#resistankara").

Three days after the mothers' chain at Gezi, women found another occasion to protest restrictive discourses related to mothers and motherhood. On 25 July, on TRT, the official TV channel in Turkey, a theologian, who is respected by AKP, stated that pregnant women should not wander on the streets with such bellies; it was against tradition and definitely immoral. Women again responded with protests both on the streets and on social media. Three days later, this time #direnhamile (#resistpregnant) became a trending topic on Twitter (Tekay and Üstün).

Defining the proper behaviour for women has always been a part of the debate related to modernization in Turkey. Modernization started in the nineteenth century in the late Ottoman period and took its shape with the establishment of the Turkish Republic in 1923. Women's modernity was seen as the symbol of the modernization of the country; hence, extensive social and legal reforms were introduced by the new regime to achieve women's emancipation (Yelsalı Parmaksız, "Paternalism" 45-46). However, as Deniz Kandiyoti correctly indicates, women were emancipated but not liberated in Turkish modernization (41). More specifically, women's modernization was conditional; they had to be seen and behave as modern, but, at the same time, their control of their own bodies and sexuality was limited by the authority of real and symbolic fathers, definitely in a paternalist framework (Yelsalı Parmaksız, "Paternalism" 52). Thus, women's entry into public and political sphere was possible, as Ruth Miller (361) puts it, through the regulation of their bodies and sexualities. This control included women's reproductive capacity, so much so that the womb no longer belonged to women. Instead, it was defined as a political place (Ünal and Cindoğlu 23); in other words, it became a biopolitical space within the discourse of the nation state (Miller 365).[5] Hence, citizenship in the modern Turkish nation state is defined through gender, sexuality, and reproduction (Miller 359).

From this point of view, I suggest that the mothers' presence at Gezi Park and the circulation of the maternal issues in the protests contributed to the claiming the park as a symbolic place. By claiming the park as a symbolic place, mothers claimed the womb as individual property. In that sense, mothers have struggled against the paternal framework of the state and its representatives by using a maternal framework. According to Pierre Bourdieu, the state holds the power of using physical and symbolic violence (21). Symbolic violence is related to possession of symbolic power. However, in every society, symbolic powers are always in conflict with one another. Symbolic struggles may take place in two forms: objective and subjective. In the objective form, individual or collective entities act for their representation as they are. In the subjective form, entities aim at transforming the categories of perception of the world (Bourdieu 20) because symbolic power is the power of world making. Thus, whoever desires to change the world first has to change the ways of world making (Bourdieu 22).

As Léna Pellandini-Simányi comments, groups try to gain symbolic power, first, act according to the rules of the game, in other words "without putting into question the basis on which symbolic power is granted" (655). Second, groups attempt to change the rules. At first sight, the mothers at Gezi, by their presence in the park, seemed to confirm the stereotypes about mothers in the traditional family in Turkey, as someone who negotiates between the father and children. Relying on the traditional roles has been a way for mothers to succeed in public protests (Lemish and Barzel 166).

Yet, seemingly, the presence of mothers at Gezi protests showed that common stereotypes about mothers should be deconstructed and redefined (Canlı and Umul 29). Therefore, the mothers joining the protests were not only reacting against the governor's threatening statement but also protesting the political discourse that tells them how to deliver their babies, how many children they should have, and why they are not equal to men. In the next section, I discuss the consequences of mothers' mobilization as protesters at Gezi Park and hence evaluate the possibility of defining a maternalist frame for political action in a patriarchal and paternalist context.

MATERNALIST FRAME FOR POLITICAL ACTION
IN A PATERNALIST CONTEXT

A maternalist frame came into prominence at Gezi through the circulation of issues related to motherhood and also through the mothers' participation in the public protests. Michelle Carreon and Valentine Moghaddam define a maternalist frame by referring to "elements of motherhood, mothering, and maternal identities deployed to evoke meanings within a given context and elicit participation and/or support of collective action" (19-20). They also add that maternalist frames can also be used for conservative purposes through helping to underline patriarchal values based on maternalist sensibilities and roles of and for women; they can be used at times as "a cloak for paternalism" (Koven and Michael qtd. in Carreon and Moghaddam 20).

Paternalism implies that "the actor knows better than the person acted upon" (Cornell 1316); in that sense, it entails disrespect for them as decision makers. Because they cannot be trusted to know what is best for them, paternalism treats adults like children (Ben-Ishai 155). If the group of people who are acted upon is already a disadvantaged or a marginalized group, such as women or the poor, paternalism becomes an authoritarian and bureaucratic tool for discipline (Cornell 1327). It is not a coincidence that the first accounts of paternalism can be found in the writings of John Stuart Mill, an early advocate of suffrage, who interprets it as "the interference with a person's liberty of action" (qtd, in Ben-Ishai 152). Henceforth, paternalism is to be recognized as gender-based concept. Similar to Iris Marion Young's concept of "masculinist protection," paternalism is related to the state acting like a father to protect a society identified with femininity (Dönmez 554). In the early stages of the nation state, paternalism was an obvious political discourse of patriarchal state formation, yet in the modern state, it appears as a tool for governmentality in liberal or neoliberal contexts, which is distinctively seen in the social policy regulations of the states.

As for the use of paternalism by the AKP government in Turkey, a similar tendency is observed: the social policies the government pursues, just like those to prevent the consumption of alcohol by young people, introduces new regulations to protect people. In doing so, the AKP government asserts a religious conservative position in addition to a paternalist position (Seçkinelgin, 274). It has become more apparent since 2007 that the government has employed a moralistic and patriarchal discourse referring to religion, not only in recasting social and cultural life but also in discussing international relations (Acar and Altunok 14). In the cases even where there was no direct reference to religion; the use of moral judgments and stigmatization for the practices that the religion denounces imply neo-conservatism (Acar and Altunok 15). Nevertheless, more recently, the statements of the President Erdoğan[6] with regard to maternal issues represent more direct references to religion. In a speech on 30 May 2016, he said that family planning and contraception are not apt for Muslim families ("Recep Tayyip Erdoğan"). The evaluation of the AKP's gender politics reveals its neoliberal and conservative political discourses and policy preferences, with an increasing religious content as a source of moral judgments. The use of morality with religious, nationalist, or conservative rhetoric does not necessarily label the patriarchal use of power as paternalistic, but it does negate individual autonomy. Here, though, is why the AKP's gender politics is defined as paternalistic.

Paternalism may occur in different forms, from a simple nudge to restrictive regulations and punishment; yet in all cases it impedes the individual's ability to make choices. The political position taken with regard to mothers and motherhood represents a paternalist intervention. In that sense, mothers' participation in Gezi protests signifies a symbolic action in the face of symbolic violence of the state. Chris Samuel defines the experience of symbolic violence as the feeling of "being out of place, anxious, awkward, shamed, stupid and so on" (402). Thus women's struggle to open up a maternalist frame to claim the control of their bodies and identities should be regarded as an attempt to gain autonomy in a paternalistic context. Certainly, maternalist politics is not necessarily feminist or should be explicitly feminist, yet, not conservative or patriarchal by definition. Moreover, as Carreon and Moghaddam (22) argue, contemporary maternalist politics can embrace an antihegemonic political discourse and fight for democratic appeals.

It is for this reason that the use of a maternalist frame during the Gezi protests was linked to democratic demands. It was in such a way that mothers participation in the protests not only broadened the scope of democratic appeals but also protested the symbolic power of the paternalist frame.

ENDNOTES

[1] All Turkish-English translations belong to the author.

[2] See Tuba Demirci-Demirci-Yılmaz"s article in this volume.

[3] According to the findings of the research by KONDA, 50.8 percent of the protesters were female, and 49.2 percent were male. 48.8 percent of the population in Turkey is female and 51.2 percent male.

[4] The most recent research on the availability of abortion services demonstrates that although abortion is still legal in Turkey, abortion service at state hospitals is not necessarily available. Out of 431 state hospitals with departments of obstetrics and gynecology, 78 percent provide abortion service if there is a medical necessity, whereas 11.8 percent do not provide the service at all. Only 7.8 percent of state hospitals provide the service as it is defined in the law. As for the education and research hospitals, out of fifty-eight with departments of obstetrics and gynecology, 71.1 percent provide the service for medical emergencies, whereas 11.4 percent do not provide the service at all. 17.3 percent of the education and research universities providing the abortion service without restriction (Mary Lou O'Neil et.al, *Legal but Not Necessarily Available*). Earlier in March 2014, the Turkish Gynecology and Obstetrics Association announced controversially that the "abortion procedure that is provided free up to 10 weeks within the social protection system in public hospitals linked to the Ministry of Health [had] ended." It was because that "the online health registration code for this particular procedure ha[d] been removed from the system. As a result doctors [could not] perform the procedure without getting authorisation from the system, leading to the cessation of all relevant inspections and procedures in this area" ("Kürtaj").

[5] Miller insists that no matter if abortion is legal or illegal, in either case there is political control of womb as a political space (365).

[6]Recep Tayyip Erdoğan was elected as the President of the Republic 10 August 2014.

WORKS CITED

"30 yılın terör bilançosu: 35 bin 576 ölü." *Radikal*, 28 Jan. 2013, www.radikal.com.tr/politika/30-yilin-teror-bilancosu-35-bin-576-olu-1118893/. Accessed 4 June 2017.

Acar, Feride, and Gülbanu Altunok. "The 'Politics of Intimate' at the Intersection of Neo-Liberalism and Neo-Conservatism in Contemporary Turkey." *Women's Studies International Forum*, vol. 41, 2012, pp. 14-23.

Altınay, Ayşegül, and Yeşim Arat. *Violence against Women in Turkey: A Nationwide Survey*. Punto, 2009.

Arıkan, Saadet, et al. *Ve Hep Birlikte Koştuk: İlerici Kadınlar Derneği (1975-1980)*. Açı Yayınları, 1996.

Ben-Ishai, Elizabeth. "The New Paternalism: An Analysis of Power, State Intervention, and Autonomy." *Political Research Quarterly*, vol. 65, no. 1, 2012, pp. 151-165.

Bourdieu, Pierre. "Social Space and Symbolic Power." *Sociological Theory*, vol. 7, no. 1, 1989), pp. 14-25.

Canlı, Ece, and Fatma Umul. "Bodies on the Streets: Gender Resistance and Collectivity in the Gezi Revolts." *Interface: A Journal for and about Social Movements*, vol. 7, no. 1, 2015, pp. 19-39.

Carreon, Michelle E., and Valentine M. Moghadam. "'Resistance is fertile': Revisiting Maternalist Frames across Cases of Women's Mobilization,'" *Women's Studies International Forum*, vol. 51, 2015, pp. 19-30.

Cindoglu, Dilek, and Feyda Sayan-Cengiz. "Medicalization Discourse and Modernity: Contested Meanings over Childbirth in Contemporary Turkey." *Health Care for Women International*, vol. 31, no. 3, 2010, pp. 221-43.

Cornell, Nicolas. "A Third Theory of Paternalism." *Michigan Law Review*, vol. 113, no. 8, 2015, pp. 1295-1336.

Dönmez, Rasim Özgür. "Nationalism in Turkey under Justice and Development Party Rule: The Logic of Masculinist Protection." *Turkish Studies*, vol. 16, no. 4, 2015, pp. 554-71.

Erhart, Itır "Biopolitics and the Gezi Protests." *International Con-*

ference on the *Modern Development of Humanities and Social Science MDHSS*, edited by Atlantis Press, 2013, pp. 301-03.

Eslen-Ziya, Hande. "Social Media and Turkish Feminism: New Resources for Social Activism." *Feminist Media Studies*, vol. 13, no. 5, 2013, pp. 860-70.

Eslen-Ziya, Hande, and Itır Erhart. "Toward Post heroic Leadership: A Case Study of Gezi's Collaborating Multiple Leaders." *Leadership*, 2015, pp. 1-18.

Farro, Antimo L., and Deniz Günce Demirhisar. "The Gezi Park Movement: A Turkish Experience of the Twenty-First-Century Collective Movements." *International Review of Sociology: Revue Internationale de Sociologie*, vol. 24, no. 1, 2014, pp. 176-89.

Gedik, Esra. "Security of the Nation: Why Do We Need 'Mothers of Martyrs' in Turkey?" *disClosure: A Journal of Social Theory*, vol. 22, no. 7, 2013, pp. 23-50.

Genç Yılmaz, Ayfer. "Toplumsal Hareketin Kalbinde Bir Yeni Özne: Anneler, Türkiye'de Cumartesi Anneleri ve Arjantin'de Mayıs Meydanı Anneleri Üzerine Karşılaştırmalı Bir Analiz." *Marmara Üniversitesi Siyasal Bilimler Dergisi*, vol. 2, no. 1, 2014, pp. 51-74.

Göle, Nilüfer. "Gezi-Anatomy of a Public Square Movement." *Insight Turkey*, vol. 15, no. 3, 2013, pp. 7-14.

İnsel, Ahmet. "Haysiyet Ayaklanması." *Radikal*, 4 Jun. 2013, www.radikal.com.tr/yazarlar/ahmet-insel/haysiyet-ayaklanmasi-1136174/. Accessed 4 June 2017.

Kandiyoti, Deniz. "Emancipated but Unliberated? Reflections on the Turkish Case." *Feminist Studies*, vol. 13, no. 2, 1987, pp. 317–38.

"Konda Gezi Report: Public Perception of the 'Gezi Protests' Who Were the People at Gezi Park?" *Konda*, 5 Jun. 2014, konda.com.tr/en/raporlar/KONDA_Gezi_Report.pdf. Accessed 4 June 2017.

"Kürtaj SGK Kapsamından ıkarılabilirmi?" *Haberturk*, 13 Mar 2014, www.haberturk.com/polemik/haber/929189-kurtaj-sgk-kapsamindancikarilabilir-mi. Accessed 4 June 2017.

Lemish, Dafna, and Inbal Barzel. "Four Mothers' The Womb in the Public Sphere." *European Journal of Communication*, vol. 15, no. 2, 2000, pp. 147-69.

Miller, Ruth A. "Rights, Reproduction, Sexuality, and Citizenship in the Ottoman Empire and Turkey." *Signs*, vol. 32, no. 2, 2007, pp. 347-73.

Morgan, Kimberly J. "The Politics of Mothers' Employment: France in Comparative Perspective." *World Politics*, vol. 55, no. 2, 2003, pp. 259-89.

"Recep Tayyip Erdoğan: No Muslim Family Can Accept Birth Control." *The Guardian*, 30 May 2016, www.theguardian.com/world/2016/may/30/recep-tayyip-erdogan-no-muslim-family-can-accept-birth-control. Accessed 4 June 2017.

"Right to Abortion Campaign Launched." *Bianet*, 31 May 2012, bianet.org/english/health/138770-right-to-abortion-campaign-launched. Accessed 4 June 2017.

O'Neil, Mary Lou, et al. *Legal but Not Necessarily Available: Abortion Services at State Hospitals in Turkey*. Kadir Has University Gender and Women's Studies Research Center, 2016.

Patton, Marcie J. "Generation Y in Gezi Park." *Middle East Report*, vol. 268, 2013, pp. 30-37.

Pellandini-Simányi, Léna. "Bourdieu, Ethics and Symbolic Power." *The Sociological Review*, vol. 62, no. 4, 2014, pp. 651-74.

Samuel, Chris. "Symbolic Violence and Collective Identity: Pierre Bourdieu and the Ethics of Resistance." *Social Movement Studies*, vol. 12, no. 4, 2013, pp. 397-413.

Seçkinelgin, Hakan. "Social Policy and Conflict: The Gezi Park–Taksim Demonstrations and Uses of Social Policy for Reimagining Turkey." *Third World Quarterly*, vol.37, no.2, 2016, pp.264-80.

Sedgh, Gilda, et al. "Legal Abortion Worldwide in 2008: Levels and Recent Trends." *International Perspectives on Sexual and Reproductive Health*, vol. 37, no. 2, 2011, pp. 84-94.

Tahaoğlu, Çiçek. "Men Kill 18 Women in July." *Bianet*, 3 Aug. 2016, bianet.org/english/women/177481-men-kill-18-women-in-july. Accessed 4 June 2017.

Tekay, Cihan, and Zeyno Üstun. "A Short History of Feminism in Turkey and Feminist Resistance in Gezi." *Talk Turkey Conference: Life since Gezi*, New York City, 4-5 October 2013.

Thévenon, Olivier. "Family Policies in OECD Countries: A Comparative Analysis" *Population and Development Review*, vol. 37, no. 1, 2011, pp. 57-87.

Ulukaya, Ceyda. "Who, Where, How: Femicide Map of Five Years."

Bianet, 25 Nov. 2015, bianet.org/english/women/169543-who-where-how-femicide-map-of-five-years. Accessed 4 June 2017.

Ünal, Didem, and Dilek Cindoğlu. "Reproductive Citizenship in Turkey: Abortion Chronicles." *Women's Studies International Forum*, vol. 38, no. 1, 2013, pp. 21-31.

Yelsalı Parmaksız, Pınar Melis. "#resistankara: Notes of a Woman Resisting." *Jadaliyya*. 16 Jun. 2013, www.jadaliyya.com/pages/index/12261/. Accessed 4 June 2017.

Yelsalı Parmaksız, Pınar Melis. "Paternalism, Modernization, and the Gender Regime in Turkey." *Aspasia, International Yearbook of Central, Eastern and South Eastern European Women's and Gender History*, vol. 10, 2016, 40-62.

MOTHERHOOD
AND POLITICAL ACTIVISM

8.
On *Andariegas, Carishinas* and Bad Mothers

Challenges to the Political Participation of Indigenous Women in the Ecuadorian Andes

MARÍA MORENO

IN LATIN AMERICA, WOMEN have greatly contributed to social movements. Indigenous women have also been important participants of indigenous movements and have a central role as symbols and agents of cultural reproduction. Female leaders are breaking traditional roles, as do Latin American women who enter the masculine realm of politics. Despite their ascendance to positions of leadership, indigenous women, as well as their peers of other groups, find that their fuller role in society is accepted as long as they do not forego their maternal responsibilities. Although some traditional gender roles are eroding, "one element which has remained more constant has been the centrality of motherhood" (Craske 194). Motherhood still looms large in the lives of many Latin American women and complicates their political endeavours.

In the canton of Cotacachi, in the northern highlands of Ecuador, *Kichwa* women have participated in the local indigenous organization since its emergence in the late 1970s. To participate in politics, women leave their homes, fields, and communities and attend meetings, events, demonstrations, and uprisings, which take them to the municipal town, the capital, and other national and international locations. Within the terrains of the personal and the community, indigenous women of Cotacachi experience gender conflicts and exclusions, and face criticisms that undermine their political position. They constantly negotiate their role as leaders and their roles as mothers, wives, daughters, and community members. As they leave the domestic and community spaces to participate in politics, indigenous women transcend those spaces associated with their roles as cultural reproducers and mothers, and, in so doing, break with more conservative and traditional understandings of femininity.

Nevertheless, I argue that this exit toward the public sphere of politics is not a once-and-for-all achievement. Instead, indigenous women's mobility and leadership responsibilities conflict with their domestic and maternal roles, especially for those married women who have small and young children. Husbands, relatives, children, neighbours, and community members mobilize notions of maternal, marital, or community duty that result in tactics of shaming and a sense of guilt for women. Female leaders have been accused of being "*andariegas*," "fond of walking" or being "*carishinas*," from the Kichwa "*cari*" = man, and "*shina*" = like—"like a man." Not only do these adjectives have negative connotations of neglecting the role of mother and wife, but they also cast a doubt on the morality of the women so described. Children are also vocal regarding their mother's absence from home because of political involvement. The accusations, directly or in the form of gossip, have worked to discourage and undermine their political participation; they represent part of the daily challenges women confront as female leaders.

Indigenous women of Cotacachi have found ingenious strategies to circumvent these challenges, sometimes accommodating to the expectations of motherhood, being a proper wife, and staying at the community. Although some of their strategies may largely acquiesce to traditionalist views of the proper place of women (at home and in the community), they enable women to leave the home and the fields, walk beyond the community, and have a voice and a presence in indigenous politics.

COTACACHI, CITIZEN PARTICIPATION, AND INDIGENOUS WOMEN

Canton Cotacachi gained notoriety as a successful case of participatory democracy and decentralization after becoming in 1996 one of the first municipalities with an indigenous mayor. Located in Imbabura province in the northern highlands of Ecuador, Cotacachi includes a great diversity of climates, extending from 300 metres to 4,800 metres above sea level, and comprises diverse life zones, ranging from subtropical forests to *paramo* or plateau like upland areas ("Shuk Yuyaylly").

The canton promotes itself as a multicultural space—comprised of mestizo (population of mixed Spanish and indigenous descent), indigenous *Kichwa* people,[1] and Afro-Ecuadorian populations, and more recently a small community of expatriates from the United States and Canada. The total population of Cotacachi is approximately forty thousand; the most numerous groups are the mestizo (53.5 percent) and indigenous (40.5 percent) populations. The majority of the population live in rural areas (77.9 percent) (*Censo de Población*). The most populated area of the county (71 percent of the population) is the mountain valley and adjacent slopes, which extend from 2,600 metres to 3,350 metres above sea level, and is called locally the "Andean zone" of the canton.

Cotacachi has been traditionally known for the production of leather handicrafts. The economy also relies on agricultural production and tourism with an associated small handicraft production. The leather industry is owned by mestizos and directed toward the national and Colombian markets. The agricultural activity of Cotacachi comprises different groups from export-oriented producers to small farmers. A small group of entrepreneurs is linked to the agro-export of flowers or the industry of turkey ranching, whereas large and medium producers are devoted to livestock production and the production of cereals, vegetables, and fruits (Ortiz 64-90). These three groups combined own 80 percent of the land. The majority of producers, nevertheless, are *campesinos*, small farmers who grow corn, beans, tubers, and cereals, and are more oriented towards self-consumption than the market. Several of these small producers are *Kichwa* indigenous peoples, whose plots of land are under five hectares and do not permit self-sufficiency. Seventy percent of the families of this group of agricultural producers are below the poverty line (Ortiz 88).

In this context, *campesinos* diversify their economic strategies. Opportunities for remunerated jobs are limited to seasonal work in some agricultural estates, and many migrate to urban areas for jobs. In Cotacachi, 60 percent of indigenous people migrate for wage work and 35 percent of heads of household work away from their place of residence (Ortiz 99). This migration has been defined as circular migration because it is based on "the circulation to urban areas for jobs in a context where not all needs can be met in one's own community" (Flora 273). In this pattern of circulation, migrants do not intend to relocate permanently in the urban areas where they work. Instead, people leave their communities to work somewhere else during the week and return during the weekends, or they leave their communities for the day to work in nearby cities and towns, and return to their communities at the end of the day (Flora 271-72). This diversified strategy and the change of occupations are central to the survival of indigenous *campesino* families (Ortiz 99), given that a permanent job is an exception for most residents of the Andean zone of Cotacachi (Flora 276).

Cotacachi has pioneered citizen participation in local government since 1996. Groups from civil society have participated in annual citizen assemblies, in defining the canton's development plan, and in participatory budgets. The participatory process has been institutionalized in the Assembly of Cotacachi Canton's Unity, an umbrella organization that brings together various political actors. Currently, the Assembly is comprised of nineteen organizations and constitutes a "public space of dialogue" for the discussion of citizen interests (Ortiz 13). In every annual meeting of the assembly, hundreds of delegates from the organizations come together to define the most important issues for the population of Cotacachi and to agree on resolutions, which are considered mandates to be addressed by the local municipality.

Indigenous women of Cotacachi take part in the process of citizen participation both through the organization that represents the indigenous communities of the canton, UNORCAC (Union of Indigenous and Campesino Organizations of Cotacachi, comprising forty five indigenous communities), and through a coordinating council of women's organization of the canton. Within UNORCAC, indigenous women have carved their own institutional space through a Central Committee of Women. The local scenario of citizen participation has allowed the inclusion of women's perspectives and the integration of formerly underrepresented groups. The most important elements in the women's agenda have been health with an emphasis on intercultural health; access to education and fighting illiteracy; attention to intrafamily and sexual violence; economic alternatives based on agroecology, handicrafts, and community tourism; access to credit; and participation in the struggles for the defense of natural resources and biodiversity (Arboleda).

Although indigenous women in Latin America and in Ecuador have had an important political role in the indigenous movement and its history (Becker), they still face challenges when participating in political life (Picq). Indigenous women in Cotacachi participate at multiple levels of politics. They are representatives in the *cabildos* (term used for the community councils and their authorities); in women's groups; in UNORCAC and the Central Committee of Women of this organization; in groups of midwives; in the coordinating council of women of canton Cotacachi; in the canton's assembly; and as elected officials in the municipality. The election of indigenous women as official representatives of organizations has increased since the second half of the 1990s in response to several factors: the ascendance of the indigenous movement in Ecuador; the experience of citizen participation in Cotacachi; the demand of development projects and nongovernmental organizations for gender mainstreaming; the national quota laws for the participation of women in elections; and the increased circular migration of men out of the area (Moreno).

Analyzing the case of indigenous women of Cotacachi offers an opportunity to examine the contention that the local level of political participation may be the most auspicious for women's participation (Ranaboldo 63). In a wider context allegedly favourable to the participation of citizens in the canton's political process, it is possible to investigate what other factors present barriers for the participation of women in political life. In this chapter, I focus on the most local levels of the personal and community dynamics that affect indigenous female leaders. I argue that local politics are still fraught with elements that thwart this group's participation and that adversely affect indigenous women. Specifically, the examination of their role as mothers and cultural reproducers makes it possible to tackle discourses that aim to "domesticate" indigenous women and make them return to those spaces where they are supposed to enact the practices necessary for cultural continuity. By making an appeal to idea of "the mother," family and community members put pressure on politically active women to return to the proper spaces of home, fields, and community, which they are supposedly abandoning or neglecting because of their involvement in politics.

METHODOLOGY

The information presented comes from ethnographic research conducted in Cotacachi, which combined participant observation, interviews, and archival research. The methods used elicited data on the participation of women in their indigenous organization; their historical achievements; the factors facilitating or limiting their participation; their current political agenda and priorities; and the strategies they used in different forums. The emphasis of this ethnographic research is on the interpretations, perceptions, and understandings of indigenous women about their participation in diverse formal and informal political arenas. Fieldwork was conducted for fifteen months during two fieldwork seasons between 2009 and 2011.

Interviews were conducted with diverse actors in Cotacachi, which allow for understanding the variations on viewpoints regarding indigenous women's participation. I conducted a total of eighty-six interviews, fifty-five of which were with indigenous women, both leaders and nonleaders. Thirty-three of the total interviews were conducted specifically with former and current indigenous women leaders. Interviewing women who were both past and present leaders and rank-and-file members of the communities was intended to represent variation on women's experiences regarding participation, or lack thereof, in projects and politics. Additionally, interviewees included indigenous men, mestizo and indigenous staff at UNORCAC, officials of the Municipality, members of the Assembly of Citizens, and staff of NGOs working on or funding projects for indigenous women in Cotacachi.

During the fieldwork, I resided in an indigenous community with one of the female leaders of the indigenous organization. Living in the community and learning the *Kichwa* language helped me negotiate the tensions arising from my mestiza identity. Participant observation allowed me to attend activities, events, and meetings of the *Kichwa* women participating in leadership and projects in

UNORCAC. I attended the monthly meetings of the Committee of Women; meetings of the indigenous organization; activities and workshops of projects involving midwives and health volunteers, microcredit, and agricultural projects for indigenous women; and meetings of indigenous women with other organizations of women from different areas of the canton. As I followed the women to the diverse political arenas in which they were active, I also partook in activities related to the local government and canton-level organizations, such as periodic meetings and the annual grand meeting of the Citizen Assembly. I had the opportunity to travel with some leaders to meetings and workshops in other areas of Ecuador.

Participant observation allowed me to observe the interaction between indigenous women and a myriad of actors with whom they interrelated—local officials, NGO staff members, indigenous peoples from other parts of Ecuador, foreign volunteers, researchers and students, and members of feminist organizations, among others. In these encounters, I paid attention to decision-making processes and the involvement or displacement of the indigenous women's voices in those processes. Along with my attendance to these events, I also participated in the day-to-day life of the women and the community: baptisms, weddings, funerals, religious and secular rituals, birthdays, and inaugurations of infrastructure, among others.

Participant observation may prove critical to understanding discrepancies between discourse and practice during research on gender dynamics. In this research project, participant observation provided a source of information to be contrasted with interviews (Fernandez and Herzfeld 96). For instance, indigenous leaders may speak of an egalitarian, complementarity-based version of gender relations in the Andes while their daily interactions contradict such an ideal. Participant observation also granted the opportunity of informal talks on gender relations, or let me witness people's commentaries, which sometimes touched sensitive subjects (Spradley). The narratives I present here come from the interviews and fieldnotes of broader research on the political participation of indigenous women of Cotacachi (for further elaboration on the methodology, see Moreno 206-12). Names and identifying information have been changed to protect the participants of this research.

MOTHERHOOD: ITS POSSIBILITIES AND TRAPS

When speaking about women in politics in Latin America, one soon stumbles into the trope of motherhood. Women either have entered politics under the banner of their maternal identity or have been excluded or marginalized because of it. Moreover, motherhood remains central to the construction of women's identities in Latin America, whether women embrace it or contest and challenge it. For instance, simplified depictions of female gender roles in Latin America, such as *marianismo*, point specifically to notions of motherhood (Stevens 91). This concept also entails the notion of a submissive and selfless mother who sacrifices for the family. *Marianismo* has been thoroughly critiqued as an over-generalization constructed on data limited to middle-class, urban Mexican women. The concept does not account for historical context, cultural change, and the experiences of the peasant, poor, and working-class women of Latin America (Navarro). Although *marianismo* as a concept for ideal womanhood has been contested, motherhood itself continues to be seen as a primary role in the lives of many women.

On the one hand, motherhood has been the basis for the political participation of some women in Latin America. At times, women's involvement in the political arena has entailed an extension of their domestic and maternal roles. In this line, Elsa Chaney has characterized women in politics as "supermadres"—"super mothers" who assume maternal roles in the supradomestic realm of public affairs. Chaney argues that by entering the world of politics in their supermadre role, women are relegated to subordinate positions in the political system and to sections of politics that deal with welfare and feminine concerns (22). On the other hand, women qua mothers have also become political actors without necessarily entering the formal arena of politics. One paradigmatic example is the case of the Mothers of Plaza de Mayo.[2] Between 1976 and 1983, the military regime in Argentina perpetrated heinous human rights violations, including torture, disappearance, and murder. Amid a prevalent atmosphere of secrecy, denial, and fear, a group of mothers demanded to know the whereabouts of their children. Organizing under the banner of motherhood, these women represented the first responses to the human rights violations in Argentina and were able to raise the world's awareness of such violations.

This group of women emphasized their identity as traditional mothers and bearers of higher moral standards, willing to sacrifice anything for finding their disappeared children. At the same time, they redefined motherhood as political, public, and collective, as mothers of all the disappeared (Guzmán Bouvard), complicating and defying the binaries of the private-public and housewife-political activist. In other countries of Latin America, committees of mothers have also confronted authoritarian regimes seeking the truth about the disappearances of sons and daughters (Maier; Schirmer). Even if they mobilize around traditional motherhood, women went beyond some of its limitations and became political actors. For some mothers, this very same political participation revealed discriminatory gender dynamics as tensions arose with their husbands and children for their being away (Guzmán Bouvard 13).

Motherhood, even if political, is a double-edged sword as it enables but also impedes. Some women have used maternalist notions to their advantage and become supermadres in the political system or the voice of the disappeared in authoritarian regimes. Nevertheless, in the daily life of women, motherhood continues to set limits to their political participation (O'Connor, *Mothers Making* 4). Motherhood reproduces female subordination in the family and beyond, positioning women disadvantageously within the gender status quo and locating them in the private rather than the public sphere. Part of the reasons why feminists question the invocation of the institution of motherhood for public and political participation is that it works to ensure that women and their relation to reproduction and to children remain under male control. Additionally, the responsibilities of care work complicate women's public endeavours, sometimes ending, interrupting, or deferring their action (Jelín).

The limitations set by motherhood are also connected to the specific emotional reactions that it elicits by virtue of its continuing central role in the construction of female identities. As Lindal Buchanan asserts, "due to its role in subject formation and collusion with the gender system, the Mother is easy to invoke, but difficult to resist" (7). That is, the persuasive force of motherhood encourages

identification and an emotional response while discouraging critical distance and reflection. Politically active women may find that
their motherhood is put into question and used to discredit their
activities (Buchanan 7). Thus, women may be pressured to conform
to maternal values in order to deter criticism for abandoning their
maternal duties and to live up to the subjective compliance that
"the mother" demands. Mexican anthropologist Marcela Lagarde
argues that women have a "captive subjectivity"—one that is based
on the "being-for-other," a relation of vital dependency on *the
others* through maternity, filiality, and conjugality" (Lagarde 38).[3]
Based on an ethic of care, women prioritize others' interests over
their own. Motherhood continues to have cultural and symbolic
gravity in Latin America as well as in the individual's construction
of worth. Consequently, motherhood is useful for examining "the
reproduction of power and the power of reproduction" when
analyzing the women's involvement of politics (Joan Scott qtd. in
O'Connor, *Mothers Making* 8).

INDIGENOUS MOTHERS, GUARDIANS OF CULTURE

In Latin America, national and ethnic movements have positioned
women as signifiers and carriers of national and ethnic identity
(Crain; Gutiérrez; Muratorio; Radcliffe and Westwood). In their
bodies, choice of costume, language, practices, and socialization
of children, indigenous women play a paramount role in the
construction of cultural difference. It is not only in their roles as
cultural bearers but also in their roles as mothers that indigenous
women are vital to the continuity of their cultures. Leaders of
the movement explicitly emphasize this connection when they
associate women in their role as mothers with Pachamama, the
Mother Earth: "We are the carriers, conduits of our cultural and
genetic make-up; we gestate and brood life; together with men, we
are the axis of the family unit and society. We join our wombs to
our mother earth's womb to give birth to new times in this Latin
American continent" ("Manifesto").

Gender in the indigenous movement plays an important role at
both the symbolic level and the level of the practical and everyday
relations and interactions between men and women (Vásquez

García). The indigenous movement and its leaders have adopted the concept of complementarity to characterize male-female relationships as interdependent and harmonious, wherein men and women are different but both equally needed in the construction of indigenous communities. In certain communities of the Andes, gender relations may follow a more egalitarian arrangement in comparison to mestizo populations (Hamilton). However, the discourse of complementarity has been questioned. Complementarity does not necessarily imply egalitarian relationships and may actually entail hierarchies and exclusions (Harris; Prieto et al.). The critics of the concept view it as a discourse that essentializes indigenous identity for political mobilization; it fails to recognize gender inequality and disregards women's interests (Cervone; Picq). For some, though, it offers a mobilizing force that can be used as an ideal state of gender relations, which indigenous women can employ to denounce violence and exclusion at the level of the everyday relations and interactions (Méndez Torres).

In a similar way as how the discourse of complementarity may open space for legitimate action for some women, the role of guardian and reproducer of culture may provide opportunities for the political participation of indigenous women (Prieto et al). For instance, one of the main annual activities of the indigenous organization of Cotacachi is a seed fair intended to rescue and exchange native seeds. Indigenous women are seen as the ones who conserve these seeds, and their work is considered critical because the defense of agrobiodiversity is one of the main elements in the mission of the indigenous organization. The organization has also worked to revitalize indigenous traditional medicine. Midwives and health volunteers have played a central role in the creation of an intercultural health system in Cotacachi. Participating in health initiatives has been pivotal for female leaders in Cotacachi, as many of them became politically active as health representatives elected in the organization.

Despite the symbolic value of the figure of the guardian of culture and its usefulness for some female leaders, the gender gap in politics within the movement indicates the marginalization of indigenous women at the level of gender practices and relations (Picq; O'Connor, *Gender*). In some cases, the defense of culture becomes a mechanism of control and a system of oppression: the guardians become the guarded (Picq). Even in a figure that purportedly exemplifies Andean complementarity, the *chacha-warmi* or political couple among the Bolivian Aymara, women stand only in nominal equality vis-à-vis men, but in the practice men occupy most of the leadership positions and take more advantage of indigenous organizations (Arnold and Spedding 37). In Cotacachi, although women have increasingly been selected for the important offices of president and vice-president, they are still overrepresented in more supportive roles, such as secretaries and treasurers.[4] Moreover, in the water boards of fourteen communities that have community managed water systems, only one woman was president in 2010. Additionally, interviewees related that women used not to voice their opinions in the community assemblies until recently. Indigenous women leaders of Cotacachi also expressed that their proposals are not always heard in the indigenous organization. Thus, indigenous women are increasingly present in the community councils and the indigenous organization but still find barriers to effective participation and decision making (Moreno).

That indigenous women are symbolically important but politically marginalized has important implications for the indigenous movement. First, these movements may not incorporate in their agendas the demands of women; they, therefore, may not be in favour of emancipation at all levels (Canessa). Second, the movement may be legitimizing discriminatory practices and essentialized identities, which could foreclose discussions of gender violence (Picq). Finally, the responsibilities related to cultural reproduction complicate the participation of indigenous women in politics. Motherhood, in specific, implies responsibilities that may limit women's attendance to meetings on a regular basis (O'Connor, *Mothers Making* 206).

Not only do many indigenous women find themselves too busy with domestic responsibilities, but some male activists also express concern when indigenous women abandon their homes and their role in maintaining cultural identity. O'Connor argues that motherhood simultaneously makes indigenous women central to the indigenous movement and marginal within it, and, thus, it is not surprising that some prominent indigenous women leaders choose to either remain single, as in the case of Nina Pacari in Ecuador, or to postpone maternity to commit to political causes, as in the case of Rigoberta Menchú in Guatemala (*Mothers Making* 206).

Indigenous women's role as guardians and reproducers of culture also highlights their maternal role, one that has the "Janus-like capacity to generate compelling persuasive means while buttressing restrictive gender roles" (Buchanan 6). In examining indigenous women's political involvement, consequently, it is useful to interrogate the practices and everyday relationships of female leaders in intimate and community spaces. In what follows, I explore the ways in which "the guardians become the guarded" (Picq 44) and some of the challenges that indigenous women face for their mobility and participation in politics. The analysis will concentrate in the terrain of the personal and the community to explore the gender exclusions women face when going beyond the proper spaces they should inhabit as cultural reproducers.

ACCUSATIONS AS *ANDARIEGAS, CARISHINAS,* AND BAD MOTHERS

By asserting that women are more Indian, Marisol de la Cadena argues that indigenous women's mobility beyond the community is more restricted than that of their male counterparts in a community near Cuzco. This is the case for the indigenous women of Cotacachi as well. Their political participation demands that women attend a series of events, meetings, and training opportunities for which they need to leave their homes and communities and sometimes go back late at night. Indigenous women leaders reported that they are accused of being "*andariegas,*" meaning "fond of walking." This epithet has several negative connotations beyond that referring to mobility itself. One is that of being lazy. Not only husbands but also other women, such as mothers, sisters, or neighbors, have accused women leaders of it. Lolita, the president of the Committee of Women of the indigenous organization during my fieldwork, commented: "my husband told me that I spend the time strolling, that that is because I'm lazy, that I do not want to do the house chores."[5] The accusation of being *andariega* points to local ideas about the proper place for women: women stay within the community; they care for their husbands and children; they work in the house, fields, or community. In short, their place is in the domestic spheres of home and community in their role as guardians of culture. Invoking the figure of the *andariega* serves to restrict women's mobility by tapping into local ideas of proper female behaviour.

Beyond being lazy, being *andariega* also implies neglecting children and husbands. In an argument that a leader had with her husband, her own sister sided with him claiming that the leader *"dejaba botando la casa y a los hijos"* ("she left the house and children abandoned"). The blaming of indigenous women leaders for the tragedies of their families is pervasive. In one occasion, this happened with the death of the husband of the elected representative of the midwives. The husband was a construction worker, and his death was the result of an accident in which he fell from a building. At the funeral, a man commented that the wife had neglected her husband because of her multiple commitments as the president of the midwives: *"las mujeres callejeras, ¡qué van a cuidar del marido!"* ("women who love to be out, no way they can take care of the husband!").

A former community female president recalled how her father used to scold her when she was young and left home to attend meetings of the local indigenous organization. In his scolding, he emphasized proper female behaviour and implied the moral failure of not following it: "You are a woman; you must be here with your mother, together working in the house, helping to do the household chores, helping with the animals, helping to wash the clothes, helping to cook. Where do you come from? What were you doing out of the house? *Carishina*, you are like a man. Only men can go out of the house or arrive late."

The adjective *carishina* is used against women in several contexts in which they transgress female gender roles and feminine behaviour. *Carishina* could describe a girl who is physically active, similar to the idea of a tomboy. *Carishina* also refers to women who do not know how to cook or do household chores. In this context, *carishina* refers specifically to the idea of *andariega*. The accusation of *andariega* is not limited to neglecting traditional gender roles and proper (domestic) places for women. In its connection with *carishina, andariega* establishes that the proper place for women is the home, and when women go out of it, they are behaving like men. This adjective is especially harmful and hurtful for indigenous female leaders because it casts doubts on women's morality and affects their reputation. "*Has de tener mozo*" ("you probably have a lover") is an accusation waged against politically active women.

Indigenous female leaders affirmed that domestic conflicts arose from this specific association of politically active women and their supposed infidelity. In the case of a few members, domestic conflict had escalated to physical violence. In one conversation among indigenous women and mestiza women in the coordinating council of women of the canton, the president of the council commented on her busy agenda and jokingly said: "*buscaránme otro marido*" ("you'd better start looking for a new husband for me"). Accusations of being *andariega* and *carishina* compromise women's reputation and may result in significant domestic conflict with their husbands.

Even when the accusation of *andariega* or *carishina* is not explicitly used, failure to live up to the maternal ideal is used against female leaders. A former community president recalled that her responsibilities required that she arrive late at night, and she did so several times with her children accompanying her. Coming back at night took a toll on the children's health. The arguments with her husband at home escalated until he launched the ultimatum: "*los guaguas o la comunidad*" ("our children or the community"). Distressed with the situation at home, the president decided to discuss her situation with other community authorities. The vice-president proposed that she resign her position, and then he would take her place as president for the rest of the term. She was not certain about the option. At a community assembly, she asked people whether she should resign, but the assembly did not accept it. They told her, "'you have to finish. You have had good work initiatives. You are doing fine. We know and we understand about your family, but it is only one year. Make the effort." She commented that those words raised her morale: "I felt stronger. I accepted. All right." In this example, although the community supported the female president in her political role, her domestic conflict originated in her attempt to simultaneously attend to her leadership responsibilities and to her maternal responsibilities. Her husband framed the problem in terms of traditional gender roles, viewing her political activity and her maternal responsibilities as not compatible.

Their husbands and family members, or other members of the community questioned women's absence from home because of their political activities, but so did their own children. Research with women in indigenous movements has documented a sense of guilt associated with not fulfilling traditional understandings of motherhood. In the case of the few female presidents of munici-palities of Oaxaca, for instance, the internalization of the maternal ideal was manifested in a sense of guilt expressed by women lead-ers, as their absence from home prevented them from living up to it, even when their children were older or independent (Vásquez García et al.). Some women leaders in Cotacachi also expressed their concern and feeling of guilt when their children complained about their absence from home. Many took their small children with them to the meetings.

At a meeting of the Committee of Women, I asked why one of the members was absent that day, and I was told that her adolescent son has told her that she was wasting her time with the organi-zation and was neglecting her home and fields. The president of the Committee of Women had similar issues. Her nine-year-old daughter and seven-year-old son at times protested her being away from home. Some leaders felt pressured by their families, both spouses and children, as well as members of the extended family and community, to conform to traditional gender norms—namely, being a good woman equated to prioritizing her role as wife and mother, and staying within the community confines, where women perform their role of the a hard-working community member in the fields and in communal work. Too often, women get chastised for their disruption of traditional gender roles, for moving beyond the house, fields, and community required to carry out their lead-ership responsibilities.

JUGGLING MULTIPLE ROLES:
LEADERS, COMMUNITY MEMBERS, AND MOTHERS

In their homes, fields, and communities, indigenous women of Cotacachi have extensive responsibilities. The changes associated with circular migration have resulted in the reassignment of responsibilities to the women who stay in their communities (Flora). The feminization of agriculture has been associated with a general decline of the peasant economy has increased the burden of agricultural activities and the care for livestock for those who stay in the community, especially women, young people, and elders (Larrea 37). This reconfiguration of livelihoods places significant demands on the time of women, whose subsistence agricultural work subsidizes the local economy (Larrea 58). Considering that women's time is not elastic, their political participation requires a considerable time commitment that significantly extends their working day.

Women leaders must manage these multiple responsibilities. The increased burden of agricultural responsibilities has not changed the traditional assignment of household chores to females. Cooking, for instance, is still one of the main elements associated with female responsibilities and identity in the Andes of Ecuador (Weismantel). Many women leaders complained that they had to wake up earlier to leave breakfast ready before they left for activities or meetings related to their leadership. Also, during meetings women excused themselves and left earlier because they had not left anything at home for their children or husband to eat. The president of the women of the indigenous organization of Cotacachi, Lolita, was repeatedly late to meetings in the morning because she needed to cook breakfast, walk the children to school, and feed the animals before she left to town.

Additionally, women take part in initiatives and projects of their indigenous organization related to agro-ecological production: diversification of home gardens to improve the family nutrition; raising small domestic animals, such as guinea pigs, poultry, pigs, and sheep; organic production of goldenberries and blackberries for national and international fair trade; participation in an annual fair for exchange of seeds; production of medicinal plants, etc. It is no coincidence that women play a significant role in these projects—first, as members of an indigenous community and second, as responsible for cultural continuity in the organization's agenda of ethno-development, development based on cultural identity.

Caring for small animals and for herds was considered one of the most demanding activities. Lolita was constantly worried about the caring of her cows and the need to herd them daily. This was an activity that she enjoyed, as she wandered through the community, but it was at odds with her need to be away, in Cotacachi town, or visiting other communities that belong to the organization. In 2010, a sustained drought affected the availability of grass, and, consequently, Lolita needed to herd the cows farther and farther away from home. Since her children were still relatively young, they could not help her with this daily responsibility. On one occasion, her ox fell into a ditch when she was at a meeting in Cotacachi town. Her daughter called her in desperation asking her to come back to the community. Other community members tried to help the ox out of the ditch, and they finally rescued it. Lolita recounted that the community members were angry with her for not having been there. Her husband argued that this happened because she was attending a meeting instead of being home.

In the indigenous organization UNORCAC, only the president of the organization received a salary. As president of the Committee of Women of the indigenous organization, and as all other leaders in the communities, Lolita received no salary. The women of the organization considered that not only the president of the organization but also the president of the Committee of Women should receive a salary. The rationale was that the role of president of the women necessitated that Lolita attend multiple activities and meetings as the representative of the indigenous women of Cotacachi. For the women of the organization, Lolita's work, though not totally commensurate with the role of president of the organization, made a considerable demand on her time. However, during my fieldwork this proposal received limited attention, and the organization reimbursed transportation expenses but did not approve the request of a salary. Part of Lolita's husband's complaints was that her prolonged absences from home or her hard work for the organization was not justified because she did not receive a salary or that her political activity did not directly benefit the specific community where they lived but generally all the communities that belonged to the indigenous organization.

ACCOMMODATING TO TRADITIONAL ROLES IN ORDER TO TRANSGRESS THEM

At the level of the family, women leaders used a variety of tactics that helped them continue with their political participation as they tried to live up to their roles as mothers, agriculturalists, and community members. Tactics are acts that depend on time and seizing opportunities. They depend on "clever tricks, knowing how to get away with things, 'hunter's cunning,' maneuvers, polymorphic simulations, joyful discoveries, poetic as well as warlike" (Certeau xix). Women's ability to move out from the spaces of the home and the community to the public spaces of their political participation is predicated upon a series of small acts that acknowledge the power of the husband to control their mobility.

Considering that most of the women I interviewed were or had been leaders of formal organized structures in their communities and beyond, their acquiescence to traditional gender roles may seem at odds with their political roles in public arenas. At the micro level of the family and community, indigenous women display their agency in ways that do not necessarily resist gender power configurations, in the sense that they do not oppose them overtly. This does not necessarily mean that they condone them either. For those adhering to traditional gender roles, husbands are still seen as having the final authority in families, with the capacity and the right to control their wives and children.

In order to deal with their absence from home, women leaders resorted to several tactics that to a great extent comply with traditional gender roles. In doing so, the leaders strived for fulfilling their maternal, household, and agricultural duties and complying with the image of the good mother and caring wife. For example, women leaders negotiated their political activities by taking into consideration when the husband was present or absent from home. During days in which her husband was at home (in the in-between

time of the end of a construction contract and a new one, for instance), the president of the Committee of Women was more likely
to stay at home and miss leadership activities. Another leader left
early from one of the meetings because her husband had told her:
"*volverás pronto m'ijita, porque voy a estar acá temprano*" ("come
back soon, my little daughter [form of endearment], because I am
going to be here early").

Additionally, indigenous women relied on relatives or other
people to take care of the children while they were busy with
their political activities when the help was available. However, the
leaders often took small children with them to their activities and
meetings, especially when they were babies and toddlers. Foreign
development workers and volunteers used to evaluate the presence
of children as negative for women's political participation. They
considered children's proper place to be at home or at school,
whereas in Ecuador, and more generally in Latin America, children
are present at several events and spaces with the adults. Thus,
someone, either from his or her own communities and families or
other people external to the community, always commented on
the leaders' mothering, whether they had brought their children or
they had left them behind. Bringing the children to the meetings,
though, made possible the participation in meetings and activities
when help was not available.

At times, women humored their husbands so that they were
on good terms before they informed them that they needed to
attend activities that required them to travel away and be absent
for more than a day. Many women reported that their husbands
were "*comprensivos*," or understanding, and not only let them
participate but also "helped" them at home when they had to leave.
Nevertheless, there are limits to this help, and, when there is the
perception that an indigenous woman's political activity jeopardizes
her motherly duties, even an understanding husband may press
the leader to abandon her political roles. This was, for instance
the case of the woman who put her resignation to the presidency
into the consideration of the community assembly.

The need for women to ask for permission to participate in
political activities reinforces the role of the husband as the patri-
arch of the family. In that sense, these micro tactics are forms of

accommodation to dominant values. Nevertheless, they "should not be viewed as the simple acceptance of dominant ideals or of the partner's power" (Alcalde 35). These quotidian accommodations to and negotiations with established traditional gender roles ultimately allow women to take their public leadership roles, and these political roles do transgress the traditionally "appropriate" place for women. Therefore, for these leaders, a foot in the door of the public depends upon accommodations in the private.

Nevertheless, in other instances, women leaders did not avoid conflict but continued with their participation despite it. One woman who had been an important leader recalled: "*así me machuque, me iba*" ("even if he smashed me, I went" [to go to activities as leader]). I also heard from others that this woman had experienced increased domestic violence during the high point of her political activism. Other leaders also commented that they participated even if it implied escalated conflict at home, especially when their presence in a meeting or activity was indispensable. Though not necessarily a situation reported by the majority of the interviewees, political participation and absence from home were seen as possible triggers of domestic violence.

CONCLUSIONS

Indigenous women have played an important role in the indigenous movement and are symbolically central as guardians of the culture. In canton Cotacachi, Ecuador, indigenous women have increased their participation in politics in their communities, local indigenous organization, and local processes of citizen participation and governance. They figure prominently as cultural reproducers within the indigenous organization's mission of promoting development based on indigenous culture by being the guardians of native seeds and the main practitioners of indigenous medicine in the intercultural health system of the canton.

Although indigenous women in Cotacachi have taken on new public roles as formal leaders in their communities and local organization, for many of them their maternal role complicates their political participation. Husbands may not necessarily be openly opposed to indigenous women's participation in politics, and may even be *comprensivos* regarding the demands that leadership place on women, but they, as well as other members of the family and the community, may use ideals of proper motherhood to limit the transgression of traditional gender roles that their political activity entails.

The political commitments of indigenous women add new responsibilities to their already long days, and their mobility beyond their homes and communities may also provoke negative reactions from their husbands, children, family, and community members, and even accusations that put into question their reputation. Invested in maintaining a respectable position as committed mothers and wives and hard-working community members, indigenous women use strategies that at times reproduce the traditional understandings of motherhood and proper female behaviour.

The difficulty of reconciling political participation and maternal, agricultural, and community responsibilities shows that domestic arrangements have largely remained untouched, even if the place of women in society is being redefined. Even when women do not necessarily condone this state of affairs, the weight and legitimacy of "the mother" compels them to use strategies that largely comply with or accommodate to traditional gender roles. The complaints of husbands and children and the gossip in the community may restrict the mobility of women, and discourage them from leaving their homes. The added responsibilities have high cost given that the leaders' time is not elastic and their leadership positions not remunerated, but the highest costs for the indigenous women leaders may be emotional when they are accused of being *andariegas*, *carishinas*, and bad mothers.

ENDNOTES

[1]Indigenous peoples of Ecuador are populations that recognize themselves as descendants of the groups that inhabited the land prior to the Spanish colonization, and have been historically marginalized by the dominant mestizo population. The Ecuadorian indigenous movement is a social movement that comprises the indigenous grassroots organizations, federations, and national confederations, and has struggled for cultural recognition and

collective rights. The Constitution of 1998 declares Ecuador a multicultural and pluri-ethnic country. The *Kichwa* are the biggest indigenous linguistic group comprising several ethnicities and peoples of the highlands and Amazon regions.

[2]There is a vast literature on the Mothers of the Plaza de Mayo. Among the most important works are Arditti; Guzmán Bouvard; Navarro; and Mellibosky.

[3]My translation from the original in Spanish.

[4]Data I collected in the archives of UNORCA Cindicate that in 2008, 26 percent of the presidents of the communities represented by the organization (46 communities) were women. In 2009, this figure decreased to 11 percent, whereas in 2010, it recovered to 23 percent (for more information in percentages related to vice-presidents, treasures, and secretaries see Moreno 125).

[5]My translations from interviews in Spanish and Kichwa.

WORKS CITED

Alcalde, M. Cristina. *The Woman in the Violence: Gender, Poverty, and Resistance in Peru.* Vanderbilt University Press, 2010.

Arboleda, María. "Género y Gobernanza Territorial en Cotacahi y Cotopaxi." *En las Fisuras del Poder. Movimiento Indígena, Cambio Social y Gobiernos Locales,* edited by Pablo Ospina, Instituto de Estudios Ecuatorianos, 2006, pp. 151-214.

Arditti, Rita. *Searching for Life. The Grandmothers of the Plaza de Mayo and the Disappeared Children of Argentina.* University of California Press, 1999.

Arnold, Denise Y., and Alison Spedding. *Mujeres en los Movimientos Sociales En Bolivia 2000- 2003.* CIDEM, 2005.

Becker, Marc. *Indians and Leftists in the Making of Ecuador's Modern Indigenous Movements.* Duke University Press, 2008.

Buchanan, Lindal. *Rhetorics of Motherhood.* Southern Illinois University Press, 2013.

Canessa, Andrew. "Soñando con los Padres: Fausto Reinaga y el Masculinismo Indígena." *Género, complementariedades y exclusiones en Mesoamérica y los Andes,* edited by R. Aída Hernández and Andrew Canessa, Abya Yala, British Academy, and IWGIA, 2012, pp. 99-116.

Certeau, Michel. *The Practice of Everyday Life*. University of California Press, 1984.

Cervone, Emma. "Engendering Leadership: Indigenous Women Leaders in the Ecuadorian Andes." *Gender's Place: Feminist Anthropologies of Latin America*. Ed. Lessie Jo Frazier et al., Palgrave Macmillan, 2002, pp. 179-96.

Chaney, Elsa M. *Supermadre: Women in Politics in Latin America*. University of Texas Press, 2014.

Crain, Mary. "La Interpretación de Género y Etnicidad: Nuevas Autorepresentaciones de la Mujer Indígena en el Contexto Urbano De Quito." *Antología de Género*, edited by G. Herrera, FLASCO-Junta De Andalucía, 2001, pp. 353-81.

Craske, Nikki. *Women and Politics in Latin America*. Rutgers University Press, 1999.

De la Cadena, Marisol. "Women Are More Indian: Ethnicity and Gender in a Community near Cuzco.: *Ethnicity, Markets, and Migration in the Andes: At the Crossroads of History and Anthropology*, edited by Olivia Harris, Duke University Press, 1995, pp. 329-48.

Fernandez, James, and Michael Herzfeld. "In Search of Meaningful Methods." *Handbook of Methods in Cultural Anthropology*, edited by H. Russell Bernard, Altamira Press, 2003, pp. 89-129.

Flora, Gabriela. "Circular Migration and Community Identity: Their Relationship to the Land." *Development with Identity: Community, Culture and Sustainability in the Andes*, edited by Robert E. Rhoades, CABI Publishing, 2006, pp. 271-86.

Gutiérrez, Natividad. *Women, Ethnicity, and Nationalisms in Latin America*. Ashgate, 2007.

Guzmán Bouvard, Marguerite. *Revolutionizing Motherhood: The Mothers of the Plaza de Mayo (Latin American Silhouettes)*. Scholarly Resources Inc., 2002..

Hamilton, Sarah. *The Two-Headed Household: Gender and Rural Development in the Ecuadorean Andes*. University of Pittsburgh Press, 1998.

Harris, Olivia. "Complementarity and Conflict: An Andean View of Women and Men." *Sex and Age as Principles of Social Differentiation*, edited by J.S. La Fontaine. Academic Press,1978, 21-40.

Censo de Población y Vivienda 2010. Instituto Nacional de Es-

tadísticas y Censos, www.ecuadorencifras.gob.ec/wp-content/
descargas/Libros/Demografia/documentofinal1.pdf. Accessed 1
October 2015.

Jelín, Elizabeth. "Engendering Human Rights." *Gender Politics
in Latin America: Debates in Theory and Practice,* edited by
Elizabeth Dore, Monthly Review Press, 1997, pp. 65-83.

Lagarde, Marcela. *El Cautiverio de Las Mujeres: Madresposas,
Monjas, Putas, Presas y Locas* Universidad Nacional Autónoma
de México, 1990.

Larrea, Sissy. "Género, Cultura y Ambiente: La Agenda Ambien-
tal de Cotacachi y la Ausencia de los Saberes y Prácticas de las
Mujeres Rurales." MA thesis, FLACSO, 2009.

Maier, Elizabeth. *Las Madres de los Desaparecidos: Un Nuevo Mito
Materno en América Latina?* México, Universidad Autónoma
Metropolitana, Colegio de la Frontera Norte, 2001.

"Manifesto of the First Continental Summit of Indigenous Women."
Abya Yala Net. 22 Jun. 2009, www.abyayalanet.org/node/22.
Accessed 1 October 2015.

Mellibosky, Matilde. *Circle of Love over Death: Testimonies of the
Mothers of Plaza de Mayo.* Willimantic. Curbstone Press, 1997.

Méndez Torres, Georgina. "Miradas de Género de las Mujeres
Indígenas en Ecuador, Colombia y México." *Participación y
Políticas de MujeresIindígenas en América Latina,* edited by
Andrea Pequeño, FLASCO, Ministerio de Cultura del Ecuador,
2009, pp. 53-71.

Moreno Parra, María S. *Warmikuna Juyayay! Ecuadorian and
Latin American Indigenous Women Gaining Spaces in Ethnic
Politics.* Dissertation, University of Kentucky, 2014.

Muratorio, Blanca. "Indigenous Women's Identities and the Politics
of Cultural Reproduction in the Ecuadorian Amazon." *American
Anthropologist,* vol. 100, no. 2, 1998, pp. 409-20.

Navarro, Marysa. "Against Marianism." *Gender's Place: Feminist
Anthropologies of Latin America,* edited by Lessie Jo Frazier et
al. Palgrave Macmillan, 2002, pp. 257-72.

O'Connor, Erin E. *Gender, Indian, Nation: The Contradictions of
Making Ecuador, 1830-1925.* University of Arizona Press, 2007.

O'Connor, Erin E. *Mothers Making Latin America: Gender,
Households, and Politics since 1825.* John Wiley & Sons, 2014.

Ortiz, Santiago. *Cotacachi: Una Apuesta por la Democracia Participativa*. FLASCO, 2004.

Picq, Manuela. "Trapped Between Gender and Ethnicity: Identity Politics in Ecuador." *Identity Politics in the Age of Globalization*, edited by Roger A. Coates and Markus Thiel, First Forum Press, 2010, pp. 31-56.

Prieto, Mercedes, et la. "Respeto, Discrinación y Violencia: Mujeres Indígenas en Ecuador, 1990 2004." *De lo Privado a lo Público: 30 Años de Lucha Ciudadana de las Mujeres en América*, edited by A. L. Bolles et al., Siglo XXI Editores, 2006, pp. 158-80.

Radcliffe, Sarah A., and Sallie Westwood. *Remaking the Nation: Place, Identity and Politics in Latin America*. Routledge, 1996.

Ranaboldo, Claudia. *Participación Política de las Mujeres Indígenas en los Procesos de Gobernabilidad Local y en los Gobiernos Locales: Bolivia, Colombia, Ecuador, Guatemala y Perú*. UN-INSTRAW, 2006.

Schirmer, Jennifer. "The Seeking of Truth and Gendering of Consciousness." *Viva: Women and Popular Protest in Latin America*, edited by Sara Radcliffe and Sallie Westwood, Routledge, 1993, pp. 30-64.

"Shuk Yuyaylly, Shuk Shungulla, Shuk Makilla. Un Solo Pensamiento, Un Solo Corazón y Una Sola Mano. Propuesta Política y Plan Estratégico UNORCAC 2008- 2018." UNORCAC, 2008.

Spradley, James. *Participant Observation*. Holt, Rinehart and Winston, 1980.

Stevens, Evelyn. "The Other Face of Machismo in Latin America." *Female and Male in Latin America: Essays*, edited by A.M. Pescatello, University of Pittsburgh Press, 1973, pp. 89-102.

Vásquez García, Carolina María. "Miradas de Las Mujeres Ayuujk. Nuestra Experiencia de Vida Communitaria en la Construcción del Género." *Genero, complementariedades y exclusiones en Mesoamérica y los Andes*, edited by Aída Hernández and Andrew Canessa, IWGIA, 2012, 319-28.

Vásquez García, Verónica, et al.. "Entre el Cargo, la Maternidad y la Doble Jornada. Presidentas Municipales de Oaxaca." *Perfiles Latinoamericanos* vol. 39, 2012, pp. 31-57.

Weismantel, Mary J. *Food, Gender, and Poverty in the Ecuadorian Andes*. University of Pennsylvania Press, 1992.

9.
Between the Private and the Public

Paradoxes of Motherhood and Politics in Brazil

NATHALIE REIS ITABORAÍ

IN THE LAST DECADES, Brazilian women have experienced substantial changes in their experience of maternity, with a remarkable reduction in fertility rates and an expressive diversification of family arrangements. The transformations in their private lives, however, were not accompanied by a significant improvement in female political representation. Despite the fact that a woman has been president of Brazil since 2011,[2] the presence of women in positions of power continues to be very small (around 10 percent).[3] In this context, some researchers believe that the advances in women's rights were obtained more from advocacy than from an increase in the presence of women in Congress.[4] Furthermore, the scarce data available on the characteristics of female politicians suggest that they are married and/or mothers in a smaller proportion than men, and usually they are not mothers of small children.

Women have a long and diversified tradition of political participation in Brazil, including resistance against dictatorship, participation in popular movements, and defending women rights, along with specific demands for rights related to motherhood and childcare. This chapter analyzes interviews with women who are mothers and who participate in varied political arenas, some official and some not, and asks them about their political and private trajectories.

In this chapter, I analyze some aspects of women political participation, relating them to the familial life, especially motherhood. The first section presents the methodological approach of this research. The second section offers a brief historical review of the political participation of women, especially mothers, since the

1970s. The third discusses the difficult insertion of mothers in the political field and considers cultural and institutional aspects. The fourth section considers some mothers' perception about family and politics, their possible reconciliation, and the challenges of being an unstereotypical mother and participating in politics. The chapter concludes by summarizing some questions about mothers in politics and then looks beyond their participation in politics to discuss the inability of the public sphere to accommodate them. This research does not intend to be representative of women's political participation in Brazil but to propose some questions based on information collected in dialogue with the literature on women in politics in Brazil.

METHODOLOGICAL APPROACH

This analysis results from interviews and observation in the contexts of women's[5] political participation, including the participation in a regular meeting of a policies management council and a municipal conference about policies for women.[6] As a strategy to approach and identify mothers in politics, I subscribed to participate in a local conference on women in politics. During this conference, I participated in the group about women's political representation in which two women who had been candidates for city council were present.

I undertook eight long interviews (approximately one hour in length) and had several shorter discussions (between ten and twenty minutes) during the conference. There was no posterior contact after the interviews. Respondents had to be a mother and to be a member of a political organization (political parties, trade unions, social movements etc.). The participation during the conferences allowed me to confront the discourses of the interviewees and to observe political meetings, which, in fact, did not accommodate mothers.

The data were collected between July and September 2015, in two cities over 300,000 inhabitants, both located in the Southeastern region, one of the most developed in Brazil. The proposal was to conduct the main fieldwork in a city (1), which included interviews and participant observation in political events, and complementary fieldwork in another city (2), which included only interviews. In a huge and socially unequal country like Brazil, studies suggest the importance of several kinds of variations (regional, socioeconomic, ethnic etc.), such as the fact that female political participation differs in local and national spheres (Miguel and Queiroz). Although this analysis does not intend to be representative of those regional and context differences, I attempted to obtain some diversity in data. And even though the data gathered are not enough for a systematic comparison, the choice of two different contexts aims to broaden the range of views.

In the first city, where I attended the conferences, it was possible to identify and contact the respondents in public spaces. The long interviews were conducted in reserved, isolated spaces. During the conference, I held short interviews in spaces of common use, such as restaurants and halls. In the second city, the first contact with respondents was mediated by another person who had previously identified women who are mothers as well as political activists. One interview was held in the house of the participant, and the other was in a cafe of a mall. To maintain the anonymity of the interviewees, I have not named the cities, as some of the researched women occupy public positions and could be identified. This protection permitted them to provide information about the occupied positions, which is relevant to situate the historical and social context of the interviewed mothers.

Women from different socioeconomic conditions and with different political experiences, such as activists of popular movements and politicians, were counted in the analysis. These case studies are considered in the perspective of the challenges of articulation between family life and the mothers' effective political participation. As proposed by Lucia Avelar in *Segundo Eleitorado*, it is important to have an enlarged conception of political participation in order to analyze other political spheres in which women participate more actively (86). She proposes that political practice consists of a variety of participatory acts (vote, be voted for, and other nonelectoral participation) and political arenas, each of them with different costs, so women can choose forms of political participation that are more viable for them in each stage of life. For Avelar, it is important to analyze the female political activities considering women's life cycles and the role of motherhood.

Of course, women's participation in politics in Brazil occurs in several other ways beyond the role of mother. In the conference on women policies, for example, there were debates about transsexual and transgender demands of specific rights. I could observe a tension between these new identities and traditional ones of mothers in politics, but there were, simultaneously, women that had not been mothers who were surprised when I and other women discussed the difficulties that familial responsibilities posed for women to enter the political realm. At this moment, one woman talked about her responsibility of taking care of her old mother, highlighting that care demands are not only restricted to children.

Gender studies problematizes inequality in different dimensions, and political space is one with more resistance to changes (DeVault 32). The political arena is a male domain par excellence. The description of this field is masculine, and the interference of private life in politics is described as a disturbance. According to DeVault, feminist methodology seeks an "'excavation,' shifting the focus of standard practice from men's concerns in order to reveal the locations and perspectives of (all) women" (32). Despite all the stereotypes that female politicians are motherlike, this excavation is much more necessary and difficult in the case of mothers.

Feminist thinkers develop numerous approaches for undertaking studies on women and gender—reflecting about knowledge production, reviewing dualisms, and rejecting the separation between subject and object. Several studies explore the ethical dilemmas of fieldwork in general and in feminist methodology specifically, including the risk of methodological essentialism and the limits of claims by intersubjectivity and reciprocity in feminist research (Stacey). Recognizing these dilemmas and the inherently asymmetrical situation of research, I interacted with research participants in a respectful, supportive, and empathetic manner, with friendliness, not friendship (Kirsch).

Answering some questions posed by the interviewee, I offered previous information about my university education and research project, explaining that I needed information about their familial and political trajectories. Some interviewees knew that I am a mother too, and once in an interview carried in a mall, two of my children appeared, so I and the interviewee greeted them. It was for us a funny situation. I suppose that the fact that I am a mother was a factor of identification in some situations.

Gender studies also questions the pretension to universalize female experiences, and pays attention to diversity. In these aspects, some reflections are useful concerning my being a woman who has a certain empathy for the participants, whereas my being a white and middle-class person probably was not a crucial difference, since the majority of the respondents belonged to the middle class (including high and low occupational groups, such as teachers and public servants). It should be noted that the circumstances of the conference (performed in business hours) represent a limitation for the presence of women of lower strata that work in less flexible conditions. In a next stage, I would like to expand this research by interviewing a more diverse range of mothers, including black, younger, and poorer ones. Although few respondents had these profiles, reflections about social cleavages in political participation emerged explicitly in the interviews. Many middle-class women commented that their activism is possible because of their domestic employees who free up time for them to participate in political activities.

A BRIEF HISTORICAL VIEW OF MOTHERS
IN POLITICS IN BRAZIL

In this section, I present some information about women's participation in the political sphere in Brazil. I emphasize the diversity of such political acts and some aspects in which motherhood is an interesting dimension to be analyzed in female political participation. The aim is to consider some turning points in the political landscape since the second half of the twentieth century in which motherhood and political activism walked more clearly side by side.

Suffragist movements began in Brazil in the final decades of the nineteenth century, and women have voted in Brazil since 1932. Therefore, since the nineteenth century, there have been organizations defending women's right and female workers participating in labour unions (Hahner), but it was only from the dictatorship period (1964-1985) on, and especially with redemocratization in 1985, that there were more intensive and visible women movements as well as more information about women in politics in Brazil.[7]

According to Maria da Glória Gohn, since 1975, women have been in the public sphere in different social roles. Many of those roles are familial ones, as mothers of disappeared political activists, and mothers who fight for better living conditions for the suburbs and workers. Ana Maria Colling discusses the family tensions that women experienced during the Brazilian dictatorship—such as the disruption of family ties, threats against the children of political prisoners who were mothers, and the struggles of the mothers for the liberation of their sons and daughters. The author shows the challenges of being a political woman during the dictatorship because of the patriarchal values of the time and the repressive political environment. By the perspective of the repressive state apparatus, women were classified into two deviant categories, prostitutes or communists. They were also seen as only an appendix of male activists because it was supposed that women activists were incapable of political decisions. Women who became politically active during the dictatorship faced prejudice from not only the police but also men engaged in left-wing movements. Male militants on the Brazilian left also had their prejudices during a time with so many social changes, especially in sexual behaviour, which threatened the traditional family institution.[8]

In this context, it is not surprising that the entrance of many women to political life often occurred through the Church, since it was a way of legitimate mobilization at that time. As an interviewee commented: "In military dictatorship we would in fact be tied to the Church's apron strings. There was a more progressive church, which worked with neighbourhoods with the most excluded population, a church of the liberation theology."[9]

Liberation theology has been developed in Brazil since the 1970s, and it proposes an interpretation of Christianity that favours poor and marginalized people, and helps them politically organize around social justice demands. Avelar notes in *Segundo Eleitorado*, however, that the majority of Brazilian women during 1980s have, in general, identified with traditional Catholicism and not with the vindictive side of liberation theology, and there is evidence

172

that traditional Catholicism reiterates traditional female roles and imposes obstacles to individual autonomy.

At same time, it is recognized these critical religious viewpoints, inspired in liberation theology, helped to organize some political movements, including the case of mothers' clubs (Sader). According to Eder Sader, there have been housewives associations since at least the 1950s, which were often sponsored by benevolent religious or social institutions. The purpose was to transmit skills of housework (such as sewing and embroidery) and hygiene and health notions to poor women. These relations of paternalism enclosed a relationship of gratitude and suspicion (due to latent class conflicts) of assisted women toward the upper-class ladies who were attending them.

In contrast, self-managed movements of lower-class mothers emerged in the 1970s and provided a social space for these women to evade the oppressive routine of family responsibilities; they learned new abilities and generated income. Sader emphasizes the importance of the Church in the constitution of these movements, not only in terms of material support but in terms of legitimacy. Such assistance was absolutely necessary in the face of two then socially condemned forms of political activism: the right wing, with its unreliable politicians, and the left wing, with its subversive protestors. These mothers' movements mobilized around questions about the cost of living reiterated the tradition—which was analyzed by E.P. Thompson in Europe—of women's movements around everyday demands of working families, reaffirming traditional care roles of mothers, in an approach very different from the modern feminist claims for female autonomy, including the sexual domain. Nevertheless, Sader shows that in the Brazilian mother movements of the 1970s, the politicization of everyday life helped to question the traditional domestic roles assigned to homemakers.

Mothers also fought for children's education in the context of increasing female participation in the labour market. In the 1970s and 1980s, there was a flourishing of women's movements that demanded kindergartens and infrastructure to facilitate the work of mothers (Rosemberg). The usual response to the pressure from these popular movements was the community nurseries, which emerged from the collaboration between government and community organizations. The Brazilian fight for nurseries has persisted with advances and new tactics in the recent decades (Marcondes et al.).

Nowadays, it is also established that women who are mothers, through their moral force, can resist violence, especially in Brazilian slums (Machado da Silva; Leite). The moral force of mothers appears especially in situations where they are forced to defend their families. Fabio Araújo analyzes the case of the "Mothers of Acari" who mobilized against the state and military police officers accused of extortion, and the torture and murder of their young sons. Araújo demonstrates that it is from the traditional mother role that these women find legitimacy to enter the public sphere, but other senses are intertwined in the process of transition from mothers who suffer (because their families were victims of public violence) to mothers who struggle. Employing a policy of emotions and feelings in their manifestations in public spaces, walking in circles, or remaining silent with photos of missing children hanging from their bodies, they seek for their personal tragedies not to be forgotten and to convert them into units of collective situations for which they expect solidarity, justice, and repair. In this process, these women have created a collective identity and have transformed their self-images and the historical significance of motherhood.

These examples of the political participation of mothers in Brazilian history illustrate its force and capacity for political action, but in general there are many difficulties facing mothers who participate in the political domain, especially the representative one. Therefore, it is important to analyze the difficulties that mothers tackle in their political participation.

DIFFICULTIES IN WOMEN'S ENTRANCE INTO THE POLITICAL FIELD

In the last decades, Brazil has experienced an expansion of women's participation in various spheres, but the political field remains very masculine. To some extent, inequality in political representation reproduces social inequality, affecting not only women but also other oppressed groups, such as lowest classes and excluded ethnicities (Phillips, "De uma política"; Santos; Campos and Machado), all of them underrepresented in political spheres. As emphasized by

Avelar in "Mulher e Política," there is a gap between, on the one hand, increasing women's participation in the labour market and in civil society organizations and, on the other hand, their small presence in the spaces of formal representation and political parties. Avelar affirms that women are involved in politics but not as officials, since most are not elected.

Avelar in "Dos Movimentos" points out that women's participation in political movements and NGOs has expanded, but there are still restrictions on their participation in parties and formal politics. Avelar shows that in 2007 women at the summit of the major parties ranged between 7 and 16 percent—they attain 30 percent in the Workers' Party (PT), which she attributes to the increased presence of social movements at the base of it. According to Avelar, the best example of the difficulties facing women in parties is their small political representation in official leadership roles ("Dos Movimentos" 109).

Attempts to increase the feminine presence in representative positions have not had the expected impact. The Brazilian quota law increased the number of female candidates but not the percentage of women elected. Parties can include female candidates, to be adjusted to law, without providing the conditions for women to be elected. The fact that parties should fill a quote of 30 percent of women candidates creates some paradoxical situations. One activist said that after her children had grown, she became a candidate for councillor several times just to bargain, with the party, to support the social actions that she was developing: "I applied in exchange for a building site, but not even I voted for me," as she did not believe in her electoral possibilities. According to her, women need to be above ideological conflicts between parties to advance their agenda: "I cannot be political; I am apolitical. If I need an action, I cannot choose between party A or B. I stand for all parties according to my need to promote women claims." On the distribution of resources in the parties, she explained the following:

> They [political parties] only give [money to finance political campaigns] to men. Political party is money.... I did not have money to cover everyone who knows me in the

campaign. In the day that women shall receive the same amount as men they will win.... The woman has less friendship. The political man has a manager who likes him, a man in the industry who helps his campaign. For the woman it is more difficult.... [The party] distributes more [for male candidates] because a man has more potential. They imagine that the woman does not have any, but she would, if she had the money.

Therefore, the inequalities in the distribution of resources in the parties is compounded by the fact that women have less social capital, an essential resource in the fight to obtain power and performance in the public sphere (Avelar, *Mulheres na Elite* 76). According to Teresa Sacchet in her work "Capital Social," women participate more in popular councils and have a more private social capital, whereas men have a more public social capital, which favors male electoral performance.

Some interviewees reported that the entrance in the political spheres is more demanding with women, as Avelar shows that female professional qualifications and huge fighting spirit are the essential requirements for their professional and political advancement (*Mulheres na elite* 69). These problems of reconciliation become more severe to mothers who are activists. One interviewee said the following:

A woman has to work much harder than men in order to have a reasonable professional life. You always have to show yourself more hardworking than men. I have no doubt, I think for women today to compete on equal terms with men, they have to be more. You have to devote much more; it also has the working time at home, a working time with the children. My son, I think he had very little of me. Not only is the quality of time that matters, I think the quantity as well.

In *Mulheres na Elite*, Avelar argues that women make a difference in politics because, regardless of party, they tend to pay more attention and to give more priority to women's rights policies and subjects, such as family, children, health, and reproduction. However, women experience a division of labour that directs them to less prestigious political areas in Congress. Patricia Rangel notes that besides the low political representation of women among congress members, women are directed to committees for social protection, consumer protection, and education, and this is partly caused by their typical professional profile, such as teachers, health professionals, and social assistants. The authors Luis Felipe Miguel and and Fernanda Feitosa note that the female deputies handle human rights (which are present in 14.5 percent of their speeches compared to 4.1 percent of the speeches of men), family, reproductive rights, children and adolescents (9.9 percent for women versus 2.9 for men), whereas men show a greater concentration on economic policy and taxes (15.4 percent for men versus 9.2 percent for women) and in tribute and commemorative speeches (19.1 percent against 13.7 percent). Therefore, maternalism echoes in the profession profile (which is also a reflection of occupational segregation by gender, see Soares and Oliveira) of women who are elected and also in their areas of political action.

During the conference, participants cited, among the problems of political representation, the fact that although women are the majority in some movements, they themselves vote for men for positions of leadership. Women are the basis of many movements, but they do not ascend to leadership positions. Some of the interviewed women mentioned facts related to this lack of participation in leadership positions in areas such as teachers union, human rights, and public safety. One woman said, "Those who dedicate themselves to services in the area of human rights consist invariably of 95 percent of women, while men composed a great portion of the coordination of the programs, and all of this [stressing how paradoxical it is] considering that the human rights area is very active in the struggle for women's rights." Another woman said, "I am from a union in which 80 percent of the members are women, teachers, and much of the leadership is men. And we had to do a very great job in the union to create the secretariats of women in order to have women questions analyzed and discussed. So today, we have unions chaired by women, women in most relevant positions, but there is still great resistance."

The inclusion of women in politics frequently had the form of a partially accepted (but in fact a segregated) group, which is visible in the fact that parties created female sectors. Avelar notes that it was only in 1978 that the parties authorized the creation of women's sections in their organizations. She observes that rather than women being naturally absorbed into party organizations, a special sector was created that incorporated them yet also isolated them; their difference was recognized more than their equal condition (*Segundo Eleitorado* 42).

An additional problem is the use of gender stereotypes to explain the participation of women in politics. Motherhood can and has been mobilized politically. Daniela Peixoto Ramos notes that private roles, particularly the roles of mothers, can be dignified and opposed to political roles considered unworthy. In a situation that Ramos calls "benevolent stereotype of virtuous womanhood," it is supposed that women would behave in politics as they do at home, as honest and sensitive mothers, more concerned with societal well-being. The mobilization of this mother stereotype can essentialize the political participation of women as a way to bring private mothers' virtues into the political sphere, but it also acts to discourage women to participate in politics by arguing that it is necessary to protect them from the corruptive logic that rules political activity.

The view that women add more honesty and concern for social question to politics leads, however, to the expectation that women occupy political positions in the social sector that are less valued in the political field. Motherhood eventually has an empowering aspect, once the condition of mothers in certain contexts leads women to political activity and raises their mobilization, as highlighted in the case of Mothers of Acari and the paradigmatic example of the Mothers of Plaza de Mayo in Argentina. Nonetheless, the stereotype of the maternal woman is also questioned by women in politics. During the conference, a woman who had been a candidate for councilor questioned the fact that her party asked her to bring a pretty tablecloth to a reception, as if women were in parties only to perform a caregiver role, and she refused to attend. Therefore, women also resist practices that attempt to reify their subordinate role in politics and society.

Although in reality women politically act more in social areas, the essentialist view that women bring feminine virtues to the political sphere is an argument employed to alienate and marginalize women from the political sphere.

CHALLENGES OF FAMILY LIFE AND POLITICAL LIFE BALANCE

Given that our societies are structured around the separation of the public and private spheres and that there is a sexual division of labour not only in families but also in the public sphere, it is possible to consider that inequalities within the family are aligned with inequalities in economy and politics. As argued by Anne Phillips ("Does Feminism"), the fact that women are the primary caregivers has huge effects on the structure of the labour market and on political power. The interactions between motherhood and politics are marked by restrictions, as the burden of domestic and care work hinders the political participation of women and especially of mothers.

During the conference, young women pointed out that some parties and social movements have "*cirandas*," spaces with caregivers that take care of children during the meetings. Not all parties and social movements have this kind of structure though. One interviewee—a mother of two children aged five and eleven, who participates in three different movements: neighbourhood associations, black movement, and solidarity economy—said that when her children were born, she became less dedicated to the movement, but later she resumed her activism. She always brings her children to political activities with her: "I come and put two chairs and leave the children sleeping ... just ... I did not know other moms who do it, people think it is strange, but I do it anyway."

She heard criticism from people saying that she should be caring for her children instead of at the movement. She counts on the help of her mother and her husband to care for children. They have an equal division of housework, and she relies on her husband's support in her political participation, although he usually does not participate in political meetings. As she works during the day and studies at night and her husband comes home earlier than she does, he is the one who cooks and cleans the house. Even with more support of family members than other mothers, she highlights the need for better public childcare to allow mothers to dedicate themselves to paid work and politics.

Many of the interviewees have relied on the help of their mothers, some with the help of their husbands, and for those with better economic conditions, there is the option of hiring maids. The interviewees highlight the lack of childcare and other care services as a complicating factor of political participation of women, especially because many of the meetings occur at night. One interviewee had this to say:

> But we do not have public instruments that facilitate the woman in this role, you see that the number of day care centres is very small; it is one of the claims of almost all women.... So the state is lacking policies that could favour women. Even if there were enough kindergartens operating in daytime, most political meetings are at night. How do you deal with this? Where do you leave your children? That is it ... There are not public instruments that strengthen the role of women, you just do not have it.

Sachet discusses the limits of the notion of universal rights recalling Philips's reflections about the limits of usual conception of citizenship to incorporate the needs of women, especially those who are mothers (*Which Equalities*). In the opinion of Sacchet, the neglect of the demands from specific groups implies special treatment for hegemonic groups ("Representação"). I have found evidence that taking small children to political meetings is seen as disruptive of public-private boundaries. A black and popular activist, who was a candidate, said that in a political party event someone complained about the presence of a small child, saying that it was no place for children—in the face of that, she reacted publically saying that "yes, politics is place for children." This episode, as well as the episode of a health community agent that took her children to political meetings, suggests that women from lower classes, who cannot afford paid childcare, are more aware of the limits of political spheres to accommodate mothers, and they are more active in enlarging political spaces for mothers.

Several respondents pointed out party meetings are held at night, which creates difficulties for political participation because of women's responsibility of looking after not only children but also the elderly. In Brazil, any family responsibilities are predominantly assigned to women. Mothers who bring their children to political activities are rare, which is confirmed by the fact that during the conference I saw only one child, who was there only because she had been invited to do a musical performance. Even in a conference about women politics, children were not accommodated, which would have allowed the participation of their mothers. I also observed that among participating women, ones with older children or younger without children predominated. It was difficult to interview activists who were mothers of young children.

The unions and parties that do have daycare facilities only do because of the political pressure of female members: "In the party, we also have this concern to ensure you have daycare, but sometimes we have to fight with many companions, even in left-wing parties, even in a union that has a progressive posture and advanced one, to get spaces of power, so that women can participate, and it is still not satisfactory."

It is common that women who have managed to reconcile family life and political life understand themselves as atypical mothers. One interviewee explained it in the following way:

> I had the experience of being a mother when I was twenty and then when I was forty years old. My daughters miss me, but they understand that their mother is that way. Sometimes when they complain a lot I say, "you could have chosen another belly; you could have chosen a sedentary belly, but you chose a nomadic belly." It is complicated, but I think ... in the first place I believe we create our children to the world; we have to go over many barriers. A father goes out and leaves the child, people understand, but if a mother goes out and leaves the child, people say that the mother is denatured. People say: "How could she not think about the girl? She will grow up and become what?" ... I

have an example that the presence of quality is worth more than the presence in quantity, because my daughter gave demonstration of seriousness, commitment ... but I also do not enter the parameters that are put to mothers because then you have stereotypes of what a mother should be, I do not fit these stereotypes, but it's hard.

Despite these restrictions, the importance of political participation of mothers is highlighted, given their understanding of the specific demands that motherhood brings. Another woman had this to say:

I think when you're a mother it creates a sensitivity, an experience that I did not have, because before it was easy for me to attend a meeting. I could stay there up to 10 p.m. or 11 p.m. When I became a mother, I knew I would have to take her with me. So I think that motherhood also brings the experience of situations that if you are not a mother, you do not pass through them. So that is why having women in politics is important because even if the man has the intention of making a transformed society, an egalitarian one, he does not live the experiences that the woman lives. So that is why women have to participate; you cannot give their representation to a man. Women are really needed in politics, so they can speak in fact what they feel. The fact of being a mother made me even more aware to things that I was not aware of before.

To some extent, mothers have the potential to give visibility to issues previously excluded from the political agenda, for example, the subject of public care—care of children, the elderly, the sick, and disabled people. The experiences of mothers eventually encouraged more political activism in defined areas, such as children's and women's rights. Asked about eventual changes in their political participation after being a mother, some interviewees responded with the following:

I turned a lot to the struggle for children's rights. It reinforced the idea I have always had. Before it was more a political struggle; it was a fight for rights in a wider sense. It was not a change in population niches. Then [after becoming a mother] it became a fight for the rights of women, and for children's rights.

[Becoming a mother] is always going to affect you. From the moment you make the choice of motherhood, you give yourself to this care. When I was not married and did not have small children, I had no time restrictions. I was much more available for meetings, often meeting at night, participating over and above the work in other areas in a more systematic way. In fact [after motherhood], I focused more on engaging in the struggles in the workspace [she works as a social assistant]. Then I participated in political councils [as a representative of government, an official form of participation that is considered part of her work as a social assistant and that is accounted as working time].... Motherhood changes our look. As much as you have studies or critical discussion, when you talk about a place that you do not live, it is not the same thing. And when you live, you also measure many things because you exercise that place, you pass from the field only of ideas, academic discussion, to experience the place of motherhood.

Some of the interviewees only became devoted to politics after their children had grown. It raises the question of the reconciliation between familial life and political life in a similar fashion as the debates about family-work balance, since the existence of services that enable women (or people with familial responsibilities in general) to participate in social and political life is relevant for both issues.

The arrangements of reconciliation between family life and political life are very unequal. In *Segundo Eleitorado*, Avelar notes that there are not only inequalities between men and women but social inequalities among women. She observes, for example, that lower-class women have greater family responsibilities, whereas the upper classes can hire domestic services, which encourages their political participation over that of poorer women.

Similar to the child penalty at work, in politics women need to "masculinize" their routines. For example, women who occupy major positions in either the political or the work world are often not mothers, and if they are, their children are looked after by a domestic worker.

An interviewee clearly recognized the importance of a good domestic worker to permit her to balance work as political official and family life:

> I was lucky that in Brasilia I had a lady [house cleaner] who lived in my house. Then I realized that these women make it possible for other women to go to the fight too. This woman was a blessing for me, Dona Maria, a struggling woman. We can work or study thanks to the work of other women. I think that there should be services to take care of children. Today it is easier because there are the nurseries and schools, but they did not exist previously. Women became more independent due to the work of other women [domestic workers] who achieved labour rights only recently.[10]

When Avelar critically reviews the thesis of female apoliticalism, she points out that there are different processes of socialization for men and women, and they unequal access to economic resources for political campaigns (*Segundo Eleitorado*). The problem of women's political participation has a cultural dimension, related to gender inequalities in political socialization, and an institutional dimension related to difficulties of party organization, which suggests that the adoption of quotas is not enough because they can be applied only as a formality and not as an effective instrument to promote female representation. Additionally, there is little infrastructure to promote female engagement in political activities.

FINAL CONSIDERATIONS

This study shows that there are several possible relationships between motherhood and politics in Brazil. On the one hand, there are difficulties related to maternal responsibilities, wherein politics exacerbates the problems of family-work balance. In this context, if paid work is essential to survive, then political participation becomes unessential in the context of so many demands. Many women can decide to dedicate time to political participation before having children, or after they grow, or by not having them at all. This is related to the problem of the structure of care in society. On the other hand, the representations of political themes or areas suitable for women are still very much associated with a mother's place or an ethic of care, which reflects the practices of the division of labour by gender, now applied to politics.

It is necessary to escape the essentialist argument that women are more capable of representing female claims only because they are women, but, at the same time, it is desirable to recognize that women who are mothers can bring new political demands, such as care policies, once they have different experiences of social relations. Philips advocates special rights policies (through quotas) as a means of equalizing the political access of members of oppressed groups, and not as a representation of a specific group. The two dimensions seem important to me in all analyzed data. In addition to the challenges mothers face to participate in the political game, there is the task of representing the demands of the mothers in the political arena, as illustrated by the rarity of work-family reconciliation policies in Brazil.

Karolyne Romero and Celia Lessa Kerstenetzky show that despite the various studies about the ineffectiveness of quotas for political representation of women (Araújo and Alves), little is known about how the existing female representation affects Brazilian legislative life. The authors intend to fulfill this gap by focusing on the impact that the presence of women parliamentarians has upon the quantity and quality of propositions to reconcile family and work obligations. They show that the power of parliamentary women is very low and that propositions concerning reconciliation between family and work are uncommon. Furthermore, these propositions generally have more conservative content; they often focus on children's well-being and not on gender equality.

In this context, the importance of mobilization and political pressure is evident. One interviewee made a suggestive comparison between government that after pressure of women's movements finally attended their demands, and a mother who ends up giving in to tantrums of a child:

> I usually joke that the both executive and the legislative powers are similar to a mother who brings the child to the market. Sometimes you are going with ten reais [Brazilian currency] to buy potatoes and something else for lunch, then the child does such a great tantrum, you end up taking something for the child to stop crying. Social movements generally do not need to do tantrums but if they do not manifest, the government will not serve them because the priorities will be established by the government, and not the demands proposed by the social movements. Therefore, the participation of the population is essential to obtain more correspondence between the public priorities and the demands of the population. Moreover, even the idea that politics is not for women—that is, politics is dirty, politics is bad—this idea turns women away from participating in politics.

Described in social imaginary as mothers devoted to public causes, or as children making tantrums to get resources and rights, women still have not overcome condescending attitudes in Brazilian politics. Although they have been able to advance many rights by advocacy, underrepresentation of female issues in Brazilian policy expresses a significant gap of the gender revolution in this country, which has become stagnant because of the institutional inability of the quotas arrangement to increase the number of women elected. And it is now further threatened by a new conservative atmosphere.[11]

The uncomfortable situation of women in politics in Brazil can be seen in the opinion of one interviewee who worked in the capital coordinating a national public safety program. She noted that women always must mark and build their place in politics, unlike men, whose place in politics is recognized beforehand. She realized, however, that overcoming this uncomfortable place of women in politics has the potential to broaden the spectrum of issues and public included in politics:

I felt people staring at me ... a woman who is in a place of risk that was expected to be occupied by a male police officer. It was subtle. In daily life, people were surprised to know that they were nationally coordinated not by a truculent man, but by a woman.... People tend to have less respect. I am not sure if it is the proper way of saying that, perhaps recognition of women's work. The woman has to be marking this space in daily life, or she ceases to be recognized as authority, this place of leadership. If she slows down, if she is not at all times checking this space, it ceases to exist, which is not the same for men. Men come to a place, and it their place; it is the right place. Women come and it is more difficult, but I think we learned to deal with it, and fighting for these rights, we learned a lot more to fight for the rights of all.

This research is not intended to be conclusive, but it raises some hypotheses about the low representation of women who are mothers in Brazilian politics. Moreover, in some social movements that mothers participated, it was actually common for them to assert themselves as mothers who attend the traditional expectations of care to family members. In those situations where their maternalism was considered a political weapon, they were not elected candidates, but they acted in defense of their families. Such critical situations include protesting violence against children during the military dictatorship, opposing more recent police violence, and fighting since the 1970s for daycare to increase women's participation in the labour market.

The study sheds light on inequalities in the political field that intersect with inequalities in the family sphere, in this case investigated from the point of view of motherhood. This category is particularly interesting because against all the evidence of low political participation of women who are mothers, there is the assumption that women in politics are maternal. This essentialism proves to be a lie because the inequalities experienced by women in general in politics are no doubt even more intense for mothers. Even political participation in local politics lacks care structures for children and other dependents, which, if they existed, would allow the political participation of mothers and other women who have care responsibilities. Political representation is a restricted dimension of political participation for women and mothers, but it illustrates some of the challenges of shifting from descriptive representation to substantive representation in order to increase the number of women in formal politics and to meet their demands.

ENDNOTES

[1] I am very grateful for all the women who shared with me their experiences, allowing this research to be possible. I also thank the valuable help of my sister and my brother-in-law, Natércia and Eden Silveira, in the organization of the fieldwork, and Mayara Peixoto with the English language.

[2] Dilma Rousseff is a mother, grandmother, and the first woman to be a Brazilian president. She suffered an impeachment process in 2016, orchestrated by a congress recognized as conservative and full of male politicians who are themselves involved in large scale corruption scandals, who accused her of corruption. During this tumultuous period of her second elected government, she was the object of sexist provocations by politicians and the media. One conservative congressman, in his vote for her impeachment, paid tribute to the colonel that tortured Dilma when she was a political prisoner during the Brazilian dictatorship.

[3] Data from Inter-Parliamentary Union (2016) are available at http://www.ipu.org/wmn-e/classif.htm.

[4] Brazilian legislators have approved laws of affirmative action for women in politics and some political parties have taken measures to support female participation. However, in the context of small female political participation in Congress, women's rights have advanced because of the advocacy of women's movements that were able to influence public policies and political parties (Avelar, "Mulher e Política"). Rangel shows the impact of actions of feminist movements on the legislative production in Brazil. Although the Constituent of 1988 counts a very small percentage of women among the members of the Parliament, these members joined in a nonpartisan way to advance women's rights; there was a strong

advocacy (at the time known as the "Lipstick Lobby"), which allowed 80 percent of female claims to be incorporated in the 1988 Constitution (Rangel).

[5]All the interviewees are mothers. The use of the term "women" is to avoid repetition.

[6]In Brazil, there are public policy conferences in local, regional, and national levels in several areas in order to promote popular participation in definitions of the government goals. I accompanied the two days of a public policy conference and an ordinary meeting of a municipal council, both in the area of women's rights. There are also other public policy conferences and councils about social assistance and children and teenagers' rights and health.

[7]Since the 1980s, women's political participation in different social movements has been gaining prominence. Uriella Coelho Ribeiro notes that the spaces of expanded democracy—the settlements of the Landless Movement, participatory budgeting, and associations of civil society—are more receptive to female participation. Nevertheless, women tend to be concentrated at the base of such movements, and the positions of power are still occupied by a majority of men. The pluralization of female political representation has been facilitated by new forms of representation established by the 1988 Constitution, among which the policy councils have been created to promote rights in many areas. These councils are composed of representatives of public administration and civil society. In her analysis of Health Councils, Ribeiro notes parity in the number of male and female representatives, but she emphasizes a higher frequency of men talking and that women participated more as government officials, bearers of a technical knowledge, and not in the condition of users of the Health Services like the majority of men.

[8]Moreover, if in the 1970s women participated in clandestine left organizations, the dominant question was the revolutionary fight, and not the women question. As an interviewee commented: "It was a bit like that: you first change the structure and then human rights and women's rights would come naturally, as if it were the nature of the revolution ... one did not speak about the specific struggle for women's rights, but only about structural change; there were no specific rights. Those came later."

[9]All the interviews were carried out in Portuguese, and I provide the English-language translations.

[10]In Brazil, domestic workers labour rights were regulated only with constitutional amendment number seventy-two, passed on 2 April 2013.

[11]Nowadays, Brazil experiences a wave of political conservatism, which includes campaigns against the use of the term "gender" in political documents.

WORKS CITED

Araújo, Clara, and José Eustáquio Alves. "Impactos de indicadores sociais e do sistema eleitoral sobre as chances das mulheres nas eleições e suas interações com as cotas." *Dados: Revista de Ciências Sociais*, vol. 50, no. 3, 2007, pp. 535-77.

Araujo, Fábio. "Falta alguém na minha casa: desaparecimento, luto, maternidade e política." *Antropologia e Direitos Humanos V*, edited by Roberto Kant de Lima, Booklink, 2008, pp. 165-225.

Avelar, Lucia. "Dos movimentos aos partidos: a sociedade organizada e a política formal." *Política & Sociedade*, vol. 11, 2007, pp. 101-16, out. Print.

Avelar, Lucia. "Mulher e política em perspectiva." Congress of Brazilian Political Science Association, 2012, Gramado, Brazil.

Avelar, Lucia. *Mulheres na elite política brasileira: canais de acesso ao poder*. Konrad-Adenauer, 1996.

Avelar, Lucia. *O segundo eleitorado: tendências do voto feminino no Brasil*. Editora da Unicamp, 1989.

Campos, Luiz Augusto, and Carlos Machado. "A cor dos eleitos: determinantes da sub-representação política dos não brancos no Brasil." *Revista Brasileira de Ciência Política*, vol. 18, 2015, pp. 121-151.

Colling, Ana Maria. *A resistência da mulher à ditadura militar no Brasil*. Rosa dos Tempos, 1997.

DeVault, Marjorie L. "Talking Back to Sociology: Distinctive Contributions of Feminist Methodology." *Annual Review of Sociology*, vol. 22, 1996, pp. 29-50.

Gohn, Maria da Glória. "Mulheres—atrizes dos movimentos sociais: relações político-culturais e debate teórico no processo democrático." *Política & Sociedade*, vol. 11, 2007, pp. 41-70.

Hahner, June E. *Emancipação do sexo feminino: a luta pelos direitos da mulher no Brasil, 1850-1940.* Ed. Mulheres, 2003.

Kirsch, Gesa E. "Friendship, Friendliness, and Feminist Fieldwork." *Signs: Journal of Women in Culture and Society*, vol. 30, no. 4, 2005, pp. 2163-172.

Leite, Márcia Pereira. "As mães em movimento." *Um mural para a dor: movimentos cívico-religiosos por justiça e paz*, edited by Márcia Pereira Leite and Patrícia Birman, 2004, pp. 141-190.

Machado, Da Silva, and Luiz Antonio. *Vida sob cerco: violência e rotina nas favelas do Rio de Janeiro.* Nova Fronteira/Faperj, 2008.

Marcondes, Mariana Mazzini, et al. *Olhares de gênero sobre a Política de Creches no Brasil: Mudanças e permanências das práticas sociais de cuidado.* São Paulo, 2015.

Miguel, Luis Felipe, and Cristina Monteiro Queiroz. "Diferenças regionais e o êxito relativo das mulheres nas eleições municipais no Brasil." *Estudos Feministas*, vol. 14, no. 2, 2006, pp. 363-85.

Miguel, Luis Felipe, and Fernanda Feitosa. "O Gênero do Discurso Parlamentar: Mulheres e Homens na Tribuna da Câmara dos Deputados." *Dados: Revista de Ciências Sociais* vol. 52, no. 1, 2009, pp. 201-21.

Phillips, Anne. "Does Feminism Need a Conception of Civil Society?" *Alternative Conceptions of Civil Society*, edited by Simone Chambers and Will Kymlicka, Princeton University Press, 2002, pp. 71-89.

Phillips, Anne. "De uma política de idéia a uma política de presença?" *Estudos feministas*, vol. 9, no. 1, 2001, pp. 268-90.

Phillips, Anne. *Which Equalities Matter?* Polity Press, 1999.

Ramos, Daniela Peixoto. "A família e a maternidade como referências para pensar a política." *Revista Brasileira de Ciência Política*, no. 16, 2015, pp. 87-120.

Rangel, Patrícia. *Movimentos feministas e direitos políticos das mulheres.* Tese (Doutorado), Instituto de Ciência Política, Universidade de Brasília, 2012.

Ribeiro, Uriella Coelho. "Saúde é assunto para as mulheres: um estudo sobre a dinâmica participativa de Conselhos Municipais de Saúde do Brasil." *A dinâmica da participação local no Brasil*, edited by Leonardo Avritzer, Cortez, 2010, pp. 215-52.

Romero, Karolyne, and Celia Lessa Kerstenetzky. "Entre o altruísmo e o familismo: a agenda paramentar feminina e as políticas família-trabalho (Brasil, 2003-2013)." *Revista Brasileira de Ciência Política,* vol. 8, 2015, pp. 119-46.

Rosemberg, Fúlvia. "O movimento de mulheres e a abertura política no Brasil: o caso da creche." *Cadernos de Pesquisa,* no. 51, 1984, pp. 73-79.

Sacchet, Teresa. "Capital social, gênero e representação política no Brasil." *Opinião Pública,* vol. 15, no. 2, 2009, pp. 306-32.

Sacchet, Teresa. "Representação política, representação de grupos e política de cotas: perspectivas e contendas feministas." *Estudos feministas,* vol. 20, no. 2, 2010, pp. 399-431.

Sader, Eder. *Quando novos personagens entram em cena: experiências, falas e lutas dos trabalhadores da Grande São Paulo, 1970-80.* 2nd ed., Paz e Terra, 1988.

Santos, Fabiano Guilherme Mendes dos. "Um elogio ao Tiririca: o perigo da oligarquização ronda nossa democracia." *Insight Inteligência* no. 54, 2011, pp. 80-90.

Soares, Cristiane., and Sonia Oliveira. "Gênero, estrutura ocupacional e diferenciais de rendimento." *Econômica,* vol. 6, no. 1, 2004, pp. 5-33.

Stacey, Judith. "Can There Be a Feminist Ethnography?" *Women Studies International Forum,* vol. 2, no. 1, 1988, pp. 21-27.

Thompson, E. P. *Costumes em comum: estudos sobre a cultura popular tradicional.* Companhia das Letras, 1998.

"Women in National Parliaments." *Inter-Parliamentary Union,* 1 June 2017, www.ipu.org/wmn-e/classif.htm. Accessed 13 June 2017.

10.
Before Boston's Busing Crisis

Operation Exodus, Grassroots Organizing and Motherhood, 1965-1967

JULIE DE CHANTAL

IN 1965, ELLEN JACKSON, a thirty-year-old Black working-class mother living in Boston, founded Operation Exodus.[1] The first volunteer busing program launched in the city, Exodus addressed overcrowding issues that had long affected Boston's predominantly Black schools.[2] These schools—located in the Boston neighbourhoods of Roxbury, Dorchester, and the South End— enrolled between ten and twenty more children per classroom than white schools across the city. At its peak in 1967 and 1968, Operation Exodus transported over six hundred students daily, and extended its mission to welfare reform, urban renewal, and community protection against police brutality. Yet the work of the organization and of its founder remains fairly unknown in the history of civil rights in the United States.

When studying the civil rights movement in Boston, historians have predominantly focused on the outburst of white violence against Black children, which emerged in response to Judge Arthur W. Garrity's federal order to desegregate Boston's public schools in 1974 (Formisano; Lukas; Tager; Nutter; Delmont). Their focus is understandable given that these events were an anomaly in Boston's relatively harmonious racial history. Boston, after all, did not fit within the conceptual framework through which historians typically understand the civil rights movement. The city was not located in the South, and it did not have a history of open racial conflict; the activism seen within its city limits did not fall into the chronological boundaries of the "classic period" of the civil rights movement—1954 and 1964 (Theoharis). As a result, studies on the busing crisis have focused on race and class—the main protagonists being white and working-class Bostonians—but have failed to examine the role of Black activists, men or women, in the years leading to the events (Formisano; Lukas; Tager; Nutter). In this sense, their historical narratives only tell half of the story and perpetuate the idea that Boston was on the margins of the civil rights movement, both geographically and chronologically.

If the Boston busing crisis challenges the ways in which we understand the civil rights movement in the North, the work of Operation Exodus forces us to also rethink the significance of organizing in the years leading to the busing crisis and the assumptions made on the role of women, and especially of mothers, within civil rights organizations. Some historians have argued that the patriarchal structure of the civil rights movement confined women to "lower-level organizational tasks" (Marable xiv). It is true that few Black women shared the spotlight with Martin Luther King, Jr., Malcolm X, or Stokely Carmichael at the national level.[3] However, at the local level, organizations such as Operation Exodus demonstrate that women created associations on their own and took on leadership roles in successful large-scale initiatives in their communities (de Chantal; Sanders; Orleck; Orleck and Gayle).

Operation Exodus was a continuation of a longstanding tradition of working-class and women-led grassroots organizing, which emerged in Boston in the early twentieth-century. Examples include the following: the Kindergarten Club and the Friendship Club, formed under Melnea Cass's auspice in the 1920s; Lucy Mitchell's Ruggles Nursery School and the Robert Gould Shaw House Nursery School, which opened in 1922 and 1931 respectively; and Freedom House, which was founded in 1949 by Otto and Muriel Snowden (Cass 37; Mitchell 21; Snowden 11). As grassroots leaders, many Boston Black working-class women entered the political arena through childcare and education. Once their group was firmly established in the neighbourhood, they expanded the mission of their organizations to address other needs within the community. Over time, all of these institutions became political centres where working-class mothers organized and drew upon their networks to legitimize their intervention in the city.

This chapter examines how Black working-class mothers volunteering for Operation Exodus used their organizing knowledge to circumvent the constraints of city politics. It demonstrates that, as members of nonprofessional, women-led, grassroots organizations, these Black women worked outside of traditional political channels to answer the needs of their families and their community. It further argues that because of this strategy, Black working-class mothers were more successful at effecting change in the city and in their community than other Boston professional civil rights organizations. Furthermore, it shows that their different goals— Operation Exodus attempted to secure equal opportunity for all of Boston's Black children, notwithstanding the setting, instead of adopting the desegregation strategy of the National Association for the Advancement of Colored People (NAACP)—also contributed to the mothers' success.

Through studying oral histories, newspapers, and official sources, this chapter first looks at Ellen Jackson's background and her path toward founding Operation Exodus. It then examines the ways in which the Boston School Committee deflected the conversations about segregation, educational resources, and school overcrowding. Finally, it analyzes how Operation Exodus allowed Black mothers to circumvent the political quagmire that the School Committee had fostered.

Born in Boston in 1935, Ellen became an activist at a young age. She received her education in Boston's public schools and joined the ranks of civil rights organizations when she was a teenager. As a young adult, she went to college to become a teacher, one of the few professions accessible to Black women in the 1950s (Jackson 55; Shaw). Yet she married young, and by age thirty, she was the mother of five young children.[4] Through her childbearing years, Ellen did not hold a fulltime job. To compensate, her husband, Hugo, held two jobs, working both day and night shifts to make ends meet (Jackson 60; "Ellen Jackson, Housewife-Crusader").

Like many women of her generation, Ellen claimed membership to both traditional civil rights associations, such as the NAACP, and grassroots organizations (Jackson 21). Most traditional associations offered Black working-class women a place to mobilize. However, the organizational structure and procedures of these groups often restricted their members' activism (Jackson 21). Members had to follow the associations' preferred channels, pay dues, or abide by their expectations in terms of organizing strategies. In contrast, the grassroots organizations offered a more democratic approach to organizing and placed fewer restrictions on the member's activities. They did not require those who joined to either pay dues or commit a specific amount of time and resources to the association, and for the most part, they did not require a member to sponsor or introduce a prospective member (Cass 67). Furthermore, grassroots organizations encouraged members to think creatively about solutions to the problems that the community faced. By working with both traditional and grassroots organizations, the women learned different models of organizing strategies and attained a high level of political sophistication.

In 1965, Ellen learned about Head Start, and knew that volunteering for the program would enable her to help her children and her community ("Ellen Jackson, Housewife-Crusader"). Part of Lyndon B. Johnson's Great Society campaign, Boston's Head Start was an eight-week summer program that targeted low-income five- and six-year-old children who planned to enter the school system in the fall. Head Start authorities hired educators, nurses, physicians, dentists, and social workers to offer a comprehensive program, which included educational activities, medical care, supplemental nutrition, and parental involvement (Zigler; Vinovskis; Sanders; Jordan). In many cities across the nation, Head Start also created educator positions within the community (Peters; Jordan). Many saw these jobs as a way out of poverty and as an opportunity for advancement. Yet unlike mothers in other cities, Boston's Head Start mothers did not necessarily seek out paid employment. In Boston, educator positions went to Job Corps members who also benefited from poverty relief initiatives ("From Pre-School to Dropouts").[5] As a result, most Head Start mothers in Boston volunteered time and resources to the program, planned activities, secured additional funding, and acted as liaisons between Head Start and their community (Jackson 35).

To Ellen and many of her neighbours, the lack of employment bonds between them and Head Start was a blessing in disguise. It allowed them to organize more freely and to openly discuss their role in the education system, the shortcomings of the city's public schools, and the ways in which they could improve the system. Head Start embodied community control over education—the federal initiative served communities directly—with the program allowing mothers to shape the education of their children without having to confront the red tape of city politics (Jackson 28-35). However, since Head Start was only a summer program, the mothers began to wonder how they would maintain this control when their children transitioned into the city school system in September. Progressively, Head Start became a political centre where working-class mothers could organize their next step in resolving the public school system's overcrowding and underfunding issues. In early August, these mothers started meeting, almost daily, at the Northern Student Movement's office, on Blue Hill Avenue (Jackson 35).[6]

At the time, most schools in Roxbury, Dorchester, and the South End—the neighbourhoods where Black Bostonians lived—enrolled between thirty-five and forty students per class, compared to the average sixteen to twenty in predominantly white schools (Jackson 42). The over-enrollment strained the available school facilities and often forced classes into improvised meeting spaces. It was not rare for a class to share a large auditorium with other classes or with school-sponsored activities, such as glee club (Kozol 9-14). In these conditions, teacher retention faltered, and those who left were frequently replaced with less qualified candidates, who only stayed for a short while. School buildings were in disarray and lacked resources to teach even the most basic subjects (Kozol; Snowden 54). Unsurprisingly, Black children lagged behind their peers enrolled in properly funded schools in predominantly white neighbourhoods.

Since the early 1950s, Boston's School Committee had adopted a policy of denial and avoidance in its interactions with civil rights organizations on education concerns. Throughout the 1950s, Black parents fought to gain representation on home and school associations without success (Snowden 53; "School Principal"). In the early 1960s, the NAACP demanded that the School Committee admit that it maintained de facto segregation, but the Committee simply dismissed the claims ("The School Impasse"; "Mrs. Hicks"; "School Bd."; "Board May Hear"; "NAACP Plan Tabled"; "Board's

Position"). Petitions to the mayor and the governor, marches in the city, and boycotts of the schools were all unsuccessful at getting the School Committee to acknowledge the issues of segregation, inadequate resources, or over-enrollment in Boston's Black schools.

When the School Committee finally did acknowledge the over-crowding issue in 1964, it negotiated in bad faith and proposed ludicrous solutions. For example, members of the Committee proposed to transfer a number of Black students to another school in the neighbourhood ("Negroes Lose Effort"; "Negro Parents Fight"). The solution sounded promising at first, but parents soon realized that the target school was surrounded by construction sites, which would put children at risk of injuries. The Committee then proposed the installation of portable classrooms in various school yards. Portable classrooms were a better option than the transfers but would reduce the space available for the children's outside play. Mothers raised additional concerns about the use of these classrooms during the winter, when snow and low tempera-tures would compromise their functionality (Jackson 42; "Busing Plans Topic").

When the Black mothers proposed the rent or purchase of a vacant Hebrew school, the School Committee proved again that it was not interested in resolving the situation ("Buying Temple School"; "Board Votes"). The school, like many other buildings in Roxbury, was unoccupied, as Boston's Jewish residents had moved from Roxbury to the suburbs of Newton and Brookline (Gamm 11-29). Some of the Black mothers had noticed that the school was conveniently located between two schools that their children already attended. Despite the mothers' argument, the School Committee was lukewarm to the idea. It delegated the decision to Boston's Municipal Research Bureau and Financial Committee, which ultimately rejected the plan.

In August 1965, the School Committee offered its last proposal. It would institute a double session system in which children would be divided into two groups, half of the students attending school in the morning and the early afternoon, and the other half going to classes in the late afternoon and early evening (Double Sessions Threaten"; "Eisenstadt Proposes School Plan"; "Double-Session Foes"; "Kiernan 'Appalled'"). Perhaps a sound idea on paper, the double session solution would end up creating greater hardship for working-class families (Jackson 47). Mothers, and especially single working mothers, would disproportionately bear the burden of such proposal. Being the primary caretaker for their children, they would have to arrange for twice the childcare that they usually needed. In an era when childcare subsidies did not exist to help working mothers, very few of Roxbury families could afford such expense.

On 24 August, only a few days before the school year started, Ellen, with the help of twenty other mothers, organized a rally to meet with United States Attorney General Nicholas Katzenbach during an official visit in Boston ("Katzenbach Hears Hub"; Jackson 47). Their goal was to secure an injunction to halt the double session plan before its implementation. Katzenbach was a civil rights defender who had confronted Alabama Governor George Wallace when he tried to stop the desegregation of the University of Alabama in 1963.[7] The Attorney General was their last hope. "We have done all the things that we feel should have been done, in terms of going through the channels, presenting positions, presenting petitions, appearing in person before the School Committee, appealing to the governor, appealing to the mayor," Ellen explained. "Now you are the only person who we have left to turn to" (Jackson 48). As she exposed the burden that the double session would put on the community, the attorney general remained attentive. He had been through a similar situation in his home state of New Jersey where school committees also attempted to institute a double session system to resolve overcrowding issues. Katzenbach ended the conversation with the mothers on a note of hope. "I promise you when I get back to Washington," he said. "I will look into it" (Jackson 48). Ellen remembered leaving the venue convinced that the issue was resolved (Jackson 49).

Considering Katzenbach's history, the mothers expected that he would speak with the School Committee, like he had done with Governor Wallace, and would force its leaders to abandon the idea of a double session. However, days passed and the mothers did not hear anything back from either the School Committee or from the attorney general's office. They "checked the mail every day, and nothing." They "looked in the newspapers, and there was nothing" (Jackson 49). They felt let down by the man who had been their last hope.

A few days after their meeting with Katzenbach, Ellen received an anonymous phone call. Her interlocutor claimed to have secured a copy of the race census conducted in 1964 on the Boston public school system (Jackson 51). In February of 1964, the NAACP had proposed to boycott Boston's public schools and asked then State Attorney General Edward Brooke for his opinion on the legality of the action. Bound to abide by the law, Brooke had no choice but to inform them that a school boycott would indeed be illegal in Massachusetts, where daily attendance was mandatory for all children under the age of sixteen (Whittelsey and Hadley 9-34). Although the NAACP leaders understood the law, they still saw his position on the issue as a betrayal. Brooke, the first Black Attorney General to be elected in any state across the nation, had seen firsthand the conditions in which the public schools operated. They had expected him to support the boycott, notwithstanding the legality of the action. Instead, Brooke suggested a different approach to the issue. Believing that hard numbers would force the School Committee to acknowledge the *de facto* segregation system, he recommended that the Department of Education conduct race census within the Boston schools. Ellen knew that as of 1965, the results of the census result had not been released publicly, and her interlocutor was quite clear. "Now," the person said, "if you ever say who you got it from, we will deny it," hinting at the fact that their jobs could be at stake (Jackson 51). Katzenbach, Ellen realized, had not let them down after all.

The census served the professional and grassroots organizations in different ways. Since the NAACP worked to secure desegregation nationwide, the census provided its leaders with data to use in confronting the issue from a legal standpoint. It showed that Boston's schools were effectively segregated, despite the lack of laws preventing Black students from attending predominantly white schools. By assigning schools along neighbourhood lines, the schools became increasingly segregated as the city's Black population grew and solidified in Roxbury, Dorchester, and the South End. The race census provided Ellen and the members of

Operation Exodus with the tools necessary to mobilize parents on a larger scale toward addressing the overcrowding issues.

The report gave Operation Exodus a comprehensive picture of Boston public school system by breaking down each school into facilities, furniture, and equipment. It listed the number of classrooms and administrative offices, the number of seats in each room, and the type of equipment available. If the school had an auditorium, a music room, or a sewing laboratory, the report described its configuration. The census also described the student body, breaking it down by race, gender, age, and grades, and listed the number of students with special needs (Jackson 51).

Furthermore, the report demonstrated that the overcrowding issue was endemic in Black neighbourhoods only. While classes in Roxbury and Dorchester enrolled between thirty-five and forty-five students, most of the predominantly white schools were listed as having more than five available seats per classroom. Some classes only enrolled sixteen or seventeen students. As they continued to analyze the census data, the number of empty seats grew steadily and with it, the mothers' anger. Three empty seats here, four there, ten in another classroom, the numbers were appalling. After tallying approximately thirty thousand elementary school and sixteen thousand junior and high school seats, Ellen and her colleagues were outraged and determined to find a solution.

With the information in hand, the group launched another mobilization campaign. They prepared signs to hang at all points in the neighbourhood. The signs asked, "do you know how many vacant seats there are in the city of Boston School system?" They gave parents the numbers that the members of Exodus had compiled. The group then asked more difficult questions. "Why is your kid sitting in a classroom with forty-five kids?" the sign questioned. "Don't you want to do something about that?" (Jackson 52). The group prepared leaflets and distributed them in the neighbourhood. Exodus members had one idea in mind: inform and mobilize. The numbers spoke for themselves. As days passed, the message became more forceful. "School is near. Do you want your kid sitting back in classroom...?" (Jackson 52).

Mobilizing parents, however, took a great deal of effort. Working-class mothers, in particular, wanted to enjoy the last weeks of summer vacation without having to think about lunches, books, or homework (Jackson 52). During the summer, they did not have to think about costly childcare either, as older children were home from school and could take care of younger siblings and of other children in the neighbourhood. As Labour Day approached, however, the atmosphere changed. Parents became increasingly nervous about their children going back to school. During the last week of August, Ellen received a "sudden surge of inquiries"; parents wanted to know what they could do to help (Jackson 53).

The mothers' leadership challenged the NAACP's, Urban League's, and Freedom House's perceived monopoly on the civil rights movement in the city (Jackson 53). Historically, Boston's Black community had been rigidly stratified with very little opportunity for upward mobility (Thernstrom 176-219). From the nineteenth century on, the Black elite joined white progressive circles and civil rights organizations. In doing so, they gained legitimacy as the voice of the community (Schneider; Cromwell). Ellen later explained that these organizations felt that they were "the ones that were supposed to be speaking on behalf of the communities, speaking on behalf of the parents, and the consumers of the black community" (Jackson 53). Some of the civil rights leaders felt that the mothers did not know what they were doing, or were afraid that they would "get themselves in trouble" (Jackson 53). Black working-class women did not have the experience, the prestige, or the polish of the mainstream organizations. They were, as historians argue, on the margin of the movement (Kelley 4-5). Yet even from the fringe, these women challenged the cohesion of the movement. They embodied the "forms of resistance" that Robin Kelley describes as "remain[ing] outside of (and even critical of) what we've come to understand as the key figure and institutions in African American politics" (Kelley 4-5).

In some ways, the growth of the mothers' leadership caught the NAACP, Urban League, and Freedom House by surprise. "All of a sudden," Ellen explained, there was "this little small group of inexperienced amateur parents coming up here and making these waves, and making these noises" (Jackson 53). Through their organizing, Black mothers voiced the concerns of Black working-class parents and realigned their protest toward the idea of equal access to education and opportunities for all children, rather than focusing their energy toward desegregation. This shift in priority, and the possibility of attaining some measure of success, was what Roxbury residents needed to rally behind the group.

From a few mothers at first, the group grew to more than forty or fifty within a handful of days. They met every night of the week, discussing solutions to the issues at hand. With each passing day, more joined, filling the meeting space on Blue Hill Avenue to capacity. Quickly, attendees spilled out in the streets, unable to get into the overfilled office. Some of the activists installed a sound system to allow those who could not enter to hear what was discussed inside (Jackson 53). Grassroots organizing, with active mothers recruiting their neighbors through phone calls or casual encounters at the grocery store or at the mall, proved to be the strongest mobilizing tool of the organization.

Night after night, the mothers listened to anyone who wished to share their experience and suggestions, which made the movement one of the most open and democratic in the city. Night after night, though, they ended the evening at a loss for a true strategy. More than once, they caught themselves thinking, "now, what the hell are we going to do?" as they listened to yet one more person speaking (Jackson 56). Finally, in the middle of one of the meetings, one of the mothers had an epiphany. Ellen could not remember who came up with the idea, but she remembered that it was promising. Someone spoke out: "Damn it, we ought to do it. Let's take the damn kids to their school." The answer had been in front of them all along (Jackson 56).

In 1965, Dr. Owen Kiernan, commissioner of education for Massachusetts, was tasked to study the effects of segregation on both Black and white students across the state (Advisory Committee 4). Noting the ill effect of the system on young children, the report proposed several solutions. First, it proposed to establish a busing system between predominantly white and predominantly Black schools, located less than three miles from each other (Advisory Committee 40). The report also proposed that parents use the open enrollment policy on an individual basis (Advisory Committee 8-9). The policy only required that a seat be available within the target school and that parents provide transportation for their children to and from school daily. The women realized that they could use this policy to launch community action. The mothers already knew which schools had available seats across the city. "Motorcade," one mother said, "get a motorcade going" (Jackson 56). Using parents' or friends' cars to get the children to their new schools would indeed satisfy the requirement imposed by the School Committee itself.

As they began drafting their plan, the mothers realized once again that mobilization would be important to the success of the operation. They could only force the School Committee into action if a large number of parents participated. Knowing that they would need to lead by example with such a seemingly improbable idea, they each agreed to commit their own children to the plan. They also realized that the element of surprise would be necessary to the plan's success, and remained as vague as possible as they called upon neighbours and friends to register their children. "We've got a plan," they announced to the parents in attendance the following night (Jackson 57). They made big signs encouraging parents to register, rallied Black business owners who quickly agreed to collect names on behalf of the organization, and continued to talk with parents in the neighbourhood.

On 8 September, the night before the beginning of the school year, parents assembled at the Jeremiah E. Burke School. Ellen expected to see no more than one 150 parents, at the most, but nearly 800 people came to the event. Several other activists prepared the crowd for Ellen's speech, and the audience was already "riled up" as she approached the stage (Jackson 60). When Ellen reached the curtain, she saw that Marguerite Sullivan, the deputy superintendent of the schools, was standing at the edge of the stage. Earlier that evening, the School Committee had once again rejected a proposal to institute a busing program in the city ("Showdown Tonight"; "Hub Busing Out"). "Mrs. Jackson, I must talk to you," Sullivan said, continuing on to explain that she was there to announce the results of the busing proposal. "You know, I hope you all are going to be very careful," Sullivan warned her. "I don't know what you are going to do, but I think we ought to talk about it." Ellen could not help but point out the irony. "You had your chance to talk about it," she replied. "They took the vote, they made the decision, there's nothing really to talk about" (Jackson 60). Ellen knew that the deputy superintendent had been tipped off that the group was organizing a protest. Yet she also knew that their full plan had remained a secret. If the School Committee leaders had already known the mothers' true strategy, they would have dispatched someone other than Sullivan to the meeting.

That night, mothers, who had nothing to lose, signed up nearly two hundred students, without knowing what would happen to them the following day (Jackson 61). Between 11:30 p.m. and 3:30 a.m., Ellen and her group organized Operation Exodus (Jackson 62). They booked six buses and assigned children, a parent, and a civil rights observer to each bus (Jackson 64). The parent was given a sealed list and instructed only to look at it once the doors of the buses were closed. They could then give directions to the bus driver.

Unsurprisingly, the principals of the target schools had been alerted to the possible arrival of Black children attempting to transfer to their schools. To hinder the efforts to enroll the children, four of the principals required the school district's yellow transfer slip upfront, despite the standard practice of filling out the paperwork after the child joined his or her new classroom ("Overcrowded Schools"). Most parents had not been able to secure the slips, since the schools were not open on the previous day, as they should have been. Some mothers were still able to rush back, obtain the proper documentation, and then return to the buses in time.

As word of Operation Exodus spread, some principals used creative ways to prevent the enrollment of Black children into their schools. One of them unbolted the unused seats and desks in the classrooms, physically lowering the number of seats available for open enrollment. Others filled rooms with boxes, audiovisual material, and other items so to render the rooms unusable for teaching (Jackson 68). In addition to the manipulation of the physical environment, some principals used the system itself to keep their schools segregated. Parents and civil rights monitors learned that a large number of the elementary students in Hyde Park, West Roxbury, Roslindale, and South Boston—all Irish Catholic neighbourhoods in Boston—did not actually attend the schools at which they were enrolled. Instead, these children attended parochial or private schools at their family's expense (Jackson 68). By keeping these children enrolled on the books, corrupt administrators secured money and peace of mind in the process.

Despite the attempts to prevent Black students from transferring, Black mothers persisted in finding empty seats. On the first day, eighty-five children enrolled at predominantly white schools in Mattapan and Dorchester. Fifty children, who had been turned away, finished their day at one of the Freedom Schools organized for that purpose in the city (Jackson 68).[8] On the second day, more than a hundred joined a new classroom ("But Bus Problem Looms"). The community action grew into a full-fledged community program, and the number of students who registered for the operation grew steadily over the next several years. From the initial 250 students in 1965, 425 were bused in 1966, and 600 were the following year (Jackson 74). These numbers, however, did not include all of those who had transferred schools on their own or who were driven to school by their parents once established at their new schools. Since Operation Exodus remained entirely community funded, its members capped the number of children at six hundred to maintain the organization's financial health. Overall, Operation Exodus was a success because of its focus on accessing educational resources for the children and not on the desegregation of the Boston public school system. Although it had very little effect on the School Committee, it successfully forced the State of Massachusetts into action. In 1966, the Massachusetts Department of Elementary and Secondary Education created the Metropolitan Council for Educational Opportunity (METCO), a state-funded busing program to supplement Operation Exodus.

In 1967, Exodus leaders expanded the organization's mission to health care and welfare reform, urban renewal, and community protection against police brutality. During the Boston riots of 1967 and 1968, Exodus acted as a liaison between the city, the traditional civil rights organizations, and the community. Because of lack of funding, Operation Exodus ended in 1969. Over time, a large number of Exodus mothers became fulltime activists and reform workers, continuing the longstanding grassroots organizing tradition. In 1972, Ellen joined the Department of Education task force in charge of creating a desegregation plan, and in 1974, she joined Freedom House as a community organizer. From 1978 to her retirement in 1997, she was dean and director of Affirmative Action at Northeastern University. Ellen Swepson Jackson passed away in 2005.

When looking at Boston's civil rights movement, historians have traditionally focused on the events surrounding the 1974 federal desegregation order and the violence associated with the Boston busing crisis. By examining the role of Black mothers in Operation Exodus, we expand the civil rights narrative from a story of violence within a narrow period of time to one of women-led community and civil rights organizing over several decades. Although these women did not share the spotlight with the prominent figures of the civil rights movements, Operation Exodus shows us that Black working-class mothers became important political leaders within their own communities, and were more successful at affecting change in the city and in their community than other Boston professional civil rights organizations.

ENDNOTES

[1] Operation Exodus was first used to describe the first day of busing that took place on 9 September 1965. The organization later took on the name of the operation. I use the term "Operation Exodus" in this chapter to simplify the text.

[2] Members of Operation Exodus usually simply called their organization "Exodus," instead of using the organization's full name.

[3] Although some women have led minor organizations, only men were chairs of the Student Non-Violent Committee (SNCC), the Congress of Racial Equality (CORE), the Nation of Islam (NOI), the Southern Christian Leadership Conference (SCLC), the Urban League, and the National Association for the Advancement of Colored People between 1960 and 1970. During this period, Black women led women-centric organizations, such as the National Council of Negro Women (NCNW), which played a minor role during the period.

[4] Her children followed each other quickly—with her first born

in 1955, her second in 1956, third in 1957, fourth in 1960, and fifth in 1964 (Jackson 25).

[5] An anti-poverty initiative, the Job Corps program was formed in 1964 as part of Lyndon B. Johnson's Great Society. It was and still is a no-cost vocational and academic program which aims to train youth age 16 to 24 to improve their quality of life.

[6] Ellen become a member when her first daughter Ronica reached elementary school. The organization, whose members were often college students, offered tutoring to Boston's children, organized lectures, and helped with other educational opportunities.

[7] Katzenbach was the United States deputy attorney general from 16 April 1962 to 28 January 1965. He was appointed United States attorney general on 11 February 1965.

[8] Freedom Schools first developed in Boston in 1963 to provide children with education during the first city-wide boycott. The schools—set up in community centres, churches, or other locations—offered a curriculum coupling academic activities and activism. The concept was used in Mississippi, New York, and Chicago, in similar circumstances and as organizing tools. The most widely known Freedom Schools were used in Mississippi during the Freedom Summer of 1964 (Perlstein).

WORKS CITED

Newspapers
"Board May Hear NAACP." *Boston Globe*, 14 Feb., 1964.
"Board's Position: Nothing to Study." *Boston Globe*, 26 Feb., 1964.
"Board Votes to Buy School." *Boston Globe*, 27 June, 1964.
"Busing Plans Topic Friday of Schoolmen." *Boston Globe*, 4 Aug., 1965.
"But Bus Problem Looms; Exodus Plan Settles 100 More Students." *Boston Globe*, 11 Sept., 1965.
"Buying Temple School Criticized by Financial Committee." *Boston Globe*, 7 Dec., 1964.
"Double-Session Foes Beset School Committee." *Boston Globe*, 27 Aug., 1965.
"Double Sessions Threaten." *Boston Globe*, 7 Aug., 1965.
"Eisenstadt Proposes School Plan." *Boston Globe*, 25 Aug., 1965.

"Ellen Jackson Housewife-Crusader." *Boston Globe*, 30 Jan., 1966.

"From Pre-School to Dropouts, Mass Attack on Poverty." *Boston Globe*, 4 Apr., 1965.

"Hub Busing Out—Parents Map Fight." *Boston Globe*, 8 Sept., 1965.

"Katzenbach Hears Hub School Gripe." *Boston Globe*, 24 Aug., 1965.

"Kiernan 'Appalled' Double Sessions Blasted." *Boston Globe*, 20 Aug., 1965.

"Mrs. Hicks Bids Negroes Study." *Boston Globe*, 5 Feb., 1964.

"NAACP Plan Tabled for Good." *Boston Globe*, 21 Feb., 1964.

"Negroes Lose Effort to Halt School Shift." *Boston Globe*, 29 July, 1964.

"Negro Parents Fight Student Transfers." *Boston Globe*, 7 Aug., 1964.

"Overcrowded Schools' Enrolment 472 Off." *Boston Globe*, 10 Sept., 1965.

"School Bd., NAACP May Resume Talks." *Boston Globe*, 7 Feb., 1964.

"School Principal Elizabeth Cloney Asks Retirement: Claims Supt. Haley Supported 'Agitators' in Roxbury Dispute." *Boston Globe*, 1 June, 1951.

"Showdown Tonight on Busing." *Boston Globe*, 7 Sept., 1965.

"The School Impasse." *Boston Globe*, 1 Feb., 1964.

Oral Histories

Cass, Melnea A, and Tahi Lani Mottl. *Interview with Melnea A. Cass: February 1, 1977.* Schlesinger Library, Radcliffe College, 1982.

Jackson, Ellen, and Cheryl Gilkes. *Interview with Ellen Jackson: June 26, and August 24, 1978, April 19, and June 26, 1979.* Schlesinger Library, Radcliffe College, 1989.

Mitchell, Lucy Miller, and Cheryl Gilkes. *Interview with Lucy Miller Mitchell: June 17 and 24, 1977, July 1, 6, and 25, 1977.* Schlesinger Library, Radcliffe College, 1980.

Snowden, Muriel S, and Cheryl Gilkes. *Interview with Muriel S. Snowden: January 21, October 30, and November 20, 1977.* Schlesinger Library, Radcliffe College, 1984.

Secondary Sources

Advisory Committee on Racial Imbalance and Education. *Report of the Advisory Committee on Racial Imbalance and Education.* State Board of Education, 1965.

Cromwell, Adelaide M. *The Other Brahmins: Boston's Black Upper Class, 1750-1950.* University of Arkansas Press, 1994.

de Chantal, Julie. "If There Are Men Who Are Afraid to Die, There Are Women Who Are NOT: African American Women's Civil Rights Leadership in Boston, 1920-1975." Dissertation, University of Massachusetts Amherst, 2016.

Delmont, Matthew. *Why Busing Failed: Race, Media, and the National Resistance to School Desegregation.* University of California Press, 2016.

Formisano, Ronald P. *Boston against Busing: Race, Class, and Ethnicity in the 1960s and 1970s.*: University of North Carolina Press, 1990.

Gamm, Gerald H. *Urban Exodus: Why the Jews Left Boston and the Catholics Stayed.* Harvard University Press, 1999.

Jordan, Amy. "Fighting for the Child Development Group of Mississippi: Poor People, Local Politics, and the Complicated Legacy of Head Start." *The War on Poverty: A New Grassroots History, 1964-1980*, edited by Annelise Orleck, University of Georgia Press, 2011, 280-307.

Kelley, Robin D. *Race Rebels: Culture, Politics, and the Black Working Class.* Free Press, 1994. Kozol, Jonathan. *Death at An Early Age; The Destruction of the Hearts and Minds of Negro Children in the Boston Public Schools.* Houghton Mifflin, 1967.

Lukas, J. Anthony. *Common Ground: A Turbulent Decade in the Lives of Three American Families.* Knopf, 1985.

Marable, Manning. *Black Leadership.* Columbia University, 1998.

Nutter, Kathleen Banks. "'Militant Mothers': Boston, Busing, and the Bicentennial of 1976." *Historical Journal of Massachusetts*, vol. 38, no. 2, 2010, pp. 52-75.

Orleck, Annelise. *Storming Caesars Palace: How Black Mothers Fought Their Own War on Poverty.* Beacon Press, 2005.

Orleck, Annelise, and Lisa Gayle, editors. *The War on Poverty: A New Grassroots History, 1964-1980.* University of Georgia Press, 2011.

Perlstein, Daniel. "Teaching Freedom: SNCC and the Creation of the Mississippi Freedom Schools." *History of Education Quarterly*, vol. 30, no. 3, 1990, pp. 297-324.

Peters, Barbara J. *The Head Start Mother: Low-income Mothers' Empowerment through Participation*. Garland Pub., 1998.

Tager, Jack. *Boston Riots: Three Centuries of Social Violence*. Northeastern University Press, 2001.

Theoharis, Jeanne. "'I'd Rather Go to School in the South': How Boston's School Desegregation Complicates the Civil Rights Paradigm." *Freedom North: Black Freedom Struggles Outside the South, 1940-1980*, edited by Jeanne Theoharis and Komozi Woodard, Palgrave Macmillan, 2003, pp. 125-51.

Thernstrom, Stephan. *The Other Bostonians: Poverty and Progress in the American Metropolis*. Harvard University Press, 1973.

Sanders, Crystal R. *Head Start and Mississippi's Black Freedom Struggle*. University of North Carolina Press, 2016.

Schneider, Mark R. *Boston Confronts Jim Crow, 1890-1920*. Northeastern University Press, 1997.

Shaw, Stephanie J. *What a Woman Out to Be and to Do: Black Professional Women Workers During the Jim Crow Era*. The University of Chicago Press, 1996.

Vinovskis, Maris. *The Birth of Head Start: Preschool Education Policies in the Kennedy and Johnson Administrations*. University of Chicago Press, 2005.

Whittelsey, Sarah Scovill, and Arthur Twining Hadley. "Historical Sketch of the Labor Laws of Massachusetts: Child Labor." *Massachusetts Labor Legislation: An Historical and Critical Study*, American Academy of Political and Social Science, 1900, pp. 9-34.

Zigler, Edward, and Sally J. Styfco. *The Hidden History of Head Start*. Oxford University Press, 2010.

11.
On the Margins of Politicized Motherhood

Mothers' Human Rights Activism Revisited in Turkey from the 1970s to the 1990s

TUBA DEMIRCI-YILMAZ

WOMEN'S EXCLUSION FROM POLITICS usually signifies the interplay of multiple factors as outcomes of different socio-historical contexts. Usually referred as a "regional leader" for women's rights, Turkey has failed to make women's participation into formal politics a norm (Abadan-Unat; Kinross). The late-Ottoman and early-Republican periods in Turkey provide evidence for how independent women's organizations were suppressed (Berktay). However, women were never politically inactive in Turkey; they used alternative channels of political participation (Kasapoglu and Özerkmen). Beginning in the 1980s, women's contribution to the making of a human rights movement in Turkey was a crucial achievement, which exemplifies the use of those alternative channels by which women became politically active and resilient.

Human rights as an organizational principle entered into the political agenda of activists in Turkey in the 1940s. However, the human rights movement gained momentum in response to escalating state violence between the 1970s and the 1990s, as eradication of "dissident" leftist political circles was replaced by a mass persecution of all political activity following the 1980 coup d'état. Military influence has never been a novelty in Turkey; rounds of military coups have dominated politics since 1910 (Ahmad; Çarkoğlu and Hale). Subsequent to the September 1980 coup, violence intensified, resulting in mass arrests, disappearances and torture, further necessitating the need for human rights organizations. The 1980 putsch would also prove to be the most lethal one.

Following the 1980 coup, mothers' public search for their disappeared and detained children revived the human rights organizations, which had been short lived and precarious in terms of their activities. Various sociopolitical histories in Turkey and elsewhere have provided much on women's mobilization as mothers and how they became political actors through either praise of or reference to motherhood (Göker). This chapter, however, seeks to revisit human rights activism through the life histories of Leman Fırtına, Nebahat Akkoç and Hüda Kaya—three human rights defenders who did not use a strong moral-maternal discourse for advocacy but illustrated alternative maternal political agencies besides contributing to the longevity of the organizations they worked for. Representing different political ideologies and milieus, they were politically active mothers when mobilized against the junta and reprimanded for "mothering improperly." Yet their ability to surpass maternal identity and expand political realm for gender equality requires a comparative analysis. This chapter, thus, intends to examine the relationship between human rights movements and motherhood through revealing the experiences of these women, especially how they revisited motherhood in the course of their activism.

This chapter is based on two in-depth interviews conducted with Hüda Kaya and Nebahat Akkoç. I met with Kaya on 6 September 2015 on a busy Sunday afternoon in a secluded corner of a café in Eyüp, İstanbul. Although she was elected to the parliament from the HDP (People's Democratic Party) in the June 2015 general elections, the general elections were to be renewed in November 2015, following the ill-fated government formation process. On the very same day that I interviewed her, HDP disclosed its decision to accept her to run for the second time for the deputyship of İstanbul. We talked only for an hour because of her hectic daily routine; in addition to decades of human rights activism, she then became an MP and her duties increased more than ever.

The two-hour interview with Akkoç took place on 9 September 2015 in Şişli, İstanbul following her return from a women's organizations meeting abroad. Subsequent to our conversation, she was supposed to see an otolaryngologist for an ongoing problem in her ear, which is one of the physical marks of the torture she had endured as part of being a human rights activist in the 1990s. The original idea was to visit her in Diyarbakir in late September 2015, where she established the first feminist NGO, *KAMER*, but current political upheaval and worsening security conditions in Turkey—due to the Syrian war, the collapse of peace process with PKK (Kurdistan Workers Party), and the complications of both for the Kurdish issue in southeastern Turkey—forced us to reschedule the meeting earlier in İstanbul. Regrettably, I could not interview with Leman Fırtına; while I was busy with organizing interviews, she was hospitalized for cancer treatment and passed away in early April 2015. At the time, I had barely started archival and media research, a preliminary process required to be completed prior to meeting with her. Therefore, I had to rely on previous interviews that she gave for the press and various publishers, and her speeches in human rights campaigns. I attempted to interview her family; however, we could not schedule one for a couple of reasons. Bereavement following her death was high, as were the condolatory visitors. As I could not interview her family, my efforts to present her as she was are surely limited.

Apart from in-depth interviews with Akkoç and Kaya, I also used their various articles, book chapters, and interviews that they previously gave. I have to admit that I felt rather lucky since they have been prolific writers and speech makers. Yet I am utterly indebted to Kaya and Akkoç for talking to me despite their busy schedule. I am equally grateful to Memik Horuz, a journalist and documentary film maker for providing me his book, *12 Eylül Anneleri: Röportajlar*, a seminal collection of interviews with mothers of politicized youth in 1980s, completed in five years across Turkey, before it formally hits the bookshelves.

MOTHERS, POLITICAL ACTIVITY, AND THE HUMAN RIGHTS MOVEMENT

The feminist literature has several conceptualizations of women who become politically active as mothers in various polities and historical periods. Women's political mobilization to protect and defend their children rather than questing for their own rights is generally categorised as "motherist," and arguments regarding such activism differ widely. Human rights activism provides an important example as such. However, as part of politics and human rights activism, mothers also accentuate the "essentialist, natural and sacred" qualities attributed to mothering, which further idealize patriarchal and traditional references to motherhood and become useful public icons for their supporters (Orleck 2-4). The politicization of women as mothers, therefore, often requires the strategic uses and performances of motherhood, since speaking out and protesting as mothers can bestow public credibility to them even in strictly patriarchal and authoritarian societies.

Motherist politicization is either dismissed as not being serious enough or as "female politics," which heralds the transformation of local action into international feminist activism, or a reliable political means for women by women. There are also evaluations addressing various forms of "political motherhood" as useful in any way (i.e., mothers' peace, environmentalist, and human rights activism), since the qualities of such motherist politics have the prospect of transforming the political domain by incorporating "care" perspective into it (Van Allen 63). Besides, some feminists caution against the possible dangers inherent in maternalist activism and politics—instances of nationalism, for example, that deploy motherhood to guarantee the reproduction of soldiers for national armies as conforming mothers are lauded as "distinguished" for presenting their children as potential martyrs for the nation. Feminists similarly warn about motherist movements' wherewithal for essentializing women through coalescing mother and woman as one (DiQuinzio; Grozs). In point of fact, essentialism is the most problematic aspect of motherist movements for its potential to reduce women into mothers. It implies that women's principle role in society is mothering, thereby restricting their options and underlining the belief that all women are naturally mothers. Most feminists are critical about such biological reductionism; they argue that culture also plays a prominent role constructing gender and sex differences (Moore; de Beauvoir). Equating womanhood with motherhood is untenable, since not all women become mothers, nor should they. Thus, motherist movements' potential to encourage women to adhere to traditional gender roles is a source of tension between feminism and maternalist activism. Another cause of tension is the former's avoidance of any connection with the latter for presenting itself as a mainstream and legitimate form of political activism (Hewett). Yet feminists have been embracing many of the ideals espoused by motherist movements; they have reclaimed and reworked motherhood as a feminist concept (Dietz; Whetsone).

It is a widely held view that political motherhood must begin with and represent mothers' commitment to their "own" children and family. This opinion is often verified through mothers' activism against the forced conscription of their beloveds and militarism, the disappearance and detainment of politically active youth, the pollution of the environment, and the lack of food safety. While extending their political commitments, mothers are often expected to address the children of the group and communities of which they belong (Taylor 349-57; Ruddick, "Rethinking" 374-75). This is an inherent parochialism in political motherhood as Ruddick warns, but even under such parochialism, it becomes possible for mothers to recognize the problems and anguish of other mothers and act for others. In other words, mothers have a cross-cultural capacity that translates as an extensive commitment to other children and mothers divided along class, status, and ethnic differences. While analyzing the connection between mothering and politics, Ruddick has also argued that motherhood, a plural experience of care and nurturing, gives mothers a range of political viewpoints from which they can apply to others (Ruddick, *Maternal Thinking* 127-29).

Strongly maternalist or not, women's human rights activism surpasses the ideal of "absorbed and apolitical" motherhood because, first, it is an activism that transcends child-centred motherhood perfection by reversing its long acclaimed "calming impact" over women's political potentials (Orleck 3-4). Through engaging with human rights, politically hard-core mothers dismantle the de facto political inactivity attributed to them. Second, women's human rights activity as a political activity proves that defending human rights does not have to be an extension of maternal duties. In other words, the human rights movement has been contributed by women who were politicized prior to becoming mothers; thus, the transition to motherhood does not necessarily incite women into either acting as suffering maternal icons or using conventional forms of moral-maternal discourse for their political activities. In addition to mothers' public quest for their wronged children through the vocalization of maternal suffering, human rights activity has been sustained by mother-activists, whose political and human rights activities have indicated nonessential forms of maternal activism as well as nonconventional ways of reclaiming motherhood through activism. Hence, the history of human rights movements needs to be re-evaluated with regard to women's contribution to them. Moreover, the multiplicity of maternal practices as well as activists' motherhood attributes should be incorporated into such a history so that maternal experiences—which have been disregarded as nonessential through the homogenizing representation of women as agonized mothers in human rights activism—can be revealed and mainstreamed.

There are other contradictions that transcend the differences characterizing mothers' participation into human rights movements, such as the activism itself. Since activism can detach mothers from their children, preoccupy them with political activity for long periods, and force them to risk imprisonment or death, they tussle with their children's criticism, too (Orleck 5-6). There are activist mothers whose children understand the reasons for the sacrifices they have to make for their mothers (i.e., the children who accompany their mothers to prison and throughout their activism). Deliberating how mothers' human rights and political activism affect their children, who do not automatically understand that their mothers would not prioritize the "public good" over theirs, is another crucial dimension to be discussed for women's human rights activism in particular and politicization in general. Often caught between the political and the personal, women human rights defenders pay heavy emotional costs. The women represented here link their role as mothers to their role as activists, which helps explore how activist mothers' responsibility toward their children both stimulate and complicate activism (Taylor 141-43).

The activist women considered here knew the limits of motherhood's public credibility well, and I argue that they did not use a strong, conventionally framed maternal-moral discourse in political activism because of those limits. Yet they have contributed to the maternalist perspective on motherhood and activism by way of providing antitheses for motherhood that is often represented as a single experience. Fırtına, Akkoç, and Kaya also reverse the victimization awaiting them as mothers of the detained and tortured children or divorced and widowed mothers parenting alone through their political activity. Appearing in public as demanding and assertive, fearless and allegedly "inconsiderate" for risking their children, they recast political motherhood for the defence of human rights.

WOMEN DEFENDING HUMAN RIGHTS IN TURKEY

Conventional historiographies only trivially address the contributions by mothers and prisoners' female kin to human rights activism in Turkey. Although the sociopolitical literature has accounted for women's political activity and mobilization through motherhood (Douglas and Michaels), it largely denies activist women who did not necessarily use a strong maternal-moral discourse (Kinser). Yet such experiences outside formal political structures can inform us on the multiplicity of activist motherhoods (O'Reilly and Bizzini). Fırtına, Akkoç, and Kaya are, therefore, important examples for the fight for gender equality; they have pushed the limits of "real and genuine" motherhood and exemplified how women can sustain mothering unusually through activism.

Inclusion of mothers of the oppressed into politics through the general legitimacy that motherhood bestows, political struggles and identities formed for cooperation through motherhood has become a concern for historiography only recently (Swerdlow; Bhattacharjya et al. 277-93; Orhan 120-34). Motherhood is often said to justify gender inequalities by confining women to their home, limiting their visibility, and suppressing them as the others of social policy. But it is also a practice that functions as a potential political means with which the oppressed search for power through the simultaneous legitimacy it brings (Arendell 1192-1207; Gieve). Motherhood's transformation into an oppositional element is not a new phenomenon; despite their differences and conjunctures to which they belong, mothers have used strong maternalist-moral discourses during activism. Mother activists' emphasis on mothers' procreative and caring capacity toward others (Direk 21) and their positioning as sacred peacemakers through various discourses serve to validate them as respectable political subjects with legitimate demands (Forcey; Scheper-Hughes). Human rights activism was not an exception; it has been one of those domains in which women seem to fit with their caring and serving capacity as well as the maternal-moral responsibility that they evoke. In human rights activism, one also sees the predicament that women's caregiving traits create; for some, caring responsibilities do not necessarily make women strong advocates automatically. For others, women's human rights activism can interrupt their caring responsibilities, or it becomes a mere extension of their traditional caregiving roles. Yet mothering a victim has been a strong motive for opposing human rights violations, notwithstanding the hostility it brings to the advocates, since patriarchy requires habitual deferring to men. Despite being exposed to gender-specific threats and violence and being criticized for either neglecting their dependents or for putting them at risk as activists, women still keep defending human rights (Orleck; Taylor; Miller 17-21) and sustaining the perspective of the organizations for which they work (Bonner 1-28, 61-79).

Politicization of women as mothers and use of various maternal discourses for advocacy also antagonized them as mothers of the "terrorist" and "martyred" (Fabj; Gedik, "Türkiye'de"; Sirman; Şentürk). Although children's "propriety" with respect to the normative order legitimizes mothers' claims and confirms them as "true" mothers (De Alwis), they are often represented as agonized right owners through their emotional labour and self-sacrifice, constantly lacking individuals and monuments of grief, whose mothering is interrupted with the loss of their children. Yet such depictions provide a restricted portrayal of a plural experience. One cannot help but wonder: do activist mothers really experience motherhood in such standardized ways? Or how do they really mother during human rights advocacy? Most importantly, how do they perceive this standardized representation of motherhood themselves? Answering these questions will greatly benefit the historicization of women's relation to politics and motherhood, and mainstream the efforts to reflect plural experiences of motherhood in grassroots politics.

The term "human rights" entered into the Turkish polity in the nineteenth century; the Reorganization (*Tanzimat* 1839) and Reform (1856) decrees united the criticism of reformists and Europeans, and limited the Ottoman monarch's superpowers over property rights and freedom of expression and conscience. The first Ottoman constitutions, of 1876 and 1908 further restricted the sultan's powers over expatriation, detention, and capital punishment through the introduction of the principle of a trial (Sohrabi). Although the constitutional reform movements in the empire advanced "classical rights," military establishment both as the domain to be reformed and source from which reformists and modernization proposals rose (Arslan). The reformed military establishment would lead to violations of human rights and new constitutions with a narrow human rights perspective, through its multiple interventions (Johnson; Hale 303-36).

Unlike popular revolutions elsewhere, Republican Turkey focused on the right of the nation to self-determination while underrating the individual rights as the foundational principle of state building and reform (Ahmad). A polity embodying cosmopolitan norms of citizenship was aimed for, but the result was a restrictive, secularist-unitary nation state (Arat and Altınay 12). The modernized political elite crafted a Turkish nation and sovereignty from among the antagonized multiethnic constituents of Ottoman Empire, thus precluding extensive conceptualizations about human rights (Mardin). Republican Turkey, as a single party regime, did not enforce constitutional civil liberties during its authoritarian stance between 1924 and 1945 (Hale; Tunçay). The state bestowed masses with political rights; however, it demanded them to accord primacy to the national interest over individual freedoms, duties over rights, and state sovereignty over autonomy (Keyman and İçduygu 5-6). Consequently, a political culture that favoured state building over individual rights and liberties emerged (Cizre-Sakallıoğlu). Any group fighting for human rights would be seen as accomplices of communist propaganda. Because of this stigmatization, human rights issues and violations were handled by the left; conservatives and right wingers would abstain from such issues until the 1980s in order to solidify their allegiance to the official ideology (Plageman 433-54; Negron-Gonzales 47).

The nation state's distaste toward individual freedoms and human rights advocacy was seen in its treatment toward human rights organizations. The Democratic Party—which ruled Turkey between 1950 and 1960 and promised to democratize the country in a post-World War II climate that favoured alliance with the Western (Karpat; Timur)—did not promote human rights non-governmental organizations (NGOs). Whether a "human rights" phrase was extant in their names or not, all human rights NGOs formed between 1946 and the 1970s were shut down and declared centres for communism. Legal experts, journalists, parliamentarians, diplomats, and professors were all prosecuted as accomplices of communism (Hamdemir and Arslanel 48). Until 1986, when the well-known and long-lived Human Rights Association (*İnsan Hakları Derneği-IHD*) was formed, nearly six different human rights NGOs had existed but dissolved shortly after their creation. Women's contribution to these organizations, however, requires an independent feminist and gender history analysis.[1]

Having terminated Democratic Party rule, the 1960 coup drafted the most liberal constitution ever and advanced freedom of organization considerably. However, right-aligned governments that came to power later supported extreme right-wing organizations to curb the growing labour movement under this constitution. This, in turn, radicalized the left- and right-wing youth organizations and caused large scale bloodshed for which another military intervention was executed (Üskül; Kayalı; Hale). The coup happened 12 March 1971 and with martial law following, the human rights movement finally joined with the mothers, who flocked to the gates of prisons and police stations to find their family members.

"AUNTIE" LEMAN OF IHD

The activism of late Leman Fırtına (1926-2015) commenced after her son's arrest in 1971 and culminated in her becoming one of the several women founders of IHD and the Human Rights Foundation of Turkey (Türkiye İnsan Hakları Vakfı -TIHV). She was described as the "most prominent" and "unhesitant" activist mother among the relatives of the detained (ETHA; Temelkuran). Fırtına travelled across provincial Turkey first as the daughter of a civil servant, then as the wife of an officer. She received a better education as compared to her peers; however, she got married prior to her high school graduation. During the initial years of her marriage, she lost three of her young children because of childhood diseases (Erdoğan). While accompanying her husband for his appointments in provincial Turkey, she took part in parent-teacher's associations and surpassed the usual image of "officer's wife in the officer's club" (K.Yılmaz). She maintained her activism as the founder of the Ayancık branch of the Turkish Women's Association (Türk Kadınlar Birliği) (Tahincioğlu; Horuz and Yoleri 201). Her husband was still in the army when the 1960 coup took place; she was disgusted by the repercussions of it and defined her political stance as proleft afterwards.

The politics of late 1960s and 1970s in Turkey was polarized; left- and right-wing groups also confronted one another on the streets. The radical left, the Kurdish minority, and the Alawite Muslims were alienated thanks to Republican-Turkish supremacist ideology, and the latter two aligned together to oppose the Islamists and Turkish nationalists, although all of them opposed the Kemalist republic for their own reasons. This escalated the human rights violations in the form of political repression, reciprocal violence, extrajudicial killings, massacres, largescale detention and imprisonments, and torture, which were chiefly directed at pro-left groups and organized labour. Universities were thoroughly politicized: some of the students' opinion clubs were radicalized, and radicalization of politics was reflected into student activities. For instance, Fırtına's son, Doğan, was detained for calling a boycott in Ankara University, where he studied at the time and protested the imprisonment of his friends in 1971. Fırtına hereby became acquainted with the prisons for the first time. Her son had a gastric bleeding and was mistreated by the prison physician; his condition evolved into a coma. Fırtına's first struggle was to get the right to visit him in the military hospital in the prisoners' ward; she managed to stay there to better take care of him. Following his treatment, Doğan returned to prison for two-and-a-half years. After the 1980 putsch, Doğan had to hide away from the security forces again. Until 1984, Fırtına could not see him or learn his whereabouts; he was taken under custody for two months, tortured, and later transferred to Metris Military Prison. This restarted Fırtına's activism. She struggled for visitation rights and engaged in hunger strikes to protest against torture and horrific prison conditions. She brought the issue to the public's attention through petition campaigns and sit-ins in front of prisons. Fırtına's reason to participate in such activities was obviously her son, but the dreadful effects of the coup also motivated her (İmset 60; Zeydanlıoğlu; Mavioğlu). She also met other mothers, and they regularly travelled to Ankara to negotiate with the Ministry of Justice. She befriended diverse groups of women: wives of civil servants, officers, villagers, and especially Kurdish peasants with various disadvantages. They travelled across Turkey to visit prisons under strict military rule to keep the prison and torture issue on the agenda when everyone avoided politics (Fırtına 95-104).

She collected underwear from factories and books from publishers as donations to the prisoners; she she even sometimes tried hard to supply a tube of toothpaste to prisoners. She helped transform stay-at-home mothers into activists; they were together detained several times for protest campaigns. Fırtına called the emergence of mothers who fought for justice and proper treatment for their children a "remarkable struggle," which matched similar ones elsewhere (Fırtına 95-96). Apart from being a "prisoner's mom," she called her motive to be an activist a "a personal duty and liability," agonizing and gratifying at once, not simply a motherly duty. Called "Auntie Leman" by prisoners and activists, she became one of the founders of IHD and TIHV and worked as the vice-president for IHD after 1986. She functioned as an activist who changed the meaning of victimized mother through her resilient efforts—endless travels, dozens of petition and telegram campaigns—but she could not escape the violence inflicted on her, too. Overall, she stood as a witness for the making of human rights advocacy and IHD (Fırtına 96-104). She defines being a human rights defender and a prisoner's mom as follows:

I always contemplated struggling against injustice as a personal duty. Striving for my son and others was my liability during 1971 coup, too. I struggled for our kids, who were either arrested or wanted by police following the 1980 coup. Prior to [IHD], we used to spend almost three days weekly travelling to Ankara, then distributing tasks, i.e., visiting ministries, Land Forces Command and other units as mothers, ... so that we'd leave no stone unturned about the situation. Then such activities did not necessarily satisfy us so we embarked on to find other means for struggle ... we started working for IHD, where everyone in support of freedom would come together with every asset they had. We found many enlightened people from variety of professions who believed in democracy and freedom standing with us.... We kept fighting for our cause both under the roof of [IHD] and as families.... Having obtained the visitation rights [in1987], I personally toured all prisons. All of those prisoners were like my own children and I felt happy to talk with them... (qtd. in Türkmen 73).[2]

The unity among families was solidified into a conscious, action-oriented collective in time. People comprehended that the tyranny was not only against political detainees, so called "terrorists", but for everyone defending human rights and demanding justice. As a result, collective resistance and confrontations with the "security" forces started. Many among us were detained and arrested, also beaten up and affronted. People at the age of 60-70 also got their share from these.... At every doorstep, from prisons to police headquarters, centres of martial law to the Chief of Staff, from Prime Ministry to Presidency, we continued our struggle this way. Countless petitions and telegrams were penned and sent to public authorities collectively.... [By] 1987, the movement of the relatives of detainees and prisoners took new forms parallel to the developments in the country, embracing [...] the rising struggle for democracy; coalescing with labour, student and women's movement and the activities of the enlightened.... If we firmly believe in a bright and free future, we should demonstrate it substantially and struggle without any prejudice....

Rights, justice, human rights and democracy are all good things, but even better is to be questing and struggling for them. (Fırtına 96-104)

Another important dimension in Fırtına's activist motherhood was the fact that the grave violations and pressures she endured never curtailed her zest for life; she never stopped dressing, playing cards, or drinking a glass of *rakı* occasionally after demonstrations. Overall, she was not constantly grieving. Though devoted, Fırtına never disregarded herself as a woman human being; she had cheerfully welcomed guests and never stopped being vivacious, even in her worst days. Following a long and tiresome collective struggle, mothers received visitation rights in 1985. However, on 26 August 1985, a religious public holiday on which she was to visit her son, her husband passed away, but she was determined to see Doğan. She was transformed from a stay-at-home officer's wife into an activist, a panelist, and a poised representative to discuss prison issue with President Özal directly (Öztürk). Fırtına supported IHD's Kurdish members to address the association's general assembly in Kurdish, despite the negative climate of 1990s for any discussion of the Kurdish issue and language rights in Turkey. Undeterred by her advancing age, she collected medicine for Iraqi refugees from the Gulf War and *Al-Anfal* massacre,[3] and travelled to the southeastern Turkey under a state of emergency (Tahincioğlu; Keskin). Leman Fırtına was among the IHD activists who supported Saturday Mothers' cause from the beginning; she was one of the IHD activists and Saturday Mothers who welcomed Plaza de Mayo Mothers at the airport in June 1998.[4]

After the 1980 coup, the second group that overtly protested the junta's suppression was the feminists. The feminist movement gained impetus in the mid-1980s through emphasizing the full implementation of Convention on the Elimination of all Forms of Discrimination against Women (CEDAW), ratified by Turkey in 1985. In 1986, feminist groups initiated a petition campaign signed by some four thousand women (Kerestecioğlu; Moralıoğlu 293) among whom Fırtına also participated. In 1987, a mass rally with twenty-five hundred women was organized against domestic violence; Fırtına was also present there (Y. Arat; Tahincioğlu).

As a result of aging and ailment, her preference to stay in a retirement home, too, was unusual enough to challenge the conventional beliefs over elderly care in Turkey, where primary kin is expected to undertake elderly care as a responsibility. She never disconnected with IHD or defending human rights; after moving to Antalya, a sun-belt retirement city, she kept partaking in demonstrations about domestic violence, honour killings, and Women's Day celebrations. The last turnout of such an extraordinary woman's life also resembled a human rights rally; Fırtına's funeral coincided with the funeral of a notorious member of the Turkish army, whose military mourners faced the famous motto of human rights demonstrations—"human dignity will overcome torture." Fırtına and the general died in the same hospital, so the funeral processions for both commenced at the same point. As a matter of coincidence, Fırtına's mourners had the chance to give a straightforward response to a group of retired army generals for their habitual justification for military's role in politics (Keskin).

Leman Fırtına was an activist who gained legitimacy not solely by mothering but by being a woman; she kept supporting groups destined to end discrimination, mainly toward women and minorities. Despite her worsening health, she continued to back Saturday Mothers and various feminist campaigns; she managed to raise and defend troubled children in a tough time. Leman Fırtına was a woman who personified metamorphosis of wronged women into fully fledged activist moms. Instead of putting up with the usual reprimands like "mother of a traitor," a usual way to address politically active and radical youth's mothers, she managed to broker strong ties with mothers from various communities, from different ethnic, religious, and class backgrounds. She, therefore, reversed the conventional expectations of motherist politics by not paying exclusive allegiance to her own social circle and children; instead, she cared about other mothers and children as well. She reclaimed motherhood through her militancy of supporting life and human rights; she did not reinforce the normative identity and activities assigned to motherhood in a patriarchal society.

REAPPRAISING HUMAN RIGHTS VIOLATIONS
THROUGH FEMINISM: NEBAHAT AKKOÇ

Nebahat Akkoç is a feminist human rights advocate from the same generation of Fırtına's son, and she used to be connected with IHD. Akkoç's activism was shaped by various sociopolitical dilemmas in Turkey; she was born to an orphaned mother from the *Dersim* Massacre[5] (1937-8) and a father whose parents were orphans of Armenian Genocide (1915) (Belge 18-25; Göçek). Having acquainted with an imbricated form of otherness and not having a clear line of belonging, she was brought up in Silvan, a small town in Diyarbakır, southeastern Turkey. For her activism, those intersections of otherness were crucial; her parents spoke no Kurdish but Turkish, since they had descent other than Kurdish, such as Armenian, Alawite, and Turkish-Sunni. Nebahat had to learn Kurmanchi and Zaza dialects of Kurdish outside, through socialization in a predominantly Kurdish area. All of her sisters got married into "deep-rooted crowded and traditional Kurdish families" for "that feeling of rootlessness" in a mainly Kurdish populated region as she reports (Akkoç).

Akkoç became a teacher and started teaching at a young age in various districts of Diyarbakır. She met with her late husband, a colleague and a local ethnic Kurd of a district where she was appointed for her first post. She became a wife and mother of two at an early age. They were part of leftist politics during the 1970s: she was a member of *TÖB-DER*, a left-aligned teachers' union. Following her husband's arrest after the 1980 putsch, Akkoç became a "prisoner's wife," shouldering the full parental responsibility for her children. As a school teacher in central Diyarbakır at the time, she endured house raids and political suppression. While visiting her husband in Diyarbakır Military Prison, she met with wives and female kin of other prisoners, who faced intersecting forms of oppression—for example, Kurdish mothers and wives experienced intimidation by security forces for not knowing Turkish, everlasting agony of polygamous prisoners' (unofficial) second and third wives, and extreme poverty among peasant women. She built solidarity with these women, and her approach toward women's issues and human rights became evident (Belge 46-7). Her experience at the prison further enlightened her about a wide range of discriminations in the region, including language rights, and she began doing her advocacy work and teaching in both Turkish and Kurdish.

In the mid-1980s, the junta's persecution of Kurds increased; a national state of emergency was introduced in southeastern Anatolia to contain Kurdish left, and Kurdish nationalist-secessionist claims, which were in their infancy. Those claims became steeped following maltreatment during large scale detentions (Bozyel). Torture in Diyarbakır Prison after September 1980 radicalized a generation of Kurds to join the militant PKK, which instigated an armed struggle in 1984 for greater sovereignty (Yavuz 12; Zeydanlıoğlu 8). Meanwhile, Akkoç and her husband managed to reunite, and they kept a moderate political profile. While carrying out the Diyarbakır chairpersonship of the brand-new teacher's union, *Eğit-Sen*, Akkoç lost sixteen of her colleagues through extrajudicial killings, since the political climate was not tolerant for any organized political activity. As she taught at state schools, she was fined several times for union activities and was even threatened to be dismissed from her profession. Her husband could not teach; so he worked in commerce, while receiving many threats. Following his return to teaching in 1993, he was murdered, becoming yet another entry in the long list of extrajudicial killings. A suspect was caught in 1997 but released for lack of evidence. Her husband's murder caused her to become an activist in IHD, becoming a founding and general board member for IHD's Diyarbakır branch. She reported her participation into IHD as a survival strategy, since "the life came to such a state that she could not have any other way to live it, though she had been scared to volunteer." She described commencing advocacy work in IHD as a panacea for her rootlessness and dealing with her loss; overall, "instead of watching the aggrieved," she preferred to "be with them" believing that "being together with the grieving heals one's own wounds" (Akkoç).

She participated in IHD's fieldwork in early the 1990s. She documented torture and village destruction cases, which became part of the state's means to beat PKK, and she organized campaigns in southeast branches. The initial days in IHD were different; the work they did was legitimate for everyone, even for authorities as she reported. However, the rising civilian Kurdish casualties and use of controversial arms to suppress insurgency severed friendly the relationship between the state and IHD, and IHD discourse began to resemble PKK's. This was a problem, however not the last problem with IHD. For Akkoç, IHD was not sympathetic toward feminism, especially women's autonomy, since the association was not well-informed about the women's question at the time. Special commissions existed for women, but they could not work independently; activists, both male and female, were very conservative about forming exclusive women's commissions or autonomous peaceable activities led by women (Akkoç).

Reporting the state's role in the murdering of her colleagues and husband to the European Court of Human Rights (ECHR), as well as her speaking to press and the rumours regarding her candidacy for municipal elections for *DEP*, the Kurdish Democratic Labour Party, caused her to be detained fifteen times. During detention, she endured heavy physical and psychological torture. ECHR found Akkoç's case valid and obliged Turkey to compensate her. She used that compensation for the establishment of *KAMER*, later (Belge 86-101, 104-106, 115). She reported that her detention was awful, but it crystallized her approach toward women's human rights. Her experience showed how distinctively women were hurt for just being women, such as physical-sexual violence under detention, which awakened her about gender-based discrimination. She informed IHD co-members that she had to do something specific about violence and women, otherwise she could not continue her advocacy, but no one seemed to appreciate the seriousness of the issue. Unsurprised, she concluded working with IHD so that she could exclusively advocate for women victims of violence, despite the infamy and further isolation awaiting her. Meanwhile, she kept being threatened and scolded by state and nonstate actors because she was a mother and activist; as a politically active feminist mother appreciated by no one, she had the ordeal of not allowing her children an independent life, somewhat contradicting her own ideals as an educator, activist, leftist, and feminist mother (Akkoç). As a family, they had an unstable life as their privacy was compromised: she changed their home often, kept her children under control, and made special arrangements to reduce the impact of police surveillance (Belge 96; 113-118). Her children were well aware of the fact that she was not an ordinary mother, which caused her to have serious thoughts about her actions; they were introverted, resilient or self-censoring depending on the conditions of her detentions unhoped for their ages:

Besides me, my five year old son lived through the difficulties of 1980 coup and the violence of 1990s. He experienced his father's killing, my detentions and he got very tired.... Every time I was detained, he stood still; he kept asking the police where they were bringing me, he accompanied the house searches.... In each detention, he was sad, but careful not to reflect anything and not to collapse. (qtd. in Belge 113)

Akkoç's daughter illustrates the same notion:

I wanted to have a normal family in my own way.... I contemplated "Why we cannot be like any other normal family? ... [After losing my father], the fear of losing my mom stroke me. I knew that she was tortured. She does not know, but I still cannot watch movies containing torture scenes. [During her detentions], the weather was extremely cold. If it's extremely cold and I get chilled, I start crying.... *Akkoç versus State* is an important legal case. I am a lawyer, but I still have not read it. (qtd. in Belge 71, 74, 95)

Akkoç became a mother at a young age and raised her children through various predicaments. She had firm rules inspired by her occupation, teaching. However, she does not identify motherhood by self-abnegating praises or by censoring the heavy demands and pressures it inflicts on women. For Akkoç, motherhood is surely difficult; it often requires others' support, but it is not the sole function to define women. Motherhood is such a tiresome responsibility that one can be hurt just by being a mother and by enduring criticism over her mothering and activism, even by her own children (Akkoç; Belge 93-102). In short, Akkoç had to prove the legitimacy of her activism to her children, her tormentors, and society daily; however, her children's dismay came with huge emotional coasts. All in all, the criticism did not discourage her; having explored feminist advocacy through reading feminist literature on her own, she believed she could lay the foundations of peacemaking and for a nonviolent society. For her, building peace had to start from the private sphere and through bringing women's human rights issues to the forefront; therefore, she established KAMER in 1997.

KAMER was founded as a firm for legal complications, and became a foundation later. She set out to build a society free of gender-, race-, and ethnic-based discrimination, which was informed by feminism. In time, volunteers and women, formerly assisted by KAMER to change their violence-ridden lives, joined her. KAMER now has twenty-three provincial branches and various business operatives for women's employment and entrepreneurship. For employees, entrepreneurs, and advisors, KAMER provides nurseries; it also executes alternative preschool education projects to eliminate violence (Y. Arat and Altınay 12-19). Akkoç's motherhood and activism, her ability to be accepted by her children and society surpass the current construction of mothering, which is often marked by constant anxieties of inefficiency and quests for impeccability.

Akkoç introduces us to a path on which she set forth not only as a mother and prisoner's wife, but as a woman who managed to walk inspiringly. Her encouraging yet strenuous experience describes well the thorny and unacknowledged route taken by women human rights activists in Turkey. Akkoç's activism is exemplary for the conflicts inherent in mother activism; she had struggles with the status quo, and was looked down upon by traditional friends and some family members as an improper mother; she also endured her children's criticism and worries. She struggled with private and public patriarchy and threats of violence. She mothered without being solely confined to motherhood either and provided an alternative, though not free of regret, for motherhood during human rights activism. Akkoç described this arduous process as follows:

I constrained my kids a lot. I was scared that something bad would happen to them while receiving those threats through phone calls. I tried hard to not to let them go out. We could not have a life outside; they lurched between home and school.

I realized how much I got tired of and strained by motherhood when my children got married. I requested my son and daughter in law not to call me mother. Cause when they did so, I really felt overwhelmed by that, I could not mother four people, I was too worn out to do that. This is important. They understood it and did not let me down, I am thankful.... I told them I came to a grief.... Then I understood how difficult and arduous to take care of and protect them....

As revealed above, Akkoç's motherhood throughout her human rights advocacy had heavy emotional costs but still exemplifies a nonessential form of motherhood. She neither sanctifies nor reinforces normative motherhood even at the expense of rejecting its privileges (i.e., the power that family traditions in Turkey accords motherhood, also through mothering children-in-law). Akkoç bravely states the emotional burden of mothering and rejects a culturally enforced maternal self-sacrifice, a patriarchal entrapment. As a critical mother, she reclaims motherhood as a feminist concept through her activism and her reconstructive work in child welfare and preschool education, which is informed by gender equality and a desire to end violence.

EXPANDING THE BOUNDARIES OF
HUMAN RIGHTS ADVOCACY: HÜDA KAYA

From the 1950s onwards, Islam has become increasingly visible in Turkey, with veiling and more religious observations. Between the 1970s and 1990s, the Islamist movement strengthened, reaching its climax when the Welfare Party (*Refah Partisi-RP*) led the government in 1995. When the results of 1995 general elections were declared, it was surprising for all. No political party managed to gain majority to form a government alone; however Necmettin Erbakan's RP party was the leading one with 21 percent of the vote. This was the first time that an outspokenly Islamic party gained prominence in republican secular Turkey. The RP was dissimilar to the traditional centre-right political parties of the time. Although it supported private entrepreneurship and the free market, it gained popularity among working classes and the urban poor. With the efforts of its field volunteers, the RP built effective contact with potential voters, detecting their problems and providing support. The RP soon become more organized compared to the other parties, either left or right aligned, in 1990s Turkey. As the leading party, it succeeded to form the government after abortive attempts of other parties and arrange a coalition government with one of them, True Path Party (*Doğru Yol Partisi-DYP*).

Although the RP's rise to government was a fact, the military establishment systematically disregarded the government through refusing to cooperate with it. On 28 February 1997, the military put forward a number of measures—a compulsory eight-year education programme to prevent children from enrolling into schools for religious functionaries and a headscarf ban at universities—all aiming at banishing so-called religious fundamentalism. Prime Minister Erbakan resisted but resigned after being forced to ratify these decisions. Following this ultimatum, the Constitutional Court disbanded RP in January 1998. The RP leaders, including Erbakan, were also banned from politics. The 28 February putsch was the fourth one after 1960, but with an apparent difference: it toppled the government by an ardent secularist discourse and replaced RP-led government with an alternative civil one, not necessarily dissolving any political institution except RP. It has, therefore, been called a postmodern coup elsewhere (Özkan; Bayramoğlu).

The February coup had grave consequences, one being the headscarf issue. Modernization of society and public attire has always been interrelated in Turkey (Breu and Marchese; Aktaş). In 1925, republicans clarified their stance about appropriate public attire, which entailed hats and smart suits. Since women's employment in public offices was not prevalent in those years, few female employees and female kin of civil servants were expected to de-veil. However, regulations banned headscarf in courts, parliament, public offices, schools, and universities in the late 1920s. From the late 1960s onwards, the headscarf became a signifier of religiosity and symbolic resistance to republican modernity. Although the veil was tolerated in schools for religious functionaries until the 1980 coup, the junta revisited veiling and banned it by a new regulation for universities in 1982 (Özdalga). The enforcement of this regulation though remained ad hoc; some universities prohibited the headscarf, some did not until the February coup, which was a secularist restoration phase. The 1997 headscarf ban would be strictly implemented in both universities and schools for religious functionaries. It also created repercussions for veiled workers and female kin of civil servants. Consequently, the lives of women changed dramatically; they had to drop out of their schools and only the affluent managed to go abroad for education (Kentel; Z. Arat). Veiled workers faced demotions and job losses (Toprak and Uslu). The headscarf ban was introduced because the scarf was deemed to violate the connection between women and republican modernity for which women functioned as the markers of modernization through their rights along attire (Tekeli). The rise of headscarf donning especially among young women, professed representatives of modernization, was equated with religion's reinstatement against secular modern life and inviolable principles of the republic (Baban).

Hüda Kaya is a human rights activist from Islamic circles and experienced the severe onslaught of the 1997 February coup with her children. Born to a migrant working-class family in İstanbul, she was brought up by her father following her parents' divorce. Her family was a traditional moderate one with regards to Islam; they were believers, but not so pious apart from simple Muslim observances. She was exposed to a conservative-nationalist milieu and discovered Islam first in relation "Turkism"; the Islam she was acquainted with was a nationalistic-supremacist one. She was oblivious of other ways of observing Islam and life outside of Istanbul. Kaya then embraced a more "universalist" version of Islam through personal study over scripture; she became critical about nationalist, state-sponsored, and administered religion. Her decision to use a veil caused parental pressure over her; her headscarves, cloaks and books were destroyed by her father, who disapproved of her visible piety, but she kept improving her devotion and discovery of Islam (Kaya). As a matter of fact, she learned worship, ablutions, Islamic hermeneutics, and philosophy through personal study. The solidarity networks she had formed with Muslim circles and her family's pressures induced her to marry a refugee student from Iraq at the age of eighteen, although she had no intention to get married so early. Her marriage, a gesture of solidarity, lasted nine years, and she struggled for her five children's custody afterward.

Divorce changed Kaya's life fundamentally; her husband had turned into an oppressor. She had to hide out with her young children, since her husband attempted kidnapping them abroad. Then she had to arrange an escape with them after receiving their consent from İstanbul. The lengthy lawsuits for custody of her children created many inconveniences; she had to leave Istanbul because of her ex-husband's continuous harassment, and she moved to Malatya, an eastern Anatolian city. Residing there totally changed her life; from a middle-class mother, she turned into a working one, shouldering the responsibility of five children. She faced a negative climate for practising Islam after the post-February coup, as prejudices from within Islamic circles existed toward activist Islamist women and Kurdish issue. The solidarity she built with her children and friends in Malatya revived her Islamic activism, and financial independence transformed her life and concerns substantially.

Kaya became an activist for one of the most engaged human rights NGOs in the 1990s, *Mazlumder*,[6] and her advocacy concentrated chiefly on headscarf bans from 1994 onward. She was a veiled mom of three veiled daughters, who were attending a school for religious functionaries. She, therefore, participated in Mazlumder's petition campaign and mass demonstrations in Istanbul, and other activities framed for 1997, which was declared as "the year of freedom to headscarf." Having police records from previous headscarf demonstrations already, she supported veiled women in Malatya. The textile shop she ran was a mecca for young veiled women; she assisted young women in high schools and university to organize medical reports "verifying" baldness and sinusitis to justify their veiling. She also partook in Islamic learning meetings and relief campaigns, wrote for newspapers and magazines for Muslim masses, and engaged in radio broadcasting. Her article titled "A Night for National Excitement and Headscarf" and her activism finally caused her detention. Her underage daughters and son also became part of headscarf demonstrations following their mother's arrest; they were later detained for criminal charges. She received a twenty month-prison term. Trial and arrests were taxing on Kaya and her family; she was scolded for being an improper mother destroying her children's future, but she did not recoil:

During my imprisonment along with my daughters, particularly my closest friends and immediate family, even people from Islamic circles seriously criticized me about my motherhood. Even in my interrogation, guards in the anti-terror unit did so. During a house raid, a policeman scolded and called me to account: "You ruined the lives of these kids, all of these [raids and investigations] will be registered as their criminal past; you already tarnished their future. They will never progress in the future, what a mother you are" he said. Aww! I was accountable for my motherhood everywhere, anytime. How did I respond? I told them they did not need to worry, and I was well aware of what I was doing for my kids. I did my best for them.... As a matter of fact, everyone, including ... strangers, tried offending and suppressing me for the way I mothered.

Kaya's children were, indeed, together with her all the time; they actively supported her advocacy by becoming activist themselves at young ages; they, therefore, helped bridge the public and private gap for their activist mother's sake. As opposed to her children's whole-hearted support, few members from influential Islamic circles supported her in any way following her release. Financial difficulties stemming from unemployment combined with new legal cases brought against her family and her children's interrupted education compelled her to become a refugee in Pakistan in 2001. However, the post 9/11 climate made residing there too difficult; she returned to Turkey and went to prison to complete her three-year term in different jails across the country. Then she lost her daughter, Nurulhak, in a car accident in 2005, but the loss of her daughter did not undermine her activism. She addressed an UN meeting in Geneva about freedom of conscience and headscarf related to human rights violations in Turkey. In 2011, her son, Muhammed Cihat, was detained for "alleged affiliation with PKK; however, he was acquitted. Kaya was also critical toward the Justice and Development Party (*Adalet ve Kalkınma Partisi-AKP*), ruling Turkey since 2002 as a conservative successor to RP. AKP's indifferent stance during the 28 February hearings, its changing attitude toward the oppressed after its 2011 general election victory, and its handling of the Kurdish issue constituted her criticism. For Kaya, AKP became conformist, once representing the wronged: Muslim women and Kurdish mothers. But Kaya was most critical about AKP's handling of the Kurdish issue: she believed AKP did nothing but repeat what previous governments did. In this regard, she suffered marginalization as an "atypical Islamist woman." Her criticism against the conservative yet neoliberal and Islamist AKP government, and her approach to the Kurdish issue (i.e., the solidarity networks she brokered with Kurdish women) was seen as her breaching the alleged God-ordained submissiveness of Muslim women.

Kaya kept her advocacy work in Mazlumder intact, and then established her own association[7] while serving as Turkey's delegate for the International Muslim Women Union and as a central executive committee member in the pro-Kurdish People's Democratic Party (HDP) for two terms in the late 2000s. She became a council member in the Democratic Islam Congress in 2014. She participated into various international congresses for peace and freedom of conscience, carried out relief work for refugees together with her children, and wrote in oppositional news platforms. Her interest in Kurdish issue dated back to the time when she was a prisoner. She already organized relief work for rural Kurds residing makeshift camps following their deportation from eastern and southeastern Anatolia in 1990s, but during her prison sentence, she had the chance to meet Kurdish prisoners and gain further insight. She became especially outspoken about human rights violations against Kurdish citizens after the Roboski Massacre.[8] For Kaya, Islamists failed to prove their concern for universal human rights following this massacre. As a journalist, and to comprehend Kurdish and PKK issues better and develop an unprejudiced approach, she visited Kurdish guerrilla camps in Kandil, in northern Iraq in 2013, which infuriated Islamists and nationalists alike. Kaya believes oppression criss-crosses ethnic, national, gender differences; therefore human rights advocacy cannot discriminate against or prioritize any oppressed group.

In the June 2015 parliamentary elections, Kaya became the first veiled MP for HDP, from İstanbul, with the renewal of elections in November 2015 for the second time. She is one of the most unusual faces of human rights advocacy in Turkey. She started her political socialization with extreme right-wing nationalism, ended up working with progressive democrats questing for human rights and resolving the Kurdish question. She emphasized the sexism of the 28 February memorandum and backlashes followed; she believed the junta, the conservative Islamist government, and Muslim men altogether discriminated against women. She claimed that it was neither AKP nor Muslim men, but women with their insistence to don a headscarf and defend freedom of conscience who struggled against the February junta, concluding that no oppression is gender neutral.

Kaya reported that she had always been criticized for her "irresponsible mothering"; her activism was seen as harmful to her own children, but she argued that excluding children from political advocacy inhibited achieving results: successful advocacy is the result of children's participation in it. She had a common faith with her children from early on and was never belittled by them, even in really tough times; as a mother, she gave them the right to choose between their father and her during her divorce. Though not promising a perfect and comfortable life, she pledged a freedom built through solidarity and cooperation with them. Kaya never tried to be a flawless housewife or an impeccable mother; she aimed to be a mother who guides her children, and in return demands support and friendship from them (Kaya). For Kaya, being a mother should not be about pure self-sacrifice. It is about uniting personal strives for equality and justice at large with mothering.

Kaya as an activist mother struggled in various but often intersecting realms. She had disputes with her father about her headscarf when she was young. After becoming a mother of three daughters, she had to struggle with the junta's headscarf ban. She was one among few veiled women who protested the headscarf ban in provincial cities, whereas the majority of Islamist women preferred silence and being represented by men. While resisting the bans, her daughters, and later her sons, accompanied her. Her daughters accompanied her during her imprisonment, and she never hesitated to be joined by her children for human rights defence and relief work. Instead of treating them as minors, she perceived her children as independent individuals with opinions. For human rights defense to be effective and human rights to advance in any given society, mothers have to be in at the frontlines with their children. Such a mother-child association in human rights activism is not crucial for legitimating what is demanded, but it is essential for encouraging each party to contribute and express his or herself for a really critical issue—human rights.

CONCLUSION

As a political movement, human rights advocacy aims to save lives and to bring justice to violators. To strengthen the rule of law and change in state policies, it mobilizes large groups of women, which challenges the idea that women's role is restricted to the private realm. Despite serious setbacks, women have been an integral part of the human rights movement and community worldwide.

Women's, especially mothers', human rights defense has been subject to criticism and praise by feminists. Women's political mobilization to defend their children rather than their own rights is generally categorized as "motherist," and arguments regarding such activism also diverge. Motherist politicization is either dismissed for essentializing women's primary role as mothering and cementing compliance to patriarchy through reproducing gendered expectations from women in politics, or it is celebrated as genuinely female politics promising local and international feminist activism. Various forms of "political motherhood" (i.e., mothers' peace, environmentalist, and human rights activism) were also deemed positive thanks to their potential to transform political domain into a care-oriented one. Some feminists caution against the pitfalls of maternalist activism and politics mainly through the service that motherhood provides for nationalism, how it complies with traditional gender roles, and the biological and cultural reductionism it entails for women, even as a political activity. Some motherist groups refrain from connecting with feminism, which stands out as another problem for feminists. Nevertheless, various strands of feminism have been espousing the merits of mother movements, and they reclaim and rework motherhood as a feminist concept.

Women's human rights activism, whether strongly maternalist or not, challenges the ideal of apolitical motherhood. Women human rights activists transcend child-centred Madonna perfection by reversing motherhood's long-acclaimed "calming impact" over women's political activism and directly engaging explicitly political issues, including human rights. Moreover, mothers' human rights activism suggests that women's inclusion into politics should not have to be the extension of women's maternal duties into the public or consequent to bringing up their children all the time. Whereas mother's human rights activism can be conceptualized as one, if not the sole, channel for women's politicization, a parallel examination is required about how such advocacy transforms motherhood and how mother activists experience mothering. Women human rights activists who were politicized prior to motherhood, mother activists who were not incited into activism exclusively for their maternal identity, and the ones who neither stood as suffering mother icons nor used a strong moral-maternal discourse thus require specific attention. Not only did mothers whose quest for justice involved vocalizing their maternal suffering sustain human rights activity in Turkey, but so too did mothers whose political and human rights advocacy used nonessential forms of maternal activism and nonconventional ways of reclaiming motherhood. Therefore, the history of the human rights movement in Turkey first needs to be linked to and re-evaluated with women's contribution to it, whose involvement has remained invisible. Second, the multiplicity of maternal practices and attributes about motherhood by activist women should be incorporated into such an analysis so that maternal experiences, which have been disregarded through the homogenizing representation of women as agonized mothers in human rights activism, can be revealed and mainstreamed.

The mothers and women folk of detained and disappeared people after 1980 coup bolstered up the human rights NGOs and anchored women to this domain for further contribution. Although motherhood bestows a substantial legitimacy to the movement and advocacy, mothers' human rights activism in Turkey were circumscribed by gender-specific violations, including threats to their families and allegations relating to their "conduct" and stigmatizing them as improper women and negligent mothers.

Fırtına, Akkoç, and Kaya stand as alternative advocates who challenge various gendered stigmatizations, since they became part of the movement not simply as aggrieved mothers but as perspective-holding ones capable of transforming the domains in which they operate. They experienced motherhood and activism alternatively, without sacrificing one to the other, and defying patriarchal hypocrisy, which values motherhood only superficially and divides it into proper and improper parts. They mother without sanctifying or victimizing themselves. Their human rights work transformed the motherhood identity, which had been held standard, constant, and ahistoric, into a challenging one.

Women whose voices appear here were not formerly apolitical housewives, as opposed to the general politicization of mothers between the 1970s and 1990s in Turkey for the killing and imprisoning of politically active youth. It is true that Fırtına, Akkoç, and Kaya were moved to take political action by concern for their children and relatives, but their political criticism preceded their motherhood. Yet they believed that being politically active is a legitimate part of being mothers; they comprehended and interpreted their postmotherhood activism and further politicization along human rights as a responsible maternal reaction without belaboring essentialist and sacred notions of motherhood. By engaging with pressing sociopolitical issues— such as human rights violations, conditions of prisoners, veiling issue, and violence against women—they believed they better cared for their own children while defying the boundaries of exclusive mother-children attachment. Caring about other mothers and children while confronting pressing sociopolitical issues, these mothers changed the meaning of motherhood and their position as adult women. They gained new identities and entitlements, and a collective power and moral authority. Specifically, they mothered without being only confined to mothering; as politically active mothers; they also exemplified maternal subjectivity. Their motherhood experiences during their human rights advocacy prove the impossibility of a uniform maternal subject and multiplicity of maternal experiences. Moreover, their maternal experience highlights the fluid, divided, and always-in-process motherhood of a patriarchal society and its politics.

ENDNOTES

[1] In recent years, several case studies and memoirs were published in this respect mainly by the activists themselves see Karataş; A. Yılmaz; Akbaş; Şeşen; Çekmeci; G. Kaya; Atakul; and Gür; Göreleli.

[2] All Turkish-English translations are the author's.

[3] The Al-Anfal Massacre was the outcome of a military campaign performed by Iraqi military forces and ordered by Saddam Hussein's Ba'athist regime against the ethnic Kurds of northern Iraq between late 1987 and 1988. At least 100,000 Kurdish people were killed and some 4,000 Kurdish villages were destroyed mainly through the use of chemical weapons and aerial attacks. See Mikaberidze.

[4] The Kurdish independence movement followed the suppression of the Turkish left after the 1980s coup and evolved into an armed struggle against Turkish military forces in 1990s. The state responded with a fierce counter-insurgency campaign against the Kurdish population. The height of the campaign came between 1991 and 1996, leading to the disappearance and extrajudicial killings of more than a thousand Kurds, allegedly affiliated with the secessionist claims. Beginning from 27 May 1995, the families, predominantly mothers of the disappeared and victims of extra judicial killings as well as human rights activists commenced their silent protest on *Galatasaray* square. The relatives of the victims of state violence modelled their silent protest on the Mothers of the Plaza de Mayo (Argentina), and repeated it every Saturday at noon. They were called the Saturday Mothers (Baydar and İvegen).

[5] In 1937-38, a military campaign was organized against certain parts of the province of Tunceli, previously called Dersim, in Turkey, that had not been brought under proper state control. The campaign lasted from March 1937 to September 1938, resulting in a high death toll among civilian Kurdish Alawites- an offshoot Shia sect in predominantly Sunni Anatolia. See *Van Bruinessen*.

[6] Mazlumder was established in 1991 by activists who had an Islamic sensitivity. They felt that there had to be a human rights organization not exclusively focused on injustice against the left, but advocating for conservatives, women being discriminated against for their headscarf, Kurds, non-Muslims, Roma, missing people, and other prisoners. See Çaylak, 131-136.

[7]She established Snowdrop Association for Education, Culture and Cooperation, (*Kardelen Eğitim Kültür ve Yardımlaşma Derneği*) and functioned as its chair.

[8]In late December 2011, the Turkish military attacked a group of Kurdish men along the Turkish-Iraqi border because it suspected the group of being armed militants belonging to the PKK. The alleged militants were mainly young male civilians—performing their regular weekly round trip over the mountains to provide smuggled cigarettes and gasoline to the local black market. Thirty-four people were killed. The government declared the bombing as accidental; the smugglers had been mistaken for militants. Following the massacre, the Turkish parliament launched an investigation; however, it was curbed by limited information about what really happened. The Turkish Ministry of Interior also launched its own internal investigation. It drafted a report and classified it as "top secret," not to be shared with the public. See Eralp, 448–450 for details.

WORKS CITED

"28 Şubat'ın İdamla Yargıladığı Kadın." *Rey Haber*, 28 Feb. 2012, www.reyhaber.com/siyasethaberleri/28subatinidamlayargiladigikadin.html. Accessed 27 Oct. 2015.

Abadan-Unat, Nermin. *Women in the Developing World: Evidence from Turkey*. University of Denver Press: 1986.

Ahmad, Feroz. *The Making of Modern Turkey*. Routledge, 1993.

Akbaş, Meral. *Mamak Kitabı*. Ayizi Kitap, 2011.

Akkoç, Nebahat. Personal interview, 9 Sept. 2015.

Aktaş, Cihan. *Tanzimattan 12 Mart'a Kılık Kıyafet ve İktidar*. Kapı, 2006.

Arat, Yeşim, and Ayşe Gül Altınay. "KAMER, a Women's Center and an Experiment in Cultivating Cosmopolitan Norms," *Women's Studies International Forum* 49, 2015, pp. 12-19.

Arat, Yeşim. "1980'ler Türkiyesi'nde Kadın Hareketi: Liberal Kemalizm'in Uzantısı," *Toplum ve Bilim*, vol. 53, 1991, pp. 7-19.

Arat, Zehra F. "Educating Daughters of the Republic." *Deconstructing Images of "The Turkish Woman*," edited by Zehra F. Arat, St. Martin's Press, 1998, pp. 157-180.

Arendell, T. "Conceiving and Investigating Motherhood: The Decade's Scholarship," *Journal of Marriage and the Family*, vol. 62, no. 4, 2000, pp. 1192-1207.

Arslan, Ali. "A Different Modernization Experience: Turkish Modernization and the Army," *Uluslararası İnsan Bilimleri Dergisi*, vol. 1, no. 1, 2004, pp. 1-24.

Atakul, Bayram, and İpek Keskin Gür. *Anaların Babaların Diliyle 12 Eylül (Çile Mektupları)*. Devrimci 78'liler Federasyonu, 2012.

Aykol, Hüseyin. *Aykırı Kadınlar, Osmanlı'dan Günümüze Devrimci Kadın Portreleri*, İmge Kitabevi, 2012.

Baban, Fevzi. "Secular Spaces and Religious Representations: Reading the Headscarf Debate in Turkey as Citizenship Politics," *Citizenship Studies*, vol. 18, pp. 6-7, 2014, pp. 644-60, doi:10.1080/13621025.2013.865900.

Baydar, G., and B. İvegen,. "Territories, Identities, and Thresholds: The Saturday Mothers Phenomenon in İstanbul, " *Signs*, vol. 31, no. 3, 2006, pp. 689-715.

Bayramoğlu, A. *28 Şubat Bir Müdahalenin Güncesi*. İletişim Yayınları, 2007.

Belge, Ceren. *OHAL'de Feminizm*. Ayizi Kitap, 2012.

Berktay, Fatmagül, "Political Regimes: Turkey." *Encyclopedia of Women & Islamic Cultures*, edited by Suad Joseph, Brill, 2017, dx.doi.org/10.1163/1872-5309_ewic_EWICCOM_0127b. Accessed 23 June 2017.

Bhattacharjya, Manjima, et al. "Why Gender Matters in Activism: Feminism and Social Justice Movements." *Gender & Development*, vol. 21, no. 2, 2013, pp. 277-93.

Bonner, Michelle D. *Sustaining Human Rights: Women and Argentine Human Rights Organizations*. The Pennsylvania State University Press, 2007.

Bozyel, Bayram. *Diyarbakır 5 No.lu*. Deng Yayınları, 2007.

Breu, M., and R.T. Marchese. "Social Commentary and Political Action: The Headscarf as Popular Culture and Symbol of Political Confrontation in Modern Turkey." *Journal of Popular Culture*, vol. 33, no.4, pp. 2000, pp. 25-38.

Cizre-Sakallıoğlu, Ümit. "The Anatomy of the Turkish Military's Political Autonomy." *Comparative Politics*, vol. 29, no. 2, 1997, pp. 151-66.

Çaylak, Adem. "Autocratic or Democratic? A Critical Approach to Civil Society Movements in Turkey.".*Journal of Economic and Social Research*, vol. 10, no. 1, 2008, pp. 115-51.

Çekmeci, Sacide. *Nizamiye Kapısında*. Doğuş Matbaası, 1996.

Çarkoğlu, Ali, and William Hale, editors. *The Politics of Modern Turkey*. Routledge, 2008. 4 vols.

De Alwis, Malathi. "Moral Mothers and Stalwart Sons: Reading Binaries in a Time of War." *The Women and War Reader*, edited by Lois Ann Lorentzen and Jennifer E. Turpin, New York University Press, 1998.

De Beauvoir, Simone. *The Second Sex*. Translated by Constance Borde and Sheila Malovany-Chevallier. Alfred A. Knopf, 2009.

Dietz, Mary G. "Citizenship with a Feminist Face: The Problem with Maternal Thinking." *Political Theory*, vol. 13, no. 1, 1985, pp. 19-37.

Direk, Zeynep. "Çok Tuhaf Bir İktidar: Annelik," *Amargi*, vol. 15, 2009, pp. 21-22.

DiQuinzio, Patrice. "Exclusion and Essentialism in Feminist Theory: The Problem of Mothering." *Hypatia*, vol. 8, no. 3, 1993, pp. 1-20.

Douglas, Susan, and Meredith W. Michaels. *The Mommy Myth: The Idealization of Motherhood and How It Has Undermined All Women*. Free Press, 2004.

Eralp, Doğa Ulaş. "The Role of U.S. Drones in the Roboski Massacre." *Peace Review: A Journal of Social Justice*, vol. 27, 2015, pp. 448-55, doi: 10.1080/10402659.2015.1094325.

Erdoğan, Füsun. "Güle Güle Güzel Kadın." *Yeni Özgür Politika*, 2015, www.yeniozgurpolitika.org/index.php?rupel=nivis&id=7884. Accessed 24 June 2017.

ETHA (Etkin News Agency). "Leman Fırtına: Kendi Yolunda Yürüyen Keyifli Bir Kadın." *Etkin News Agency*, 2015, www.etha.com.tr/Haber/2015/04/05/yasam/leman-firtina-kendi-yol-unda-yuruyen-keyifli-bir-ka/. Accessed 23 April 2016.

Fabj, Valeria. "Motherhood as Political Voice: The Rhetoric of the Mothers of Plaza de Mayo." *Communication Studies*, vol. 44, no. 1, 1993, pp. 1-18.

Fırtına, Leman. "Türkiye'de İnsan Hakları Mücadelesi." *İşkence Olayı: Yolaçtığı Bedensel ve Ruhsal Rahatsızlıklar, Tedavi ve*

Rehabilitasyon, edited by Bülent Tarakçıoğlu, Belge Yayınları, 1990, pp. 95-104).

Forcey, L. Rennie. "Feminist Perspectives on Mothering and Peace." *Mothering: Ideology, Experience, and Agency*, edited by Evelyn Glenn et al., Routledge, 1994, pp. 355-76

Gedik, Esra. "Türkiye'de Şehit Annelerinin Savaş ve Çözüm Algıları." *Fe Dergi: Feminist Eleştiri*, vol. 1, no. 2, 2009, pp. 29-43.

Gieve, K. "Rethinking Feminist Attitudes towards Motherhood." *Feminist Review*, vol. 25, 1997, pp. 38-45.

Göçek, Fatma Müge. *Denial of Violence: Ottoman Past, Turkish Present and Collective Violence against the Armenians, 1789-2009*. Oxford University Press, 2015.

Göker, Zeynep G. "The Mourning Mother: Rhetorical Figure or a Political Actor?" *The Making of Neoliberal Turkey*, edited by Cenk Ozbay et al., Routledge. 2016.

Göreleli, Ayşen. *Postal ve Patik; Metris'te Her Mevsim Kış*. İlya İzmir Yayınevi, 2011.

Grosz, Elizabeth. "Conclusion: A Note on Essentialism and Difference." *Feminist Knowledge: Critique and Construct*, edited by Sneja Gunew, Routledge, 1990, pp. 332-44.

Hale, William. *Turkish Politics and the Military*. Routledge, 1994.

Hamdemir, Berkan, and M. Nazan Arslanel. "Türkiye'de İnsan Haklarını Koruma Amaçlı Sivil Toplum Örgütleri." *EKEV Akademi Dergisi*, vol. 15, no. 48, 2011, pp. 23-44.

Harris, George S. "Military Coups and Turkish Democracy, 1960–1980." *Turkish Studies*, vol. 12, no. 2, 2011, pp. 203-13.

Hewett, Heather. "Talkin' Bout a Revolution: Building a Mothers' Movement in the Third Wave." *Journal of the Association on Mothering and Feminism*, vol. 8, no. 1-2, 2006, pp.34-54.

Horuz, M., and Gülseren Yoleri. *12 Eylül Anneleri; Röportajlar*. Doliche Filmcilik & Yayıncılık, 2015.

Johnson, Maxwell Orme. "The Role of the Military in Turkish Politics." *Air University Review*, 1982, www.au.af.mil/au/afri/aspj/airchronicles/aureview/1982/jan-feb/johnson.html#johnson. Accessed 22 Mar. 2017.

Karataş, Sultan. *Metris'ten Mektuplar*. La Kitap, 2015.

Karpat, Kemal. *Turkey's Politics: The Transition to a Multi-Party System*. Princeton University Press, 1959.

Kasapoglu, Aytül, and Necmettin Özerkmen, Necmettin. "Gender Imbalance: The Case of Women's Political Participation in Turkey." *Journal of International Women's Studies*, vol. 12, no. 4, 2011, pp. 97-107.

Kaya, Hüda. Personal interview. 6 September 2015.

Kayalı, Kurtuluş. *Ordu ve Siyaset: 27 Mayıs—12 Mart.* İletişim Yayınları, 1994.

Kentel, Ferhat. "Yeni Bir Laiklik, Yeni Bir Modernite." *Türkiye'nin Örtülü Gerçeği Başörtüsü Yasağı Alan Araştırması*, Hazar Eğitim Kültür ve Dayanışma Derneği, 2007, pp.57-68.

Kerestecioğlu-Özkan, İnci. "Kadınlara Yönelik Aile içi Şiddet: Mücadele, Kazanımlar ve Sorunlar." *Birikim*, Ağustos- Eylül 2004, 184-185

Keskin, Eren. "Leman Teyze." *Özgür Gündem* 6 Apr. 2015, www.ozgur-gundem.com/yazi/130422/leman-teyze. Accessed 24 June 2017.

Keyman, Fuat, and Ahmet İçduygu. *Citizenship in a Global World: European Questions and Turkish Experiences*. Routledge, 2005.

Kinross, Patrick Balfour Baron. *Atatürk: The Rebirth of a Nation*. Rustem and Brother in Association with Weidenfeld and Nicholson, 1981.

Kinser, Amber. *Motherhood and Feminism*. Seal Press, 2010.

Mardin, Şerif. *Türkiye'de Toplum ve Siyaset Makaleler*. İletişim Yayınları, 1992.

Marshall-Aldıkaçtı, Gül. *Gender Policy in Turkey: Grassroots Women Activists, the European Union, and the Turkish State*. Suny Press, 2013.

Mavioğlu, Ertuğrul. *Asılmayıp Beslenenler: Bir 12 Eylül Hesaplaşması*, Babil Yayınları, 2004.

Mikaberidze, A. "Al-Anfal (1987-1988)." *Atrocities, Massacres, and War Crimes: An Encyclopedia*, edited by ABC-CLIO, 2013, pp.19-20.

Miller, Alice M. "Violence against Women, and Human Rights: Women Make Demands and Ladies Get Protection." *Health and Human Rights*, vol. 7, no. 2, 2004, pp. 16-47.

Moore, Niamh. "Eco/Feminism, Non-Violence, and the Future of Feminism." *International Feminist Journal of Politics*, vol. 10, no. 3, 2008, pp. 282-98.

Moralıoğlu, Aylin. "80'li Yıllarda Kadın Hareketi ve Kampany-alar." *Türkiye Barolar Birliği Dergisi,* March-April 2012, no. 99, pp. 292-96 .

Negron-Gonzales, Melinda. *East Meets West: The Politics of Human Rights Activism in Turkey, 1980-2007.* Dissertation, University of Florida, 2009.

O'Reilly, Andrea, and Silvia Caporale Bizzini. editors. *From the Personal to the Political: Toward a New Theory of Maternal Narrative.* Susquehanna University Press, 2009.

Orhan, Gözde. "Türkiye'nin Yakın Tarihinde Farklı Bir Öznelik Pratiği Olarak Annelik." *Praksis,* vol. 29, 2013, pp. 107-34.

Orleck, Annelise. "Tradition Unbound: Radical Mothers in International Perspective." *The Politics of Motherhood: Activist Voices From Left to Right,* edited by Alexis Jetter et al, University Press of New England, 1997, pp. 3-22.

Özdalga, Elisabeth. *The Veiling Issue: Official Secularism and Popular Islam in Modern Turkey.* Curzon. 1998.

Özkan, Behlül. "Turkey's Islamists: From Power-Sharing to Political Incumbency." *Turkish Policy Quarterly,* vol. 14, no. 1, 2015, pp. 74-81.

Öztürk, Fadıl. "Röportaj: Leman Fırtına: Dört Yıl Her Gece Telefon Çaldı." Bianet (Bağımsız İletişim Ağı), https://bianet.org/bianet/yasam/163519-leman-firtina-dort-yil-her-gece-telefon-caldi. Accessed 3 April 2015.

Ruddick, Sara. "Rethinking "Maternal" Politics" in *The Politics of Motherhood : Activist Voices From Left to Right,* edited by Alexis Jetter et al., University Press of New England, 1997, pp. 369-82.

Ruddick, Sara. *Maternal Thinking: Toward a Politics of Peace.* Ballantine Books, 1989.

Scheper-Hughes, Nancy. "Maternal Thinking and the Politics of War." *The Women and War Reader,* edited by Lois Ann Lorentzen and Jennifer Turpin, New York University Press, 1998, pp. 227-33.

Sirman, Nükhet. "Cuma, Cumartesi, Pazar Anneleri." *Amargi,* vol. 15, 2009, pp. 19-20.

Sohrabi, Nader. "Historicizing Revolutions: Constitutional Revolutions in the Ottoman Empire, Iran, and Russia, 1905-1908."

The American Journal of Sociology, vol. 100, no. 6, 1995, pp. 1383-1447.

Swerdlow, Amy. *Women Strike for Peace: Traditional Motherhood and Radical Politics in the 1960s.* University of Chicago Press, 1993.

Şentürk, Burcu. *İki tarafta Evlat Acısı.* İletişim Yayınları, 2012.

Şeşen, Gülten. *Tutsak Aileleri, 12 Eylül ve Tayad*, Haziran Yayınevi, 1996.

Tahincioğlu, Gökçer. "Eski Hikaye, Büyük Fırtına." *Milliyet*, 5 Apr. 2015, www.milliyet.com.tr/yazarlar/gokcer-tahincioglu/eski-hik-ye--buyuk--firtina--2039087/. Accessed 21 Aug. 2015.

Taylor, Diana. "Overview: Mothers and the State." *The Politics of Motherhood : Activist Voices From Left to Right*, edited by Alexis Jetter et al., University Press of New England, 1997, pp. 141-60.

Tekeli, Şirin. "Kadınlar: Cumhuriyetin Sevilmeyen Cinsi." *Yüzyıla Girerken Türkiye*, edited by Semih Vaner and Kitap Yayınevi, 2009, pp. 246-78.

Temelkuran, Ece. *Oğlum, Kızım, Devletim; Evlerden Sokaklara Tutuklu Anneleri*, Metis Yayınları, 1997, pp.112-118.

Timur, Taner. *Türkiye'de Çok Partili Hayata Geçiş.* İmge Kitapevi, 2003.

Toprak, Metin, and Nasuh Uslu. "The Headscarf Controversy in Turkey." *Journal of Economic and Social Research*, vol. 11, no. 1, 2009, pp. 43-67

Tunçay, Mete. *Türkiye Cumhuriyeti'nde Tek Parti Rejiminin Kurulması (1923-1931).* Tarih Vakfı Yurt Yayınları, 1999.

Türkmen, Emir Ali. *Uzun İnce Bir Yoldayız: IHD 20 Yaşında.* İnsan Hakları Derneği Yayınları, 2006.

Üskül, Mehmet Zafer. *Bildirileriyle 12 Mart 1971 Darbesi.* Tarih Vakfı Yurt Yayınları, 2014.

Van Allen, Judith. "Radical Citizenship: Powerful Mothers and Equal Rights." *Power, Gender and Social Change in Africa*, edited by Muna Ndulo and Margaret Grieco, Cambridge Scholars Publishing 2009, pp. 60-76.

Van Bruinessen, Martin. *Kurdish Ethno-Nationalism Versus Nation-Building States. Collected Articles.* The Isis Press, 2000.

Whetsone, Chrystal. *Is the Motherist Approach More Helpful in Obtaining Women's Rights than a Feminist Approach? A Comparative Study of Lebanon and Liberia.* MA Thesis, Wright State University, 2013.

Yavuz, M. Hakan. "Five Stages of the Construction of Kurdish Nationalism in Turkey." *Nationalism and Ethnic Politics*, vol. 7, no. 3, 2001), pp. 1-24.

Yılmaz, Ali. *Kara Arşiv: 12 Eylül Cezaevleri.* Metis Yayınları, 2012.

Yılmaz, Kamile. "Solcuların Anası Leman Fırtına." *Istanbul Times*, 2015, istanbultimes.net/solcularin-anasi-leman-firtina/. Accessed 15 June 2015.

Zeydanlıoğlu, Welat. "Torture and Turkification in the Diyarbakır Military Prison." *Rights, Citizenship & Torture: Perspectives on Evil, Law and the State,*edited by W. Zeydanlıoglu and John T. Parry, Inter-Disciplinary Press, 2009, pp. 73-92.

12.
The Mothers at Home to the Mothers on the Streets

Caring, Politics, and the Right to Have Rights

ROSAMARIA CARNEIRO

THIS CHAPTER AIMS TO think about the mother figure as a contemporary political actor through her strategies, representation, social upheaval, and fields of interest. The text will unweave like a spiral: it will present some situations of the recent past whereby mothers took to the streets of Brazil to fight for matters that concern them while we look for the links between those situations, which could, at first, look completely different. They will be analyzed, as such, according to the strength and the symbolic, historic, or social appeal of the mother figure and other related aspects. In order to achieve this, I will highlight contemporary situations, images, and accounts from other Brazilian studies conducted about the political practices of mothers in the Brazil today. This methodology will show the symbolic and political force of the mother figure in contemporary Brazil.

CASE ONE

In 2012, after the Regional Medical Council of Rio de Janeiro (CREMERJ) forbade physicians from supervising home births[1] in the state capital, Rio, mothers from all of the states in Brazil took to the streets carrying signs and banners in a demonstration demanding and defending the right to give birth wherever they saw fit and according to their own wishes and beliefs. With the motto "CREMERJ, no one asked for your counsel,"[2] they defended their right to give birth at home as well as the autonomy of their bodies and their choices. The women got organized and were prompted to action through the Internet, and, more specifically, through mother groups on social media dedicated to humanized birth and "attachment pareting,"[3] which signaled the presence of a strong movement of mothers surrounding what has been termed the humanized birth philosophy (Carneiro).

CASE TWO

In 2012, in August, there was a new call for action among defenders of humanized birth in defense of obstetrician Jorge Kuhn, who supported on national television the possibility of women giving birth at home in cases of low-risk pregnancies and got a severe reprimand by the Federal Medical Council (CFM) for his statement. That reprisal drove women to get organized once again and to take to the streets, now in defense of the doctor, in what became known as the "Humanized Birth March." Painted bellies, children with t-shirts that read "I was born at home," and women with signs that said "It is MY birth," "I gave birth at home," and "My body, my rules" occupied the scene in almost every Brazilian state capital (Carneiro).

CASE THREE

In 2015, around the "Out with Cunha"[4] demonstration in Rio de Janeiro, a group of mothers carrying their children on slings questioned the legislative measure that intends to forbid legal abortion in cases of sexual violence in Brazil, by means of Bill 5069/2015. Speaking for their sexual and reproductive rights, a group of mothers demanded that the president of the House of Representatives to step down from office or that the Brazilian government hinder this legal backpedaling, since legal abortion is presently a right guaranteed even within the country's unified health system. In Brazil, according to the Brazilian Penal Code (1940) and recent jurisprudence, abortion is allowed in three circumstances: rape; life-threatening conditions, and anencephaly. On paper, those women have the right to request the services of the unified health system and to get assistance in their decision for the abortion process. Those are the only situations that warrant legal abortion by the healthcare system. After the president of the House of Representatives, Congressman Eduardo Cunha, tried to suppress this right, a group of women, mothers and nonmothers, took over public spaces to demand that he step down. Within the birth rights mindset, then, mothers also began to defend and demand the maintenance of the right to abortion, expanding the idea of sexual and reproductive rights and of a spontaneous, free, and, conscious maternity (Diniz).

CASE FOUR

In 2016, demonstrations against the impeachment of president Dilma took place all over the country for the "maintenance of democracy" or "against what was (dubbed) a coup d'état." In the country's capital, Brasília, using a cellphone application, demonstrators organized "*Ciranda da Democracia*" ("Friends of Democracy Circle"), a call for families and children to occupy the mobilization spaces alongside the Museum of the Republic, areas where the protestors would march. The day of the demonstration, at the end of April 2016, saw the presence, again, of women with babies on slings and toddlers at the Monumental Axis highway in the city of Brasília as well as in other Brazilian cities.

CASE FIVE

In 2016, mothers connected through the Internet and social networks groups about maternity, childbirth, and childrearing joined forces to protest the "AnaLiz" case with a social manifesto to get her out of prison. AnaLiz, a black woman from Rio de Janeiro almost in her thirties, was arrested without a trial or legal process, accused of arranging the murder of her husband, a Belgian man who had been living in Brazil for a few years and was the father of her son. AnaLiz has been in jail since the event and has been barred from getting visits from her son. The case created huge social commotion, especially among the women and mothers who organized through the Internet to fight for humanized birth and the right for women to make choices regarding their own bodies. They even started a Facebook campaign to put pressure on the

Brazilian legal system to grant AnaLiz a proper trial and for her to get visitation rights for her son. In this campaign, protesters added hashtag #freeAnaLiz to their profile pictures and turned this particular case into a collective matter.

CASE SIX

In May 2016, a sixteen-year-old girl was the victim of a collective rape in Rio de Janeiro. She was assaulted by thirty-three men, who also shared images of her genitals and unconscious body on the Internet. Women held a demonstration on 29 May against what they called "rape culture" in Brazil. It is important to stress that "rape culture" means the permanence of sexist and misogynist ideation that leads to situations of violence as well as the process whereby the victim bestows responsibility upon herself for having been raped (Segatto). Heeding this national call for action, again triggered by feminist collectives over the Internet, a wide range of women went to the streets on a Sunday, accompanied by their children and babies, to announce their maternal presence on political spaces while demanding freedom over their own bodies, protesting gendered social violence, and fighting neglect by the state.

SITUATIONS OF PROTEST AND (IM)POSSIBLE TACTICS

The two first situations of protest revolve around the reproductive right to give birth where and when women may desire. Besides reproductive rights, the third act of contention debates the sexual right of nonreproduction, of being childfree, along with the right to have lawful guarantees and no social backtracking in the case of legal abortion and sexual violence or threats to life. The fourth protest episode sees mothers leaving aside their own interests to subscribe to a global demand for democracy. The two last cases (five and six) involve protesting against situations of violence against women. Both take place in Rio de Janeiro. The first is about a black poor mother who is put in jail, accused without the right to defend herself, and deprived of the right to see her son. The second episode is about a black poor girl who was raped by thirty-three men.

Over those myriad acts of contention, the perceived nodal or resonating points are some aspects that this chapter intends to unveil and problematize. As I see it, the strongest or more central of them, as it catalyzes the others, is the symbolic strength of the mother figure in contemporary social mobilization and protest. These episodes of mobilization bring out the interlocking or (in) separability of the public and private spheres when the political actors are mothers.

The interesting thing is that although they can be derived from each other or thought in a concatenated way, another brand brings them closer to the mother figure as a basic figure. I am referring to the mark of everyday life, the axis from which all other pleas radiate, which also organizes the agenda and behaviour of those women, considering that they seem to favour the everyday life matters. The minutiae by which they reinvent their existence, at times in silence and at times loud and clearly, leads us to think, following Pedro Pereira, about the political and investigative power of the "ordinary."

Along those lines, I intend to reflect upon those two major points by zigzagging stitches that will point out differences as well as similarities, and look for possible nodes or entanglements in order to explore exactly their intensity or density.

AMONG DIFFERENT WOMEN. OR NOT.

In the first four situations, we see groups of women who, in principle, can be considered middle class (Velho); they live in the city, most of them are white, and are seemingly in their thirties. Those are women who could "opt" for a childbirth considered humanized—they either at it home or at the hospital and had it done by a professional who subscribes to the philosophy supporting it. In Brazil, one of the criticisms directed at humanized birth aims precisely at this classist and/or racist bias, since there are few initiatives of support for natural birth without "unnecessary" interventions within the public Brazilian healthcare system, which is available to all Brazilian women. The last two cases feature black women from the poorer parts of Rio. Brazilian justice has neglected these two women: the first one for having been put in jail without trial and deprived of visiting rights, and the second one, even though she was raped by thirty-three men, for having faced resistance by the incumbent chief of police, who questioned whether the violence she suffered was actually rape. The latter case, even though the girl involved is not a mother, mobilized many mothers of girls as well as of boys to take to the streets to plead for "an end to rape culture," in their own words. And more, the girl was featured in newspapers in photographs where she was curled up on her mother's lap, an image charged with immense social appeal. After she was raped, she was also seen beside her mother, who was fighting for justice and for the prosecution of the perpetrators.

There is no shortage of Brazilian studies about the exercise of maternity among middle- and lower-class women. Generally, these studies suggest that middle-class women have fewer children and pregnancies tend to be planned; the use of contraceptives is also more frequent, and reproduction is disconnected from sexuality and usually seen as a "life project" within a supposedly more stable situation. Considering that within the middle class, childbirth, especially the so-called humanized type, is very central, the experience of giving birth is by itself valued and reflected upon, much like the subsequent childrearing, imbibed in what is being referred to as "attachment parenting." On the other hand, when it comes to women from lower-class backgrounds, such as the residents of a suburb town[5] where I conducted my survey in Distrito Federal (Carneiro), they seem to be more interested in taking care of the baby as a family, usually a large one. The mother, who is sometimes single, is a pillar of the community, which relegates childbirth to the background. While conducting the interviews, I heard women state that they would have actually preferred to undergo a Caesarean section but went through natural labour because that was the only option available. I also learned that they are much more concerned with money, with managing their time at home, and with work than with childbirth or with "how to raise" a child. Among them, then, maternity tends to be experienced as a community, as something that is shared with other women (mothers, grandmothers, aunts, and neighbours) in a network of caring that transcends the binomial (mother and baby) or trinomial (mother, father, and baby) of the middle class.

Some of the principles of attachment parenting, therefore—such as on-demand breastfeeding and a certain fusion between mother and baby for as long as possible—are farfetched for those poorer women, as they do not fit their realities. Their greatest concern centres on something else: survival.

Much the same way, the meanings of maternity, sex, and reproduction also waver depending on the social stratum of the mother. Valéria Corozacs's ethnography sets out to present those differences by exploring the perceptions from the standpoints of poorer women who attended a maternity hospital in Rio for the prenatal phase and for childbirth. In her reading, these women tend to associate sexuality with reproduction, as they have maintained "to make a baby is to make love." Having babies, then, is part of avoiding solitude, of having a network of care and caregivers, and not a matter of planning or of a previously designed life project, as mentioned by doctors from the middle class interviewed for the same study. In that sense, sex and children would come in the same line of understanding, usually more than one in single-parent families, run by single women. So perhaps many of these women, even though they know contraceptive methods, have chosen not to use them. That is why, maybe, many of those women, even though they knew about them, opted to forgo them.

> V [Valeria]: Why did you have children?
> AM [Interviewed]: I wanted to, I like them, I'm patient with kids, I think children are good for people, we aren't alone, we get company and everything. (Corozacs 241)

Klaas Woortmann has also worked with the poorer class and has delineated those women's reproductive experience. From his studies in popular contexts and poor neighbourhoods in Brazilian cities in the 1970s in the Amazon region and the Northeast, he has observed that among those groups having children meant securing an expressive number of contacts or social relationships that made it possible to expand a network of solidarity or co-maternity. There is a sort of "social calculation" among those women according to which having one child will not suffice, as it is necessary to have many in order to expand the solidarity and support network within the domestic group. Having a husband, on the other hand, would be associated with companionship and love, but those can fade away once the husband becomes a source of anguish and strife and the couple dissolve the marriage as an alternative.

In Woortman's terms, the women keep their husbands at home while they still help to support the household and the children. Regardless of whether they have a husband, they activate their relationship networks whenever they need them. The guarantees they need and investments they make lie with those children because as they grow up, the mothers become independent from their husbands and dependent on their offspring.

In the 1980s, Tania Salem explored the representation of the couple and the children among the middle class in Rio de Janeiro. She explains that this group holds the idea of the "pregnant couple," of the "two in one." Men and women turn their children into a "project," which implicates a feminization of the masculine, as the man begins to do chores that had previously been considered unseemly for his universe. Thus, they move away from the traditional family through the rejection of the patterns and rules of behaviour with which this new family would never agree. That was the experience described by Salem thirty years ago, yet according to my own research (Carneiro), this pattern seems to persist, at least partially, among the supporters of humanized birth in the 2000s. The interesting thing is that unlike the poorer classes, in which women end up becoming solo mothers, fending for themselves, here the nuclear family, at least ideologically, is trying to make do with just wife, husband, and child. As if operating like a globalizing capsule, though, according to Salem, fated to collapse into its own internal contradictions, especially during the postpartum phase, the real difficulties of the "two in one" project arise strongly in moments of crisis when it becomes evident that the trio needs the traditional original families. Estrangement between the couple also arises from the lack of space for themselves as individuals.

IN THE POORER CLASS: MOTHERS IN ACTION

Among the scenes analyzed here, we see mothers from the middle class demanding rights for themselves, for their children and other women in general. But the mobilization of mothers does not just happen among those groups, as brilliantly suggested more recently by some Brazilian studies like those by Paula Lacerda, Jurema Brites and Claudia Fonseca, and Adriana Vianna and Paula Farias.

Lacerda has visited the family of the "emasculated boys" from Altamira in Pará State in the north of Brazil. Her text tells of the suffering, the narratives, and the actions of the family members of the victims of crimes. It becomes evident in the text that the mother figure is central, especially Dona Rosa, who talks about using the death of her son (Jaenes, thirteen years old) as a "healing" strategy, but above all as a springboard for mobilization so that other boys and other mothers may avoid experiencing the pain she felt. "Emasculated" refers to boys (between eight and fifteen years old) whose bodies are found with severe signs of violence (physical and/or sexual) and without their genitalia, which are never recovered. The task of the anthropologist is to think about the suffering and pain experienced by those mothers and how both are able to create political practice. She counts on the performance of Dona Rosa, who, by talking about the death of her son, Jaenes, in official and nonofficial state premises or together with other mothers of victims, was demanding justice for those crimes and preventative measures so that others could not take place. Lacerda shows us through her pages how Dona Rosa migrates from "being powerless over it" and "having no strength to get out of bed" to meeting with other mothers and demanding punishment and investigation for the crimes. In order for that transformation to come to fruition, solidarity with the mothers' pain, seems to be, generally speaking, fundamental. Feeling the pain of others would work, then, as a propelling mechanism so that, as described by Lacerda, the "narratives of pain" turn into "narratives of fighting." In that space, then, the central speaker in the mobilization, according to the author, is the mother figure.

In several of the public speeches that I have witnessed, however, the category "mother of the victim" or just "mother" overrode other relationships and identities, as proof of the ability of those leaders in the political game to favour the relationships of mothers with their children. "All of us become 'mothers' in the speech of a law professional during a trial, including men," as argued by Vianna and Farias (85) while analyzing the political actions of the families of youngsters killed by the military police in Rio de Janeiro. Marcia Leite states that the identity and political category of "mothers of victims" draws its power from the religious allusion to Mary, mother of Jesus. Indeed, the legitimacy of the fight of mothers for the cause of their children (not always associated to deaths) is accompanied by the legitimacy of a specific way of protesting, already made routine in many Latin American cities, whereby streets, squares, and stairways are turned into scenes of the pain and suffering they go through. For Leite, the mothers protests turn pain and suffering into forgiveness and tolerance, thus (re)building the more visible and socially accepted facet of demonstrations: their pacific character (qtd. in Lacerda 63).

From this solidarity among women-mothers arises the movement of the families of the emasculated boys of Altamira, of women who relive their suffering and pain while also joining a collective, political cause, before political audiences with national representation (Lacerda 66). According to Lacerda, that means they turn "their private pain into political acts." She continues with the following observation: "From the impulse to talk, to relive, feel it body and soul, they get organized to put the state in the position of interlocutor by means of different branches: the police, municipal caseworkers, the justice system, the chamber of representatives, social workers, the National Congress, etc" (Lacerda 68).

Brites and Fonseca discuss the institutionalization of the "Women for Peace" movement, when certain actions by mothers from the poorer strata of Rio de Janeiro inspired national public policies, specifically, matters of public safety, stemming from what the authors understand as the "bureaucratization of pain." Presently, though, Brazilian society is more interested in the revival of the fight of mothers of missing children, or children killed by police violence in Rio de Janeiro since the 1990s, than in the debate about the emergence of the political side and transformation of the social practices of those women. The emblematic cases chosen by the authors are the "*Chacina de Acari*" ("Acari Mass Killing") in 1990, the "*Chacina da Candelária*" ("Candelária Mass Killing"), and the "*Chacina de Vigário Geral*" ("Vigário Geral Mass Killing") in 1993. These are situations of urban violence against children and teenagers—police violence, more specifically—which culminated in many deaths and ended up organizing mothers from marginal areas around a plea for justice and state reaction toward the incidents. History repeats itself in the three mass killings mentioned above: the victims are young residents of the favelas of Rio that have gone missing or have been killed by the police for being criminal suspects. Much like Altamira, the situation is exactly that of motherly pain getting turned into a larger movement of solidarity. The pain is no longer private, and it becomes political when they demand justice, recognition, and reparation. According to one of the women in Brites and Fonseca's work, "when you lose a child, people think you want to be alone and isolate you. But they must learn that we need them" (860). Those mothers got support from NGOs and later an audience with the Minister of Justice, which boosted their demands and proposals of national public policies for countering this kind of violence. According to Brites and Fonseca, this kind of demand and movement by women-mothers highlights the following:

> The language employed is a language of the body—tears, crying that alleviates the "pain in the heart"; of faith—"God gave us such good children that He now has the privilege having them under His care." However, it is, above all, a language of mothers. Images of everyday life are evoked—such as women who "feel it in their skin the pain of burying a child in the morning, going back to a home that was once filled with joy and, in the evening, serving dinner minus one child at the table." Insomnia creeps in, as well as an inability to get back to the "normalcy of life." It is no coincidence that the first page of the project has the subtitle "a homage to our children", and the names of the four author mothers shows up under the names of their respective murdered children (870-71).

Lastly, Vianna and Farias, much like Fonseca and Brites, analyze the mobilization of mothers from poorer the poorer classes of

Rio de Janeiro, who demand the trial and punishment of military policemen responsible for the death or murder of their children. Moreover, the authors explore the symbolic power of the mother figure in this social movement. To that end, they discuss the performances of women like Celeste, who created a lot of commotion when announcing that "they deprived me of the right to be a mother." The authors continue:

> She [Celeste] spoke of the need to "fight" as an imperative of that condition; she had the image of her son close to her body, printed on the t-shirt made for the occasion. She described the despair written in her past—the day her son died, always remembered—and the present, the worrying for her other son, but also the fight to inspire others to denounce, to prevent what happened to her son from happening to other people's children. (84)

For the authors, the mother figure has moral authority and legitimacy to connect the personal and collective spheres, feelings and the law, which expresses a moral and sentimental unity and establishes relationships between peers—in this case, between mothers of missing or murdered children in Rio and all over the country. It is in this manner that mothers are presented: they tell their stories, tell of their suffering. But while engaging in these movements, they also desingularize the case and speak not only for themselves but for all the mothers in the same situation, and even for the mothers who potentially could be in the same situation. This is the political power of the mother figure.

Vianna and Farias note that the female figure of the mother contrasts with the portrayal of the state as the entity in charge of caring for youngsters and protecting them, yet fail to do so. Whereas mothers are seen as those from whom life emanates, the state is depicted as the one that, paradoxically, takes it away.

It is also interesting to recall that, according to Vianna and Farias, as opposed to this feminine figure, that of the mother, the state is found, as a male figure, as the one who should have cared for and protected such young women, but did not. They would thus be the mothers who give life and the state, which paradoxically withdraws them. This time, according to his words. Vianna and Farias explain as follows:

> The "mothers" turned into political leaders, capable of symbolically a group all the other activists in the same movement, whether family members of victims or not, men and women, talk about a political insurgence defined by close connections to the—ever-changing—gender constructs. By speaking for a domestic order that was brutally unraveled by the murder of their children, they (and the other family members) carry the feminine not in their bodies. (93)

All authors described above deal with the fight of mothers in poorer classes who demand justice for their dead and missing children. It is a movement that takes over the justice system and demands recognition.

FROM THE HOME INTO THE STREETS AND
THE POWER OF EVERYDAY LIFE

Reflecting upon "what makes Brazil what it is," Roberto DaMatta develops the idea of "home" and "street" as spaces that are complementary precisely for being opposites. The street is the space for anonymity, for fighting, for working, a space of sacrifice, of movement and competition, whereas the home is a totalizing moral unit, in which there are people, "our people"; it is a space for affection. For the anthropologist, this division into two, complementary realms is a quintessential feature of the Brazilian culture.

In addition, DaMatta states that time and space are social inventions. Time can have an emotional measure in some cases (as aged photographs displayed in the homes), but there is also ordinary time, marked by routine (and the clock). The code of the home and the family in Brazilian society is opposed to change, whereas the code of the streets is open for business:

> From "casa" [home] we have "casamento" [marriage], "casadouro" [marriageable] and "casal" [couple], terms that denote relational acts, coherent with the space of dwell-

ing. With all that considered, "being expelled from home" means something violent, because, if we get expelled from our homes, we are deprived of a kind of space marked by the perpetual familiarity and hospitality that typify what we call "love," "caring" and "consideration." Much the same way, "being home" or feeling at home tells of situations of harmonious relationships, where strife must be avoided. I cannot turn the home into the streets or the streets into home unscathed. There are rules for that. (DaMatta 46)

Interestingly, DaMatta posits that even though the home and the street share a complex relationship, seen as opposites, they are not separate spaced, but interlinked vessels. In that sense, they operate like dimensions relating by intermediation; they communicate according to social rules whenever possible and desired.

In this configuration, the place of the Brazilian woman in this universe is the home, even though social change has been happening because of the feminist movement and many others social movements. Her roles have historically been preparing food, and nurturing and caring for children—categories tacked onto the female since the advent of modern times and social partition into the public and private realms (Laqueur). In that light, the home also operates as the space of privacy, intimacy, feelings, and emotions. It is the realm of the personal and private life.

If home is still often considered the place of women, we can see in the situations presented here the reversal: women taking over public spaces in demonstrations, marches, virtual protests and public audiences, and/or legal trials. They are taking over the streets—the space of fighting and the realm seen as belonging to males. In addition, they are dragging into this realm all their pain and mishaps, their feelings and emotions from the home. These women from the middle and poorer classes are bringing into the public scenario "our people," who are individualized and go on to occupy the realm that until then was a space for anonymity, thus subverting the classic Brazilian social order. Perhaps that is why the maternal figure is presently charged with moral legitimacy and social respect, with a powerful symbolic and political appeal.

Even though the women and their plights are migrating between spaces, the fight undertaken by mothers in the public realm is charged with the features of the home. The fight, as a rule, is peaceful, marked by images of their children on their t-shirts, by crying, by emotions, and by personal life histories. It is a fight that sends notes to judges so that mothers can have a say on trials and audiences. It is a struggle fought with scarves tied around heads (as seen with the Madres de La Plaza de Mayo in Argentina); it is a battle that mobilizes Brazilian films and soap operas and turns its history and requirements into a "social drama" (Turner).

The subversion, then, seems to be doubled. For one, women leave the home and take over the street as mothers. They carry the respectability of this female figure into the public realm. Secondly, for carrying over the themes, the pain and the practices of the home into the street, blurring both spaces, almost like a liminality (Turner), the mothers problematize social roles and labels.

This, however, happens without taking away from the emotional, sentimental, and domestic aspects of the fight, which also has to do with motherly love and family. It happens without taking away from the aplomb and social respect that the mother figure commands, which are almost unquestionable and drive the official instances to open up for their words and to let their narratives tell of the death of their children, so they can have rights over their own bodies. They can choose where and how to give birth. They have the right to be mothers. However, they also have the right not to have children, not to be a mother, when someone assaults their bodies. As such, we can see on the scenes presented in the first part of this chapter that the maternal demands in contemporary Brazil have been gravitating around sexual and reproductive rights but also around the right to be a mother (to have their children alive, safe, and close to them), or even the right to not be one. In every situation, though, the mother figure emerges wearing a t-shirt depicting her dead children or with her living children in her arms; she emerges with a painted naked body to demand control over her body and resist the many, ever-growing attempts to control her.

It is certain that the fight of poorer mothers is marked by death, violence, social inequality, and neglect by the state, whereas the fight of the middle-class mothers is against state control and excess intervention. That is how we perceive this issue according to the marches for home birth and humanized birth, the demonstration surrounding the "Out with Cunha" movement and recognition of legal abortion, as well as the AnaLiz case, in which women from the middle classes joined the movement that centred around a poor, incarcerated mother, completely bereft of her legal rights. Meanwhile, among mothers from Altamira, Acari, Vigário Geral and Candelária, among the "Mothers for Peace" and, lastly, the mother of the girl who was raped by thirty-three men, we witness the neglect, lives at the margins of the state, or, rather perversely situated there by the state itself. In all fronts, however, we can confirm the powerful symbolic appeal of the condition of motherhood in politics. Women, both mothers and childfree, have begun to gather on the streets to demand the right of abortion, of giving birth at home, of not being raped, of having access to their children, of counting on due legal process, and of getting justice in cases of abrupt and violent murders of their children.

I think that this may be because of the still-standing representation of the modern mother (Badinter) as the comforting angel, the beacon of affection, the near saint. But there is also another mother—the one who takes to the streets and churns out public politics from their private lives, their pain and their bodies, which once belonged to the home but now demand social and state attention. Maybe that is why we are going through, in Brazil, what has been called the "Feminist spring"—mothers with babies, whole families on the streets, demanding social well-being and control over their own bodies, drawing from the power of everyday life (Pereira), that is, of the slow life.

ENDNOTES

[1]Home birth is type of childbirth whereupon women opt for giving birth at home, assisted by physicians, obstetric nurses, or trained midwives. The expression, thus, refers to urban home births stemming from the philosophy of humanized birth present in Brazil since the 2000s.
[2]All English-language translations are my own.
[3]Humanized delivery is a fairly open and plural term, but it basically

means delivery with minimal medical interventions while respecting the desires of the woman and the baby. Attachment parenting is almost an educational philosophy that involves maximum contact with the baby, free breastfeeding, shared bedding, natural eating, positive discipline and non-outsourcing of childcare. It is not something typically Brazilian.

[4]The Out with Cunha March happened in November of 2015 in many Brazilian cities. The objective was to resist the amendment of the legislation on legal abortion in Brazil, which would curtail the access of women to legal abortion.

[5]Between the years 2012 and 2015, I coordinated a research project on health services of the public system. We undertook an ethnography of services for several months, through participant observation and interviews with more than twenty-five people. Open interviews sought to address how black people perceived and were treated in health services. This project received funding from CNPQ-Ministry of Health.

WORKS CITED

Badinter, Elisabeth. *O mito do amor materno: um amor conquistado*. Translated by Waltensir Dutra, Nova Fronteira, 1985.

Brites, Jurema, and Claudia Fonseca. "As metamorfoses de um movimento social: mães de vitimas de violência no Brasil." *Análise Social*, no. 209, 2013, pp. 858-77.

Carneiro, Rosamaria. *Cenas de parto e políticas do corpo*. Fiocruz, 2015.

Corozacss, Valéria. O corpo da nação. Rio de Janeiro: UFRJ, 2009.

DaMatta, Roberto. *O que faz do Brasil, o Brasil?* Rocco, 1986.

Diniz, Carmen Simone Grilo. *Entre a técnica e os direitos humanos: possibilidades e limites da humanizaçãoo da assistência ao parto*. Dissertation, Faculdade de Medicina da USP, 2001.

Lacerda, Paula. "O sofrer, o narrar, o agir: dimensões da mobilização social de familiares de vítimas." *Horizontes Antropológicos*, vol. 20, no. 42, 2014, pp. 49-75.

Laqueur, Thomas W. *Inventando o sexo: corpo e gênero dos gregos a Freud*. Relume Dumará, 2001.

Pereira, Pedro Paulo. "Violência, gênero e cotidiano: o trabalho de Venna Das." *Cadernos Pagu*, vol. 35, 2010, pp. 357-69.

Salem, Tania. *O casal grávido: disposições e dilemas de uma parceira igualitária.* Editora FGV, 2007.

Segatto, Rita. "Território, soberania e crimes de segundo Estado: a escritura nos corpos das mulheres de Ciudad Juarez." *Estudos Feministas*, vol. 13, no. 2, 2005, pp. 265-285.

Turner, Victor. *Drama, campos e metáforas.* UFF, 2008.

Velho, Gilberto. *Nobres e anjos: Um estudo de tóxicos e hierarquia.* Fundação Getulio Vargas, 1998.

Vianna, Adriana, and Paula Farias. "A guerra das mães: dor e politica em situações de violência institucional." *Cadernos Pagu*, vol. 37, 2011, pp. 79-116.

Woortmann, Klass. "Um único filho não é filho." *Respeito à Diferença: uma introdução à antropologia*, edited by E. Woortmann et al., CESPE, 1999.

13.
The Disappearing of the Disappeared in the Plaza de Mayo

Who Will Hold the Space of the Madres Once They Are Gone?

SARAH A. SCHOELLKOPF

KNOWN AS ONE OF THE more controversial and well-known human rights groups in the world, the Madres de la Plaza de Mayo began their organization through movement—walking circularly around the most public and political space in Argentina, the Plaza de Mayo, at the height of the 1976-1983 dictatorship at a time when public assembly was strictly forbidden. Through their nonviolent protest, these women cemented their claim on this public space, as they used their bodies to remind the public of their children's disappearance and lack of physical presence. Throughout their history, the Madres have resisted becoming merely photographic relics with their performativity. Their movement constituted a counter-hegemonic discourse of the body and of the mother. The Madres had to fundamentally understand the binary reasoning of the junta in order to critique and subvert its chauvinist vision of the female body, and played with prevailing notions of gender in Argentina. The Madres took motherhood to another, more spectacular and metaphoric level, publically performing gender on a national and, later, an international stage, which not only deconstructed the junta's theoretical framework but also proved its fiction. Moreover, the Madres have now moved beyond this stark polar vision in the continuation of their movement (Borland et al). But as the Madres age, no specific group seems ready to continue their ethical example or maintain their moral claims. Moreover, other public spaces have gained prominence, and the discourse that drives the Madres is mutating. When these women pass away, who will hold their space in the national collective memory? Who will remind the public of *los desaparecidos*?

MACHISMO ON DISPLAY: THE ARGENTINE MILITARY JUNTA PERFORMS RIGHTEOUSNESS

In Argentina, the country with supposedly the most psychiatrists and psychoanalysts and the most plastic surgeons per capita in the world, spectacle and psychology seem to go hand-in-hand. Argentina's last, and arguably most brutal, dictatorship took power in 1976 and were led by a series of de facto military presidents. During the dictatorship, thousands of citizens considered the "other" were hunted in the streets, their homes, their places of work, or their schools by undercover agents in Ford Falcons and then dragged off to the subterranean world of the CCD (*centros clandestinos de detención*, or clandestine centers of detention) to be interrogated, tortured, and murdered. In this rigid binary, anything female, Indigenous, non-Christian, communist, unpatriotic, weak, whorish, or leftist was perceived as the "other" by the military.

The junta framed its murderous activities in terms of a "just and holy war" or a religious crusade. According to Frank Graziano in his study *Divine Violence: Spectacle, Psychosexuality & Radical Christianity in the Argentine "Dirty War,"* a new age needed to be ushered in, and "invisible enemies: medievals, heretics, witches, and epidemics" would have to be purged (12). The collective Argentine body would be bruised and bloodied by its supposed protector, the junta. The *patria* (fatherland and father) would keep the "subversives" in line. To the military junta, those without *patria* were *apátriadas*, without a homeland (i.e., weak, country-less, and thus feminized). Men accounted for almost 70 percent of the disappeared, and the military demeaned their actions in embarrassing displays related to gender. In order to get results in the illegal prisons and torture centres, the legacy and the genetic lineage of the "barbaric heretics" had to be cleansed by the junta. Blood would be splattered and punishments would be given. The junta used the binaries already in existence in Argentina and played on a concept of "bad parents": Argentina's actual parents were not "caring" for their children, so the *patria*—fatherland and father—needed to move in and take over. Moreover, inspired by the Cold War and occidental Christian thought, the junta created a Freudian phallocentric language of power, as Graziano details in this list.

Good	Evil
Soul/Spirit	Flesh/Matter
Peacelovers	**Warmongers**
Life	**Death**
Love	**Hate/Lust**
Truth	Lies/Deceit
Protect	**Destroy**
Home/Family	**Communal binds/Party**
Mature	Immature
Political Right	Political Left (115).

I have bolded certain binaries that are key to understanding the Madres' ability to operate within the traditional norms of gender and then to expand this perception. I have added to this list—including, male-female, phallus-vagina, and Madonna-whore—as these binaries also play into the Argentine military's framing of the "other," of history, and of memory. I use this dichotomy to highlight the words that the Madres both exploited and radicalized as they formed their movement.

The macho styling of the junta manifested itself through very specific actions—public displays of guns, tanks, and bombs—and it even went so far as to shoot at the base of the central monument, or phallus, of the city, the Obelisco monument, to prove its virility (Feijoo and Gogna 136). Within the CCD, gender binaries were also set up among the captured. Binaries began to polarize prisoners: "weak-female" traitors versus "macho-male" heroes. Those who survived the torture and mistreatment were perceived as collaborators. Torture consisted of beatings, the use of the *picana* (a phallus-like cattle prod), burning, rape, drowning, and psychological torment.

Of the thirty thousand disappeared in Argentina, most were never heard from again. The military—after beating, torturing, and raping these individuals—would send them to "be transferred" (*trasladar*), which euphemistically meant, "to be killed." Victims were taken away, sometimes shot in the head, and dumped into a river, into a ditch, or into a street. In the early days after the coup, those bodies began "reappearing," which caused great concern. Although the military publically used these bodies to their advantage, often claiming that the "subversives" had killed these individuals in their "dirty war," they privately realized that they needed to perfect their methods of extermination of their perceived enemies. The military, thus, began to throw the captives out of planes into the Atlantic Ocean. As told to Horacio Verbitsky in his 1995 book, *El vuelo (The Flight)*, Retired Navy Captain Adolfo Scilingo described, in detail and for the first time to the Argentine public, how these flights worked. He also appeared on a national news show on March 9,1995, a week after Verbitsky had played the interview tapes to the Argentine public. On these tapes, Scilingo admits to throwing thirty living individuals out of airplanes into the ocean. In the book, Scilingo describes how victims were given a "vaccine" (a strong sedative to pacify them) by a military doctor, then taken up in planes, and ultimately thrown into the Río de la Plata or the Atlantic Ocean. Although Scilingo admitted that no one liked performing this terrible task, it was done and understood as "as the best way [to dispose of the bodies], no one argued about that. It was something supreme done for the good of the country. A supreme act" (my trans; Verbitsky 32). Mass murder allowed for military leaders to bathe themselves in the blood of the enemy—"a type of communion" (Verbitsky 32)—to wash away their collective sins.

LAS MADRES DE LA PLAZA DE MAYO: A HISTORY AND A REACTION TO MILITARY POWER

Perhaps because they had little prior experience in the public sphere to deter them, a group of women, mostly the mothers of the *desaparecidos,* decided to take a stand almost a year after the dictatorship began in 1977. From March 1976 until April 177, these mothers had individually visited appropriate and official locations in an effort to find information about their lost children: army barracks, police stations, morgues, churches, hospitals, official offices, and the Ministry of the Interior, where a small office had been set up near the Presidential House, or the *Casa Rosada*, to officially register those who were missing. In all of these places, these women obtained little information and were often humiliated by those officials who did speak with them. They later discovered, once they organized collectively, that they had been spied upon. Their search was proving fruitless, as no one wanted to help them, neither officially nor unofficially. Many families were torn apart by the disappearance because even relatives were afraid to help. Family members denied having a disappeared relative because they risked losing their jobs. Neighbours, friends, colleagues, and priests would look away and refuse to sympathize with the Madres. Even their own siblings sometimes stopped talking to them. Many family members and other friends assumed "por algo sera" ("there must be some reason") that their son or daughter had been disappeared. This reticence was due to the military's brilliant propaganda campaign, which created another binary to ensure inaction among the Argentine public: speaking out was equated to "subversion" and death, whereas silence was equated to "patriotism" and life. These *desaparecidos* had done something to deserve this.

In this most deadly culture war, the government-controlled media only allowed for their version of "*la Guerra Sucia*" or "Dirty War"—another indirect term that allowed the military to justify going to war against the enemy. The media tried to induce a sense of guilt among the families of the *desaparecidos* "by a barrage of slogans such as 'Do you know where your child is?' or, 'How did you bring up your child?'" (Bouvard 176). In the binary-based world of the junta, where the world was divided up as good versus evil, of crime/ punishment versus silence/ obedience, Argentine women had failed their traditional role of mothering the nation's youth (for what other role did women have?). However, the blood ties that connected these women to their children helped forge friendships and networks, which, ironically, was what the military's campaign had attempted to prevent. In their desperation, the mothers began to recognize the faces of other women who also searched unsuccessfully for the same truths and the same missing bodies. The Madres connected with one another, created community, and overcame the terrible silence and fear that the junta had imposed. While waiting in the interminable lines to speak with military officials in various bureaucratic buildings, the Madres began to speak with one another.

The Madres de la Plaza de Mayo as an organization thus emerged in 1977, responding to a need for information regarding their children's disappearance. In an effort to make their case known, on 30 April, 1977, fourteen fearful Madres—including Pepa de Noia, Haydée de García Buela, Mirta de Baravalle, Azucena de Villaflor, María Adela Gard de Antokeletz, and Antokeletz's two sisters—ventured into the Plaza de Mayo to request a meeting with the junta's first president, General Jorge Videla. Over a year after the coup, the junta would now have an active, energetic, and vocal challenger—the Madres, headed by Señora de Villaflor.

To this day, Thursday is known even in Argentine guidebooks as the day of the Madres' *ronda*, the day they circle the central pyramid structure in the Plaza de Mayo. This was not the case, however, on the first meeting in 1977. Fearful to be seen asking questions in public during the continued "state of siege," the women understood each other's anguish instantly without needing to speak words. (Meeting in more than groups of three during this time was illegal since the junta continued to label this period as *"estado de sitio,"* or a state of siege). From the first moment, going to the Plaza was cathartic. They all had the same pain and the same goal: to find out where their children had been taken. The women also realized that they had accomplished their first step in breaking the bipolar hegemony of the junta in terms of collective action. But because it was a Saturday, no one was in the Plaza, and they needed to be as visible as possible. They decided to come back during the week, this time on a Friday. As one Madre, Señora María del Rosario, explains, the women again came to a consensus that there was a better day to meet:

That Friday we prepared the wording of the letter to [General Rafael Videla, head of the junta] in our heads and decided to meet the next week to sign the letter and deliver it to Government House. One of the Mothers said, "Let's not make it Friday, Friday's an unlucky day"—they say it's the day of the witches—"let's make it Thursday." "Okay, Thursday at half past three." That Thursday we went back and delivered the letter. We arranged to meet the next week and discuss. (qtd. in Fisher 29)

According to an interview I conducted with one of the first twenty Madres, Señora Nora de Cortiñas in 2004, Friday was not necessarily associated with witches but with bad luck.

After three or four Fridays, one mother said "Today is Friday, and it brings bad luck because there is a "r" in the word [in Spanish]." Thus, we looked at each other and another mother said, "We should look for a day that has no "r" and there are only two. Monday and Thursday.... This was the superstition.... Another said, "Monday, no, because it is the day that we wash clothing." People did not have washing machines before. And the housewives washed their clothing on Mondays, not Sundays. And that is how Thursday was decided. Right there, in the Plaza, it was decided on Thursday. It was Azucena [de Villaflor] who had the idea to go to the Plaza, because it was in the center of Buenos Aires, of everything. Every day more of us went, we were more. We went to find out something. (Schoellkopf, "Resistar" 163-164)

These women had already been abandoned by society. No one offered sufficient answers to their queries regarding their missing children; they were simply marked as "terrorists." Not wanting to disrupt the delicate balance of their home life by arriving on Monday and missing their washing duties, nor wanting bad luck, the group chose Thursday to meet in the Plaza. Moreover, the connection with witches would have been doubly deadly to their persons as well as to their cause, since witches could be considered the most dangerous type of women in the hyper-masculine paradigm of the junta. From the very first moment, these women were conscious of their country's gender bias. They would take the privacy of their homes into the street, making it public for all to see because as Diane Taylor and Juan Villegas Morales argue, "the military had blurred private/public distinctions by raiding homes and snatching children in the dead of night" (296). These mothers, many of whom had never been civic minded or political, were suddenly visible and present; they demanded answers and showed concern for their disappeared children. But during the first fateful meeting, they also became engaged with other mothers' suffering. Their struggle for an answer, any answer as to why their children had been taken, had become a shared goal. Solidarity and community defined them now. When the women kept returning to sit together, this time up to sixty of them, the junta sent a policeman to tell them to keep moving. Because of the threats of the police, one of the most defining aspects of their movement began: they started their *ronda* in a silent march.

As the Madres began their organization by walking circularly around the Plaza de Mayo at the height of the Argentine dictatorship's *estado de sitio*, they performed their first indelible and revolutionary act. They imagined that they as women, and especially as mothers, would be protected to a greater extent than their husbands. As Jean Franco attests in her essay "Gender, Death, and Resistance: Facing the Ethical Vacuum," their initial resistance "would not have been possible if the mothers had not behaved as mothers. By refusing to regard their children as terrorists, by reiterating their mothering role, their particular regard for the continuation of human life, the mothers of Argentina ... were able to interrupt the dominant discourse and resacralize the body" (33). The Madres' symbols and speech acts were slyly used to combat the images that the junta propagated, that these women were unable to "mother" properly. Creating circles of memory with their own bodies, the Madres' flexible movement contrasted against the strict rows filing by in military parades. Their use of the most important political public space in the country cemented their nonviolent public protest in Argentina and the rest of Latin America. Several years after their founding, the women began wearing their children's saved cloth diapers on their heads as scarves and projected the actual truth of the murderous junta's practices. These *pañuelos,* or head kerchief, with their disappeared children's names embroidered into the cloth, named those who were absent. It is no accident that the Madres' *pañuelos* were reminiscent of the Virgin Mary's headwear in religious icons. In terms of "costume," the *pañuelo* encircled their heads, creating more loops of memory. Not only serving as a way of demanding the whereabouts of the thirty thousand *desaparecidos* and providing a common identity, the white *pañuelos* gleamed in the sun, symbolizing peace, love, life, and family—all of the things the military claimed to be protecting. The Madres used their bodies in the plaza to show the military's responsibility for the lack of bodies. Through using traditional archetypes, they reconfigured the Junta's logic.

After their tireless fact-finding and endless questioning, the Madres became savvy masters of performance against the junta's masochistic and misogynistic spectacle. Their very ability to create life through their wombs highlighted the fallacy behind the military's bipolar thinking: the desire to give new life to the country by destroying its citizens. The private sphere-public domain binary as well as the chauvinist junta's internal enemy doctrine was incredibly hard to overcome for many of the Madres, but their overwhelming grief caused them to act. As Cecelia Sosa argues, the Madres' "repetitive circles around the Plaza de Mayo ultimately reinscribed the disappeared into national history: the lives that were banished by the murderous state earned the right to be grieved as such. The disappeared reemerged from the sphere of the *abjected:* they were transformed into grievable lives" ("Queering" 70). The Madres made the *desaparecidos* an indelible scar on the national body. These private mothers took the intimacy of their homes into the street, announcing their loss for all to see. In the process, the Madres also became one of the most recognized and copied human rights organizations in the world in the process.

Eventually, the junta infiltrated the group and disappeared their leader Azucena Villaflor,, as well as two of their most vital members, Esther Ballestrino and María Ponce de Bianco, at the end of 1977. For many organizations, this would be deathblow, but the Madres kept their protest political and their bodies public by transforming traditional symbols of maternity and manipulating them for their own political agenda. As Sosa says, "although the Mothers gathered as a political community constructed through the language of kinship, the fact that their action was from the beginning attached to a public space staged their activism as exceeding the margins of a traditional family, haunting the whole nation instead" ("Queering" 70). Even though the junta called the Madres *"las locas de Plaza de Mayo"* ("the mad women of the Plaza de Mayo") in order to deprecate their struggle—something that, as Jean Franco reminds us, happens to public women in Latin America (46-65)—they continued their fight and did not relent. As international support grew, *testimonios* "reappeared" from former prisoners, and actual hard evidence in the form of bodies washed up onto beaches, the Madres pushed for information and the truth. They imposed themselves into the physical, political, economic, and cultural space.

LAS MADRES TODAY: TWO GROUPS, TWO METHODOLOGIES

Today, there are actually two Madres groups, a fact that is not widely known outside of Argentina. Both are known as Las Madres de la Plaza de Mayo, but one refers to itself as the *Línea Fundadora* (Founding Line), and the other is known as the *Asociación* (Association). The Asociación is headed by Hebe de Bonafini and vindicates the *desaparecidos'* political activity from the seventies. Less than three years after the restoration of constitutional democracy in 1983, a schism occurred within the organization: divergent views on how the group should interact with the government caused a small group of founding Madres to split from the main organization. The mothers who left the Asociación and formed the Línea Fundadora were inspired to separate by their ideological and methodological differences. A majority of the founding fourteen mothers left because there were upset by Señora de Bonafini's combative leadership style. Both groups now promote human rights but have moved past those singular goals. They frame their activities in a broader way now and speak of a progressive social change in the fight against neoliberalism as part of an expansive and inclusive struggle for human rights. Señora de Cortiñas says that their children unified them and their maternity bound the movement together, but they now have a greater understanding of the world than they did in 1977:

We picked up the battle flags of our children and we learned that we had to defend all human rights... What unified the madres, [although] we were from different social classes and educational backgrounds, was that the ideals of our children were the same. Today, I understand that human rights are all rights, economic, social and cultural, civil and political, rights of women, of indigenous people, of homosexuals, of the disabled. (qtd. in Borland 125)

After barely finishing high school, Señora de Cortiñas went back to school thanks to her work in the Madres and received her undergraduate degree in psychology. She has also aligned herself with feminist and lesbian groups, as have most of the Madres. Both Línea Fundadora and Asociación have supported the fight of the transgender community against repression, and now see the LBGTQ community as their allies based on a mutual persecution.[1]

The Madres fight now, over forty years later, is far more universal: they protest against injustice, hunger, capitalism, ecological disaster, NAFTA, the Escuela de la Americas ("No Vamos"), and military interventions around the world. They also have avidly backed the trials against the former military and police responsible for their children's and grandchildren's disappearance, and have attended the proceedings and served as witnesses for the prosecution. Their contemporary platforms expand on and modernize their message of social justice, economic reforms, and international human rights. By reframing their movement and by attempting new activities for their mission, the Madres have also expanded their goals beyond the *desaparecidos* to more varied goals. The Madres have shown elasticity in their goals and have made their arguments more complex and mature. Elizabeth Borland explains further:

Their political analysis is not just linked to motherhood and the dictatorship but it draws on the moral authority that the Madres have as people who stood up to the dictatorship, and the experience they have gained as politically savvy actors with years of activist experience to critique contemporary justice. Rather than simply adding new social issues, the Madres interweave old and new, making their claims and critiques more complex and sophisticated, more "mature." (124)

Through contemporary media, the Madres use the same vocabulary and symbols as always but to new political ends as they expand into diverse institutional contexts. For example, during the gastronomy conference "*Cocinas del Bicentenario*" ("Kitchens of the Bicentennial"), organized as part of Argentina's bicentennial independence celebration, Hebe de Bonafini, the president of the Asociación, held the first of what became weekly workshops titled "*Cocinando la política*" ("Cooking Up Politics"). Although she was in a kitchen, Hebe de Bonafini cooked up something that might be harder to digest than traditional dishes: politics. As technology has advanced and awareness has increased, the Madres have been able to add radio through their first underground and later aboveground broadcast "*La Voz de Las Madres*" ("The Voice of the Madres") and more recently, television programs, Facebook pages, and even a YouTube channel. The Asociación and the Línea Fundadora also speak regularly at schools as part of the national academic curriculum. The Línea Fundadora supports the opening of monuments in the name of the disappeared, and both groups attend national and international conferences and marches as special guests. Thus, the Madres de la Plaza de Mayo revolutionized and politicized the idea of motherhood and its cultural implications by transforming traditional symbols of maternity and manipulating them for their own political agenda. The Madres debunked the traditional binary of a loving, saintly, passive, and homebound Madonna versus the street-wise, loose, aggressive, and promiscuous whore. The Madres took their maternity to the street with their bodies and effectively blurred the binaries of the Argentine female and empowered an entire generation. Moreover, they evolved politically from a resistance group fighting against the dictatorship to a political opposition movement fighting against the concessions of a constitutionally elected government to an anti-capitalist and socialist force that was formally pro-government during the last two Kirchner presidencies. Within the political spectrum, they have defied conventional boundaries and definitions. Even during the most dangerous times of the military rule, the Madres have kept up their fight for justice, peace, and memory. Their movement in circles represents memory, community, and a hope to stop other cycles of violence and injustice.

ART, ACTIVISM, AND HIJOS: THE FUTURE OF THE MOVEMENT

Inspired by the Madres, the HIJOS (*Hijos por la Identidad y la Justicia contra el Olvido y el Silencio* or Children for Identity and Justice against Oblivion and Silence) formed in 1995 and subsequently transformed art and politics in Argentina. These young men and women, many of them older than their parents when they were disappeared, are the children of the *desaparecidos*. In the documentary *HIJOS: El alma en dos* (*HIJOS: The Soul Cut in Two*) various members explain that members do not need to vindicate their parents' fight unnecessarily: "We do not need to personalize nor humanize our parents.... We take the focus from there and place it where we want to" (my trans). They remember their missing parents with pride and celebrate their legacy while they also perform new methods of memory recuperation for the future.

At the start of their movement, the members identified as a very insular group, and essentially only those biologically linked to a disappeared person could be part of the organization. In the late 1990s, however, HIJOS created the "*escrache*" and revolutionized performance art by combining street performance, denouncement, and public service into one massive event, which led to a more welcoming environment for the public to participate in their activism. "*Escrache*" is an Argentine slang term that roughly means to reveal or expose someone to the public—to shame that person. For a month before the one-time march and performance, the HIJOS would canvass neighbours about the ex-military leader or ex-police officer who lived in a specific neighbourhood, showing identifying pictures, giving information, and publicly accusing that individual of a crime. Then, on the set day of the event, hundreds of activists, artists, musicians and *murga* troupes, and the Madres themselves would march through the neighbourhood streets, capturing public attention and publically condemning the individual's actions. HIJOS would also create yellow signs to show where the repressor lived. At their ultimate destination, the artists would then paint the repressor's name and crimes on the pavement in front of his home. The police, always forewarned, usually stayed at the edge of the march. One notorious exception was the 1998 *escrache* of Miguel Etchecolatz, the former head of Buenos Aires province police, when police tear-gassed, chased, and hit hundreds of participants with no apparent provocation. One of the most massive *escraches* occurred on March 18, 2006, a week before the thirtieth anniversary of the coup d'état. The target was Jorge Videla, former president and general, the man responsible for many of the worst crimes during the dictatorship, and many thousands attended.

As Taylor expresses, the signs used by the HIJOS, such as "Usted está aquí" ("you are here")—which shows viewers on an alternative map to the traditional city maps where they are in relation to a repressor's home or to a former CCD— "marks not only the performance space but also the collective environment of trauma that addresses and affects everyone. We are (all) here" (*Disappearing Acts* 189). All of Argentina was witness to these individuals' lack of punishment. After the lack of trials against those military and police responsible of torture and murder in the 1980s and President Carlos Menem's various amnesties for condemned military leaders during the 1990s, the HIJOS felt that this public "outing" was the only way to address past injustice and uncover truth in society. Their refrain "si no hay justicia hay escrache" ("if there is no justice, there is *escrache*") communicated their struggle for accountability for the disappeared. They also used the slogan "*Verdad y Justicia*" ("Truth and Justice") to express their demands.

But once Nestor Kirchner became president in 2003, new human rights initiatives became a hallmark of his presidency and the HIJOS' public *escraches* seemed to be no longer needed. Kirchner repealed the laws of impunity that had been set up in the 1980s, and in 2005, the Supreme Court completely nullified them. In 2004, he converted the former concentration camp the ESMA (*Escuela Mecánica de la Armada* or the Mechanical School of the Navy), where over five thousand people had been disappeared, into a commemorative space in 2004. Since 2003, hundreds of police, soldiers, and civilians have been put behind bars for their illegal and murderous activities during the dictatorship. Cristina Kirchner, Nestor's wife, furthered his reforms during her presidency from 2009 until 2015. At the end of May 2016, Argentina's last dictator under the junta, Reynaldo Bignone, was accused of crimes against humanity in Buenos Aires during the Operation Condor trial. Operation Condor was a campaign of state-sponsored terror organized by South American dictatorships in the 1970s, and the trial was considered the largest of its kind, as it prosecuted transnational crimes committed by six states in Latin America. Bignone was sentenced to twenty years in prison. There is now more truth and justice than ever in Argentina. The human rights climate has changed again, however, with the November 2015 election of rightist President Mauricio Macri, but for now the trials continue without interruption.

Sensing their mortality, the Madres wanted to make sure someone could continue their fight, and in the early 2000s, the Madres of Línea Fundadora publically bestowed headscarves on those *"hijos"* or sons deemed worthy to take up their cause. Many of those honoured were not biologically linked with the *desaparecidos,* but they had shown their passion and commitment to the Madres' message. While HIJOS seemed poised to take up the mantel of the Madres, the organization now does not possess the same zeal as the "golden age" of the 1990s and early 2000s. Between internal divides, much like the Madres, and the fact that several HIJOS members began to work within the Kirchner government, the organization has lost momentum. A number of members have left the group and no longer participate in events.

As of 2011, the HIJOS organization has relocated its headquarters to the ex-ESMA campus, thus preserving a physical presence, at least in theory. Today, they participate in large human rights marches, showing their organizational banner as they weave with other activists through the streets. The group vigorously supports and attends the ongoing trials. Online, HIJOS maintains its most active presence, with a website, current Facebook pages, and a Twitter account. But this begs the question: is a virtual space enough to maintain the movement? In terms of activities, most of what is present on these webpages are public service announcements for other, more active organizations. However, the HIJOS headquarters houses a collective radio channel, *La Imposible* or The Impossible, which offers programming which is centred on the recuperation of memory, truth, and justice. *La Imposible* includes music programs, interviews, and news programs. As the group remarks on its website, "we are a collective that works for popular communication from a space of memory: [in a space] where they sought to exterminate political organization, we declare ourselves to be PRESENT participating and fighting [for justice]" (my trans.). But the radio is a collective and not specifically an H.I.J.O.S. entity.

Sosa highlights that the number of HIJOS activists has dropped and that "most of them are no longer children of the disappeared: they do not have pedigree" (*Queering* 50). In fact, long-time members seem to have moved on to involve themselves in other political or human rights groups. Moreover, the ex-ESMA facility suffered more than thirty bomb threats from January to June 2016—a fact that constantly hinders events and scheduling for all organizations housed within the campus (Maradei). Thus, the HIJOS movement seems to remain more in the virtual realm as an inheritance from their disappeared parents and does not seem to have the same long-lasting physical stamina that the Madres have had.

At the present time, since the memory has been managed and officialized by the two successive Kirchner presidencies and by the effective reopening of trials in 2003, I am not sure who has the imperative or the biological link needed to continue the Madres' legacy. But perhaps, as Sosa seems to imply, Argentina no longer needs biology to remember. After two presidents who were young people during the 1970s, society has shifted. The Madres, who were so long forgotten or cast aside especially during the 1990s, are now protagonists again on the national stage in an official way. The Madres perhaps have truly revolutionized motherhood because now all of Argentine society shares in the loss of its children.

ENDNOTE

[1] "In Argentina, for example, gay rights activists were able to draw on the support of well-respected left-leaning human rights groups

such as the *Madres de la Plaza de Mayo* by framing their own disenfranchisement within the same discourse that described the persecution of other groups during Argentina's military dictatorship" (Donnelly).

WORKS CITED

Borland, Elizabeth. "The Mature Resistance of Argentina's Madres de Plaza de Mayo." *Latin American Social Movements: Globalization, Democratization, and Transnational Networks*, edited by Hank Johnston and Paul Almeida, Lanham, Rowman & Littlefield, 2006, pp. 115-130.

Borland, Elizabeth, et al. "Cultural Transmission and Social Movements: The Continued Relevance of the Madres de Plaza de Mayo." *Delaware Review of Latin American Studies*, vol. 16, no. 1, 2015, www1.udel.edu/LAS/Vol16-1BorlandSchoellkopfRuediger.html. Accessed 1 June 2017.

Bouvard, Marguerite Guzman. *Revolutionizing Motherhood: The Mothers of the Plaza De Mayo*. Scholarly Resources, 1994.

Donnelly, James. "The Pink Tide of Gay Rights in Latin America." *Canvas*, 21 Feb. 2013, canvas.union.shef.ac.uk/wordpress/?p=1740. Accessed 1 June 2017.

Feijoo, María del Carmen, and Mónica Gogna. "Las Mujeres en transición a la democracia." *Ciudadanía e identidad: Las mujeres en los movimientos sociales latino-americanos*, edited by Elizabeth Jelin, 1987, pp. 129-187.

Fisher, Jo. *Mothers of the Disappeared*. South End, 1989.

Franco, Jean. *Critical Passions: Selected Essays*, edited by Mary Louise Pratt and Kathleen E. Newman, Duke University Press, 1999.

Graziano, Frank. *Divine Violence: Spectacle, Psychosexuality & Radical Christianity in the Argentine "Dirty War."* Westview, 1992.

H.I.J.O.S. El Alma En Dos. Directed by Carmen Guarini and Marcelo Céspedes, SBP, 2005.

Maradei, Pablo. "La Ex ESMA Recibió 30 Amenazas De Bomba." *Clarín*, 2 May 2016. www.clarin.com/politica/ex-esma-recibio-amenazas-bomba_0_4yo1qje-Z.html. Accessed 12 June 2017.

"La Imposible Radio Online Transmitiendo Desde La Ex ESMA." *La Imposible*, 12 Nov., 2016, www.laimposible.org.ar/2016/11/12/la-imposible-transmite-desde-la-ex-esma. Accessed 12 June 2016.

"No Vamos a Mandar Gente a La Escuela De Las Américas." *Red Voltaire*, 6 Apr. 2006, www.voltairenet.org/article137526.html. Accessed 12 June 2017.

Schoellkopf, Sarah. "Resistir, combatir, y amar: La historia de una Madre de Plaza de Mayo." *Lucero: Nostalgia y memoria* vol. 15, 2004, pp. 159-164.

Sosa, Cecilia. *Queering Acts of Mourning in the Aftermath of Argentina's Dictatorship: The Performances of Blood.* Boydell and Brewer Inc., 2014.

Sosa, Cecilia. "Queering Acts of Mourning in the Aftermath of Argentina's Dictatorship: The Mothers of Plaza De Mayo and Los Rubios (2003)." *The Memory of State Terrorism in the Southern Cone: Argentina, Chile, and Uruguay*, edited by Francesca Lessa and Vincent Druliolle, Palgrave Macmillan, 2011, pp. 63-85.

Taylor, Diana. *Disappearing Acts: Spectacles of Gender and Nationalism in Argentina's "Dirty War."* Duke University Press, 1997.

Taylor, Diana. *The Archive and the Repertoire: Cultural Memory and Performance in the Americas.* Duke University Press, 2003.

Taylor, Diana, and Juan Villegas Morales. *Negotiating Performance: Gender, Sexuality, and Theatricality in Latin/o America.* Duke University Press, 1994.

Verbitsky, Horacio. *El Vuelo.* Seix Barral, 1995.

14.
"Black Protest"

Abortion Law in Poland in the Context of Division into Private and Public Sphere

EDYTA PIETRZAK AND ANNA FLIGEL

GABRIELA ZAPOLSKA, A FAMOUS Polish writer from the turn of the nineteenth and twentieth century, wrote a well-known drama in Poland titled *The Morality of Mrs. Dulska.* The eponymous character's life motto is "Don't do your dirty laundry in public." We feel that for now we are compelled to ignore this sentiment, so often repeated by Polish people, in particular by the current Polish government, the PIS party ("Law and Justice Party")—a conservative, far right, anti-liberal, populist party, with its characteristic commanding leader Jarosław Kaczyński.[1] The quote, in this case, regards the proposal of new changes to the present law on abortion, in which the right to abortion will be forbidden in any case, regardless of the woman's will. This includes cases in which even the mother's life and/or health is threatened, even when the pregnancy is the result of rape, and even when the fetus is seriously and genetically damaged.

What philosophers never dreamed possible has happened to Polish women in the twenty-first century in liberal-democratic Europe, where human rights and gender equality are the foundation of social and political order. Therefore, the radicalization of abortion law in Poland is worth a complete presentation and critical analysis. We will do this in the context of a division into private and public spheres because any attempt of radicalizing abortion law has deep roots in the public-private debate and in the role of a woman as a mother in society.

Hence, the present paper contains three parts: the theoretical background of the division into private and public spheres; the reconstruction of the course of events related to the Polish abortion law from March to October 2016; and the conclusive critical analysis in this area.

THEORETICAL BACKGROUND OF THE DIVISION
INTO PRIVATE AND PUBLIC SPHERES

The division into private and public spheres began in ancient Athens (Arendt 50-59)[2] and was developed through the Middle Ages and through the Renaissance and Modern periods. There are two positions in contemporary political thought related to public and private sphere functioning. The first one argues that in contemporary Western society all areas of social activities have been influenced by politics and that the private sphere has nearly disappeared. Politics has moved from the elites toward local communities and, as a result, has influenced all sectors of life: economics, culture, social religious, and family (Buksiński 67-97). The second position relates to liberalism. In liberal philosophy, the public-private division is of great importance.

Regarding the first position, Michel Foucault writes about the permanent presence of power in human life, which cannot be avoided. Therefore, all public institutions penetrate human interactions and control and limit people's behaviour. It is thanks to institutions that people are disciplined and social norms are obeyed. Observation, grading, punishment, and examination are used in the individual's disciplinary processes—all of this is well known in Western culture. According to Foucault, there is no room for privacy or doing what one wants in this kind of society.

Jean François Lyotard believes that although the public sphere is a common platform for discussion on matters of the entire nation, state, and society, it should disappear in favour of local and fragmentary projects. Policy is now dispersed, and reality becomes nontransparent, which clearly testifies to the weakening of the public sphere (Kwiek).

Richard Rorty, meanwhile, identifies the public sphere with the political one (73). The private sphere is dedicated to freedom and liberties. There are no rational rules there; one does not have to behave pragmatically but is allowed to live without obeying moral standards or responsibilities. Poets, philosophers, artists, intellectuals—called by Rorty "ironists"—form part of this sphere. In our interpretation, mothers and maternity are also a significant part of this area: the process of upbringing at the beginning of life is deprived of rational rules and ethical standards because it is primarily dominated by emotional attitudes. Another characteristic of the private sphere is that it is a place where new ideas, projects of change, and novel interpretations are being created. Responsibility and power are not present in it.

The public sphere, on the other hand, is full of commitments, and one has to behave rationally and according to moral standards. This is also where one is responsible for others. Politicians, reformers, manufacturers, producers, economists, and workers form part of this sphere. People seek power in it (Buksiński 67-97). According to Rorty, the private sphere is more important than the public one because of the creative abilities typical to the private sphere's representatives. Without the private sphere, changes in the public sphere would not be possible. Yet the public sphere can perfectly function without the private sphere's representatives, so they are necessary and unnecessary at the same time.

The philosopher attempts to merge the public with private through a combination of individual pursuits of excellence and a sense of belonging to a community (Rorty 13). The closest way to that approximation is to allow members of the public to be as selfish and irrational as they want, as long as they do not harm others and do not consume the resources needed by the less privileged.

Jürgen Habermas belongs to the group of supporters of the first position—the blurring of boundaries between the private and public. In *Between Facts and Norms*, Habermas shows the need for a new location of the public sphere in the state by ensuring its autonomy in relation to state power, administration, law, economy, and politics. He emphasizes the fluidity of the relationship between the public and private spheres. If in any private issue (such as family violence or the question of abortion) we perceive a universal aspect (e.g., low regulation required), this necessarily becomes a part of the public discourse and gains political significance. Therefore, even if we set the boundaries between private and public, it is dialectically open and together with the whole social context undergoes constant transformation.

Regarding the second position, in liberal philosophy, the public-private division is of great importance. The liberal-utilitarian system is based on private needs. The role of political power is to fulfil these needs. As John Stuart Mill notices, private actions are only connected to the ones that act; they guarantee the freedom of individuals (52). Public actions, on the other hand, are directed at others and are imposed from the outside, which is why in the liberal system, both religion and morality have been classified as part of the private sphere. Because of this same reason, a liberal state only allows or forbids its citizens certain actions, but it does not define what is right and what is wrong because that would then be ideology.

Contemporary liberal theories maintain this public-private division. The public sphere is defined by political actions and applicable laws. Religious and philosophical beliefs, the opinions of individuals, social ideas, and moral norms are part of the private sphere. This group of opinions should also include the beliefs represented by extremely conservative prolife organizations, according to which human life starts at conception.

What should be classified as public is decided by the arguments that have been used publicly and by their influence on the accepted social order and rules. John Rawls in his *Theory of Justice* shows that only elements that help keep peace and unity, and which are acquired through rational thinking, can be part of the public area. Moral, religious, and sexual norms are not part of this area because there is no possibility of achieving rational consensus in reaching them. Actually, they constitute reason for social tensions and conflicts, which is why they should be excluded from the public sphere. A direct example of this mechanism is the issue of abortion, which we have been observing in Poland since 1993.

In Rawl's opinion, liberalism is based on universal ideas and values that can be rationally defended in public, which cannot be said of religious dogmas or moral rules. This argument shows that ethical goods are less valuable compared to political ones. The commitment to freedom, liberalism, and ideological neutrality are more important than religious, ethical, or/and metaphysical beliefs (Rawls, *Political* 3). And—as we present the details in the next section—in the context of the "Black Protest" in Poland, we can observe the domination of political goods. It took the Polish parliament, with its conservative and Catholic majority, one day to reject the project of the new radicalized abortion law.

No matter which of the above opinions we choose, we can say that in traditional political interpretations, public sphere issues are defined as important to the state's politics and the country's population. Issues that belong to the public area have formal and legal characteristics and should be based on rules that can be accepted by all rational citizens. On the other hand, such issues as religious beliefs, family life, or entrepreneurial activity, which are part of the private sphere, do not have political importance.

Along with these two positions presented above, we can distinguish a strong tendency to criticize the private-public dichotomy. This is also done from two perspectives. The first relates to changes that took place in the centres of power and in the societies of modern democratic states because of both spheres gaining new definitions. Such changes included the emergence of late-capitalist consumer societies, which have led to new divisions, a greater role of mass media in shaping public opinion, new forms of communication, new ways of gaining more votes, new changes in power execution, and new global processes. The second perspective relates to the immanent constraints of liberal and democratic order. It turns out that transformations have led to the dichotomy's relativization, in which completely new shape of the public area has been established while the private one has been marginalized.

The crucial part of this critique is feminism, regardless of whether the feminist authors agree with the idea that the "private is political" or that the "private is nonpolitical." This feminist critique began in the 1960s when Carol Hanish used the "personal is political" slogan for the first time. Such topics as domestic violence, the division of housework, and the sex-determined division of power became part of public debate because they were part of the political process. Feminists who did not agree with the public-private division enriched the understanding of democratic equality conditions and questioned work divisions (both professional and domestic).

They undermined the belief that what takes place in the private sphere is only a private issue. Many feminist authors emphasized that separating these two spheres, similar to other contemporary control mechanisms, sustains the image of women as a submissive group, whereas men are seen as a dominant group.

With time, however, the two spheres were seen as complementary within the liberal tradition. Their legal and constitutional correlation in the state's order is of great importance if a human being is to fulfil his or her needs. In the public sphere, citizens should have the right to criticize the government and authorities as well as to share their opinions about religious, moral, ethnic, and national matters, independent of whichever political party is in power. Constraints should only be put on those ideas, opinions, or actions that are contrary to public moral standards, state order, or democracy. In the private sphere, citizens should have the guaranteed freedom to choose their own way of life, religion, and language, and to have the right to privacy without third party interference unless they violate another person's freedom or dignity. At the same time, citizens' rights and liberties cannot lead to situations in which the democratic state's interests are in danger. Nonetheless, these interests should be defined in a pragmatic way, limited only to the fundamental concerns of a democratic country in such fields as the economy, politics, and defense. Each form that tries imposing a despotic or authoritarian form of government on citizens limits their freedom.

Therefore, the public and private spheres are connected to each other in a way that the authorities' attitude to the first one influences the second one. In the liberal-democratic order, a wide variety of civil freedoms are imminently and immanently connected to liberty in the area of one's private life. These have a mutual influence. The essential features of a liberal-democratic order are social pluralism and tolerance, which are determined by the idea of secularism. Opposite to this, in despotic and authoritarian forms of government, constraints on freedom in the public sphere relate to limitations in the private area. Social pluralism and tolerance are usually neglected. Furthermore, the political order in this kind of organization is often built on national and religious ideologies.

AN ATTEMPT TO RADICALIZE
THE ABORTION LAW IN POLAND

Motherhood is a fundamental issue in every society. In the Western European culture of human rights, the concept of motherhood is linked to ideas of conscious motherhood, worthy motherhood, and safe motherhood. Therefore, the law of abortion is an important issue in this context. The topic of abortion, as in the Western culture, constitutes a difficult research subject within disciplines such as ethics and/or bioethics and represents a contentious worldview issue. The ethical positions and the general worldviews in this area are various. However, in the legal systems of most European Union member states the balance tilts toward the liberal position of a woman's right to decide about her own body (i.e., the woman's right to an abortion) because it is a woman's right to conscious, worthy, and safe motherhood.

We do not want to get into a philosophical and/or ethical analysis of the abortion issue here. Indeed, we claim that the final moral assessment of the act of abortion constitutes a totally individual issue. It depends on numerous philosophical and/or religious beliefs and is usually heavily embroiled in individual life stories. Hence, the philosophical and ethical dimensions of this topic are not our scope here, although, in some cases we will need to relate to them. In this section, we want above all to reconstruct the sequence of events directly related to an attempt to tighten abortion law in Poland, an EU country, from March to October 2016. Furthermore, we try to present the reasons for this situation as well as the consequences and reactions that it provoked.

At the end of March 2016, a Polish nongovernmental organization, "Ordo Juris," reported a legislative initiative in the form of the civil draft bill titled "Stop Abortion" to the Marshal of the Sejm, the Polish parliament. To ensure that this proposal would become applicable, the organization started to collect signatures[3] in favour of the initiative. The case immediately unleashed a storm in the Polish media and generally among Poles. Although such initiatives in Poland are carried out on average at least once every two years, the political conditions are usually not favourable enough to ensure the victory of such a battle, until that March.

The Polish episcopate almost automatically joined the initiative. Polish society quickly learned that the episcopate demands a complete ban of abortion. It is important to add that this demand was based on the Polish episcopate's support given to the PIS party and the promises made by PIS to them during the elections. Consequently, the leader of the ruling party, Jarosław Kaczyński, was indebted to the church for winning the election and confessed that as a believing and practising Catholic, he must opt for a ban on abortion, according to the episcopate's expectations. And he did this at the very beginning of April 2016.

The history of the battle for abortion law in Poland is long. We will only present the portions relevant to the current situation and present reconstruction. At the end of the 1920s, a strong campaign began to introduce no convictions for women who terminated a pregnancy because of social reasons. After a long and heated discussion, it was decided that article 233 of Polish Penal Code (1932) would legalize abortion in two cases: serious medical complications or when the pregnancy occurred as a result of rape, incest, or intercourse with a minor under the age of fifteen. During communist times, the so-called People's Poland (*Dziennik Ustaw*, 1956, No. 12, pos. 61), abortion was widespread, not only because of the reasons outlined above but because of the difficult living conditions of pregnant women.

From our point of view the most important period started in 1993, when a compromise between the Polish government and the Catholic Church produced a new law on abortion.[4] As a result of this compromise, Poland has one of the most restrictive abortion laws in Europe. Nowadays, abortion is permissible in Poland only when the pregnancy poses a threat to the mother's life or if the pregnancy is the result of rape (article 4a, 4b, 4c, of the *Law* from 1993 ["The Law"]). But now the episcopate as well as prolife organizations have recognized that they have a chance to proclaim this law as immoral and have a chance to stand against compromises and to further tighten the law. Hence, starting from March 2016, as mentioned, Poland adopted a strict abortion law, with only Malta and Ireland having tighter a one ("Abortion Worldwide"). Abortion was outlawed even if the pregnancy threatened the woman's life and even if the pregnancy was the result of violence. Abortion was now seen as the "murder of a human." We currently hear these words from the mouths of bishops, prolife organizations, and government representatives. Moreover, one can hear that all *obscure* cases of natural miscarriage would be checked by the prosecutors. The women, doctors, or any other people involved would be punished for such serious offenses if it were proven that these miscarriages were actually abortion.

In order to have a more comprehensive and objective view on the situation, we recognize that it is necessary to provide here the precise translation of the most crucial and dangerous points of the "Stop Abortion" draft. The first article states that "Every human being has the inherent right to life from the moment of conception, i.e. from the connection of the female and male cells. The life and health of the child from the moment of conception are under legal protection. Therefore art. 4a is hereby repealed; art. 4b is hereby repealed; art. 4c is hereby repealed." The essential content of these three points we presented above. They relate to the three circumstances that let Polish women to proceed with the abortion. Other important articles state the following.

Art. 24. A child conceived is a human being in the prenatal period of development, from connection of the female and male cells.

Art. 152 § 1. Whoever causes the death of a child, shall be subject to the penalty of the deprivation of liberty for a term of between 3 months and 5 years. § 2. If the perpetrator of the act determined in § 1 acts unintentionally, he shall be subject to the penalty of the deprivation of liberty for up to 3 years.

Art. 157a § 1. Whoever causes harm to the child conceived or health impairment threatening the life, shall be subject to the penalty of the deprivation of liberty for up to 3 years.

Art. 157a § 14. If the perpetrator of the act determined in § 1. [Art. 157a] is the mother of the child conceived, the court may [but it does not have to] impose on her relation

295

the extraordinary mitigation of punishment, even deciding not to apply the sentence.[5]

It was not only the leader of the governing party who quickly declared his acceptance of the episcopate's and Ordo Juris's demands. By the way, in Jarosław Kaczyński's speech related to the topic, he also said that most members of his party would vote the same as he would ("Kaczyński"). Prime Minister Beata Szydło also quickly declared her full acceptance for a complete ban on abortion in Polish law. So did many other representatives of this party (both men and women). Furthermore, for the first time in independent Poland (i.e., after 1989), the president's wife, the first lady Agata Kornhauser-Duda, tacitly supported the new law and not the rights of Polish women. Three ex-first ladies—Anna Komorowska, Jolanta Kwaśniewska, and Danuta Wałęsa—wrote and signed an open letter together on 14 April against the radicalization of the new law and in defense of the compromise law of 1993.

In response to the threat of the new law, women started to protest, supported by many men. Beginning on 1 April, girls and women started to gather around a net initiative named "Girls to Girls" (*Dziewuchy*),[6] which expanded quickly. They formed regional groups and began to protest on the streets.

In April 2016, Polish defenders of women's rights reported to the Marshal of the Sejm information on creating a civil draft bill committee titled "Save Women," (the precise title of the document was "On Women's Rights and Planned Parenthood" ["Druk nr 830, O Prawach"]). By the end of July, the two opposed drafts had gathered more than two hundred thousand signatures—double the required amount. Soon, the Sejm designated 23 September as the first reading date of the documents in the Polish parliament ("Druk nr 784"; "Druk nr 830, Obywatelski"). Within just four months, Polish society had exploded into an ideological war and into a really deep social conflict.

In the meantime, along with many protests, numerous people—professors, lawyers, constitutionalists, judges, journalists, artists, and politicians—spoke against the tightening of the abortion law and called for its liberalization. On 25 May, Salil Shetty, secretary general of Amnesty International, wrote an open letter to the prime minister of Poland. Defending the rights of Polish women, he wrote, "Amnesty International urges you to ensure, as Prime Minister, that the Polish government does not support the proposed changes to the legislation which would amount to an unauthorized retrogressive measure that poses serious implications for the women and girls who live in Poland, violating their fundamental human rights."

It must be added that different authoritative surveys taken in 2016 showed that more than 50 percent of Polish society favoured maintaining the current abortion law from 1993. Anywhere from 25 percent to 39 percent of respondents, depending on the survey, favoured liberalizing the abortion law. Instead, independent of the type of survey, no more than 9 percent of Poles favoured tightening abortion law (*Dopuszczalność*; Pacewicz; "Sondaż").

23 September was treated as if it were judgment day. The abortion conflict was discussed everywhere. Theoretically, both drafts should have been read on this day, and the vote would have only been a formality. It is necessary to know in this context that the government actually promised before the election that each civil draft bill would be directed to the Sejm Commission automatically as a citizen's draft. This way, the vote would only be a formality. But this remained purely in theory. Having the parliament majority, the right-wing governing party directed the extreme antiabortion "Stop Abortion" draft to the Sejm cCmmission instead of the liberal "Save Women" one, which they rejected in the first reading.

In the meantime, the Black Protest uproar started. By mid-September, a "Czarny Protest" Facebook profile page in Polish was founded. It called for wearing black clothes. As one 21 September FB post stated: "Dress in black and come in front of the Sejm on Thursday at 5 p.m. Let's protest together against the barbaric acts, the stripping of women of dignity and security!" (Party Razem, "#CzarnyProtest"). The reaction was immediate. Thousands of women and men responded to the appeal by posting photographs of themselves in black on social networking sites. On the 21 September, the first Black Protest took place in Warsaw in the front of the Sejm. On 22 September, the same happened in Poznań, where hundreds of people gathered in the front of the seat of the governing PIS party.

However, only after 23 September (i.e. after the vote and the government's decision to direct the radical, antiabortion draft to the Sejm's Commission) did something absolutely unpredictable start. For the first time in many years, Polish women united in a way and in numbers that had not been expected. (We need to add that they were accompanied by many men.) From 24 September, huge protests started on the streets of many Polish cities. On 25 September, there were already several thousand protesters. The following week was under the sign of the Black Protest week Poland. It was talked about and heard everywhere. The protest culminated on 3 October and was called "Black Monday." More than one hundred thousand people in over sixty cities across the country took to the streets of both small as well as big cities in Poland to protest for women's rights, but not only in Poland. There were also Black Protest marches in many European Union capital cities in the name of solidarity with Polish women. There were also several Black Protest marches outside of Europe.[7] Even the European Parliament in Strasbourg ("Women's Rights") spoke of the rights of Polish women just one day after Black Monday. Something that seems for many people in Poland and Europe to be completely private became completely public.

The Black Protest undoubtedly showed that Polish women can fight and that they can unite and appear as a real civil society. On 5 October, the case came back to the Sejm's Commission. Actually, the proceedings took the form of a total quarrel. In the final instance, the Commission decided, via vote, that the civil draft bill "Stop Abortion" would no longer proceed. Does this mean that Polish women have won the war? This would be a hasty conclusion. One can say for sure, however, that a battle has been won. Although the decision has been made, the discussion is still ongoing on both sides of the fence. And, very probably, it will not end in an easy manner and without victims.[8]

CONCLUSION

In our opinion, the case of the Black Protest is an excellent, almost textbook example of the problematic nature of the division between private and public. As we have tried to show in the first section, there are large divergences as to the theoretical interpretation of this division. In some points, it is also deeply paradoxical. Let this be our basis for the present analysis and conclusions regarding the issue of abortion in Poland. We claim that this issue is profoundly connected with such ideas as conscious motherhood, worthy motherhood, and safe motherhood. In this context, human rights should also be an additional perspective of interpretation. And last but not least, we regard another problem, which has been observable in some European countries for the past couple of years: authoritarian and antidemocratic tendencies. We focus on the case of Poland.

In the context of the liberal interpretation of private-public division, the situation happening in Poland is an illustration of the appropriation of the private sphere by the public one. This is an example of the devastating impact on the social order through the levelling of division between the private and public sphere. This is dangerous and can lead to authoritarianism and totalitarianism. Although in an authoritarian state citizens at least have a substitute for the private sphere, in a totalitarian one, they are completely deprived of it.

If we look at the events in Poland from the perspective of the opponents of separating the public sphere from the private one, from the perspective of those who recognize the interconnectedness and fluidity of these spheres, then the Black Protest shows that what is private, only seems to be such. According to Habermas, if we can extract a universal dimension in private matters, then they automatically become something public. And this is the kind of illusion that in today's world, only a purely private sphere exists.

The situation in Poland clearly exhibits that the private sphere must also be considered a public matter. Paradoxically, this is necessary to defend the private sphere and to strengthen its privacy. And, in this extent, we agree with the positions of Habermas and Rorty, as they show that the immanent and dialectical connection between these two areas. This should be an appeal to a factual argumentation for such a thesis.

There is another side of the abortion issue in Poland—so-called Polish underground abortion. This is a very important problem considering the existing restrictive abortion law of 1993, but especially in the context of the proposal of its radicalization. Poland borders with Germany and Slovakia. These countries, as many other EU member states, have liberal abortion laws that allow women to abort up to the twelfth week of pregnancy. Polish women can often find doctors (on the illegal market) who help them in Poland, but most often go to Germany or Slovakia to private clinics, and they have done so for many years. A few years ago, it was estimated that approximately a hundred thousand abortions per year were done this way by Polish women. Nowadays, reports estimate that this number may have reached even 150,000 per year. It is a staggering number. Of these so-called legal abortions, belonging to the three cases above presented, there are no more than nine hundred terminations of pregnancy per year. These two numbers clearly show that the Polish antiabortion law simply does not work. Furthermore, reliable statistical surveys indicate that one in every four adult woman in Poland confessed to having had at least one abortion in their life. Again, this means a huge number because when the data are translated into actual female citizens, it means that "abortion has been carried out by 4.1 to 5.8 million women in Poland" (Kośmiński).

The problem of underground Polish abortions is rarely spoken about. Furthermore, the Polish Catholic Church and prolife organizations do not regard this as a problem at all. One is left with the impression that this subject is better left untouched. However, when there is a proceeding on abortion law, should such a fact not be one of the key items on the agenda? How is it possible that the defenders of unborn life of the nine hundred children conceived are uninterested in these one hundred and fifty thousand?

It is important to add that it is not only Polish abortion law that is not working. Sexual education and the availability of contraception are also important issues. Sexual education is very poor in Poland and contraception is limited, as it is expensive and is available only with medical prescription. One often hears that it is the Polish Catholic Church that has hindered progress in this field. This might be true, if only because of the fact that the church is still a huge influence in Poland. However, we are convinced that this is only one side of the problem.

The authoritarian and antidemocratic tendencies constitute another side of this case in Poland's actual political context. In the perspective of the private-public split, these tendencies and aspirations increasingly fit the mould of a controlling society. Regardless of the fact that the new radical antiabortion law will not work, what matters is that power will rise along with fear within yet another sphere of life. After all, women will still carry out abortions, but their sense of fear and isolation will increase even more. So, it is a question of profound hypocrisy, but also primarily an example of civil rights violation. As it was recognized in the Universal Declaration of Human Rights innate dignity and equality, and unalienable rights of all members of the human community are the basis for liberty, justice, and world peace. The second article of the Declaration establishes the principle of nondiscrimination—equality in the use of rights set forth in the Declaration, without any distinction between race, colour, sex, language, religion, political or other opinions, national or social origins, property, birth, or other status. If we treat this seriously, there is no reason to refuse women the right to decide about their own bodies.

Hypocrisy, presented in this case by most of the so-called Polish extreme right wing (and, thus, by the ruling PIS party as well) is also expressed in professing the idea of Poland as a "messiah of nations" (Hopkin; Oleksiak). The new extremely radical antiabortion law would show that Poles are the defenders of fragile unborn life, and in Europe, only Poles have the courage to do such, which ignores underground abortion, women's rights, freedom of belief, and freedom of choice. Perhaps many people of various prolife organizations act against abortion out of their deep Christian beliefs. However in Poland, as we have shown above, they constitute no more than 9 percent of society. We have no illusions that it is not ideals that lie at the basis of the decisions of current politicians but an abysmal political calculation. Some proof of this is, for example, their almost total indifference toward refugees from Syria. One could say, somewhat ironically, that unborn beings constitute an inalienable value, yet, we, as Poles, do not care about Syrian-born children murdered and mutilated by the war in Aleppo or in any other bombed Syrian city. What lies behind the often repeated words—in the context of the current war in the Middle East—of the representatives of the currently ruling party: "we do not accept any refugees from the Middle East"?

We think that these facts confirm that regarding the case of abortion in Poland the private must become public, if privacy is going to survive. One cannot hide such huge issues, such as Polish underground abortion. This must be spoken of loudly and resolved thoughtfully and wisely. The phenomenon of the Black Protest as well as all activities taken in the last year show that Polish women are demanding the right to their own bodies and fertility and that draconian laws will not stop them from having an abortion, if they need it. This request was shouted out loudly in the Black Protest, which was a manifestation of a real civil society (Suchanow).

ENDNOTES

[1]It is worth bearing in mind that despite the fact that they won the elections resulting in their parliamentary majority, more than 81 percent of people eligible to vote in Poland did not vote for them. And, therefore, a large majority of Polish people do not agree with their professed beliefs and undertaken actions.

[2]The public sphere was modelled through citizens' discussions. The public was everything that was seen, heard, and understood by everybody and had been created in the existing world. A man could gain his identity only in the public sphere, and by participating in it, he could become a citizen who was granted rights and the respect of others. Home (*oikia*) was an obscure place, hidden from the eyes of others and full of passion. At the same time, the political arena was seen as a place full of light, in which values such as freedom, common good, justice, and equality were important.

[3]In Polish law, one hundred thousand signatures are required in order to table a motion in parliament.

[4]The full English title of the law is "The Law of 7 January 1993 on Family Planning, Human Embryo Protection and Conditions of Permissibility of Abortion."

[5]All translations are our own. The Polish version of the draft is available at orka.sejm.gov.pl/Druki8ka.nsf/0/CDB8B631C2EFE-830C1258014002A4E47/%24File/784.pdf.

[6]Perhaps, a much more precise English translation of the Polish name of the initiative "Dziewuchy dziewuchom" would be the expression "wenches to wenches."

[7]The most important TV channels around the world commentated on the Polish Black Monday strikes (Agerholm; "Black Monday"; Domonoske; "Polish Women Strike against Abortion Ban on 'Black Monday'"; "Protest in Schwarz"; Rapicetta; Siemaszko; "Women Threatened").

[8]When we were finishing this chapter, it was the beginning of November 2016. The risk of radicalization still exists as do the Black Protests.

WORKS CITED

"Abortion Worldwide: Global Incidence and Trends." *Guttmacher Institute*, May 2016, www.guttmacher.org/fact-sheet/induced-abortion-worldwide. Accessed 1 June 2017.

Agerholm, H. "Poland Abortion Strike: Thousands of Women in over 60 Cities Refuse to Work in Protest over Restrictive Laws." *The Independent*, 3 Oct. 2016, www.independent.co.uk/news/world/europe/poland-women-abortion-strike-protests-black-monday-polish-protestors-industrial-action-a7343136.html. Accessed 1 June 2017.

Arendt, H. *Human Condition*. The University of Chicago Press, 1998.

"Black Monday: Polish Women Strike against Abortion Ban." *BBC News*, 3 Oct. 2016, www.bbc.com/news/world-europe-37540139. Accessed 1 June 2017.

Buksiński, T. "Postmodernistyczna Historia, Czyli Koniec Rozumu I Wolności." *Wolność a Racjonalność*. UAM, 1993.

Domonoske, Camila. "Polish Women Hold 'Black Monday' Strike To Protest Proposed Abortion Ban." *NPR Radio on Air*, 4 Oct. 2016, www.npr.org/sections/thetwo-way/2016/10/04/496526099/polish-women-hold-black-monday-strike-to-protest-proposed-abortion-ban. Accessed 1 June 2016.

Dopuszczalność Aborcji W Różnych Sytuacjach. KOMUNIKATYZ-BADAŃ CEBOS, 2016.

"Druk nr 784: Obywatelski Projekt Ustawy O Zmianie Ustawy

Z Dnia 7 Stycznia 1993 r. O Planowaniu Rodziny, Ochronie Płodu Ludzkiego I Warunkach Dopuszczalności Przerywania Ciąży Oraz Ustawy Z Dnia 6 Czerwca 1997 r. - Kodeks Karny." *Sejm Rzeczypospolitej Polskiej*, 9 Sept. 2016, orka.sejm.gov.pl/ Druki8ka.nsf/0/CDB8B631C2EFE830C1258014002A4E47/%- 24File/784.pdf. Accessed 12 June 2017.

"Druk nr 830: O Prawach Kobiet I Świadomym Rodzicielstwie. Komitet Inicjatywy UstawodawczeJ 'Ratujmy Kobiety' Ustawa O Prawach Kobiet I Świadomym Rodzicielstwie. Marszałek Sejmu." *Sejm Rzeczypospolitej Polskiej*, 9 Sept. 2016, orka.sejm. gov.pl/Druki8ka.nsf/0/3C2A10A649B1C39EC12580290048D- CD3/%24File/830.pdf. Accessed 12 June 2017.

"Druk nr 830: Obywatelski Projekt Ustawy O Prawach Kobiet I Świadomym Rodzicielstwie." *Sejm Rzeczypospolitej Polskiej*, 9 Sept. 2016, orka.sejm.gov.pl/Druki8ka.nsf/0/3C2A10A649B- 1C39EC12580290048DCD3/%24File/830.pdf. Accessed 12 June 2017.

Dziewuchy Dziewuchom. 1 Apr. 2016, dziewuchydziewuchom. pl. Accessed 1 June 2016.

Foucault, M. *Discipline and Punish: The Birth of the Prison*. Random House, 1995.

Habermas, Jürgen. *Between Fact and Norms: Contributions to a Discourse Theory of Law and Democracy*. The MIT Press, 1998.

Habermas, Jürgen. *The Structural Transformation of the Public Sphere*. The MIT Press, 1991.

Hopkin, James. "Laying Poland's Messianic Complex to Rest." *The Guardian*, 9 Apr. 2011, www.theguardian.com/commentisfree/2011/apr/09/smolensk-po- land-messianic-complex. Accessed 1 June 2017.

"Kaczyński: Większość Klubu Pis Poprze Całkowity Zakaz Aborcji." *Dziennik*, 31 Mar. 2016, wiadomosci.dziennik.pl/pol- ityka/artykuly/516962,jaroslaw-kaczynski-aborcja-zakaz-ust- awa-pis-prawo-przerywanie-ciazy-kosciol-sejm.html. Accessed 1 June 2017.

Kośmiński, P. "Co Czwarta Kobieta Przerwała Ciążę [BADANIE CBOS]." *Gazeta wyborcza*, 31 Oct. 2016, wyborcza. pl/1,76842,13884572,Co_czwarta_Polka_przerwala_ciaze__ BADANIE_CBOS_.html. Accessed 12 June 2017.

Kwiek, M. *Rorty I Lyotard, W Labiryntach Postmoderny*. UAM, 1994.

Lyotard, Jean François. *Kondycja Ponowoczesna. Raport O Stanie Wiedzy*. Aletheia, 1997.

Mill, John Stuart. *On Liberty*. Batoche Books, 2001.

Oleksiak, Wojciech. "Being Polish: Myths and Reality Check." *Culture*, 15 Oct. 2014, culture.pl/en/article/being-polish-myths-and-reality-check. Accessed 1 June 2017.

Pacewicz, Piotr. "Sondaz Oko Press Rosnie Liczba Zwolennikow Liberalizacji Ustawy Antyaborcyjnej." *Oko.Press*, 1 Oct. 2016, oko.press/sondaz-oko-press-rosnie-liczba-zwolennikow-liberalizacji-ustawy-antyaborcyjnej/.Accessed 1 June 2016.

Party Razem. "#CzarnyProtest / Nie Dla Barbarzyństwa Wobec Kobiet!" *Facebook*. 21 Sep. 2016, www.facebook.com/partiarazem/photos/gm.1756990947907490/661396790695047/?type=3&theater. Accessed 12 June 2017.

"Polish Women Strike against Abortion Ban on 'Black Monday,'" *France 24 International*. 3 Oct. 2016, www.france24.com/en/20161003-poland-women-strike-against-abortion-ban-black-monday. Accessed 1 June 2017.

Rapicetta, Agnese. "Il 'Lunedì Nero' Colora La Polonia Di Diritti Per Le Donn: Guarda Le Immagini." *L'Unita Tv*, 4 Oct. 2016, www.unita.tv/focus/il-lunedi-nero-colora-la-polonia-di-diritti-per-le-donne-guarda-le-immagini-fotogallery/. Accessed 12 June 2017.

Rawls, John. *Political Liberalism*. Columbia University Press, 2005.

Rawls, John. *Theory of Justice*. Harvard University Press, 1999.

Rorty, Richard. *Contingency, Irony and Solidarity*. Cambridge University Press, 1989.

Shetty, Salil. "Concerns Regarding the Proposed Changes in the Laws Regulating Access to Abortion." *Amnesty International*, 25 May 2016, https://amnesty.org.pl/wp-content/uploads/2016/06/Concerns-regarding-the-proposed-changes-in-the-laws-regulating-access-to-abortion.pdf. Accessed 1 June 2017.

Siemaszko, Corky. "Polish Women Stage 'Black Monday' Strikes to Protest Abortion Law." *NBC News*, 4 Oct. 2016, www.nbcnews.com/storyline/europes-abortion-fight/polish-women-stage-black-monday-strikes-protest-abortion-law-n658776. Accessed

1 June 2017.

"Sondaż: Nie Chcemy Zmian Prawa Aborcyjnego." *tvn24*, 1 May 2016, www.tvn24.pl/wiadomosci-z-kraju,3/sondaz-millward-brown-w-sprawie-aborcji-dla-faktow-tvn-i-tvn24,640237.html. Accessed 12 June 2017.

Suchanow, Klementyna. "Czarny Protest Nie Tylko W Polsce. Ta Fala Obejmuje Kolejne Państwa: Strajk Polek Zainspirował Kobiety Na Całym Świecie," *Polityka*, 23 Oct. 2016, www.polityka.pl/tygodnikpolityka/swiat/1680376,1,czarny-protest-nie-tylko-w-polsce-ta-fala-obejmuje-kolejne-panstwa.read. Accessed 12 June 2017.

"The Law of 7 January 1993 on Family Planning, Human Embryo Protection and Conditions of Permissibility of Abortion." *Internetowy System*, isap.sejm.gov.pl/DetailsServlet?id=W-DU19930170078. Accessed 12 June 2017.

"Women's Rights in Poland Spark European Debate." *Europarl News*, 5 Oct. 2016, www.europarl.europa.eu/news/en/press-room/20160930IPR44805/women-s-rights-in-poland-spark-european-debate. Accessed 1 June 2017.

About the Contributors

Shirley Adelstein is a social policy researcher at the Urban Institute and a nonresident senior fellow at the Center for Research on Children in the U.S. at Georgetown University. Her research interests include social policy, gender and public policy, public opinion, and quantitative research methods. She holds a bachelor's degree from New York University and received her master of public policy and PhD in government degrees from Georgetown University.

Simone Bohn is associate professor of political science at York University, where she coordinates the Brazil chair and the Brazilian studies. Dr. Bohn's research focuses on political parties in South America, gender and politics in Brazil, and the study of political tolerance and attitudes toward corruption in Latin America. She is currently working on a SSHRC-funded research project titled "Evaluating Strategic Political Partnerships: The Case of the Women's Movement and the State in Contemporary Brazil." Her articles have been published in scholarly journals, such as *Politics and Government*, *Latin American Research Review*, *International Political Science Review*, *Journal of Latin American Politics*, and *Comparative Governance and Politics*.

Rosamaria Carneiro has a PhD in the social sciences from the Institute of Philosophy and Social Sciences of the State University of Campinas (Unicamp). She is a professor at the University of Brasília and is a researcher in the area of gender, health, body, and sexuality. She is the author of *Childbirth Scenes and Policies of the Body* (Fiocruz 2015).

Julie de Chantal is a lecturer at the University of Massachusetts Amherst and a research associate at the Five College Women's Studies Research Center. She is currently working on a book manuscript, titled *Just Ordinary Mothers: Black Women's Grassroots Organizing in Boston, from the Vote to the Busing Crisis,* which analyzes the role of Black working-class women in Boston's civil rights movement from the 1920s to 1974. She earned her doctoral degree from the University of Massachusetts Amherst, her master's and bachelor's degrees from the Université de Montréal.

Rebecca Deen (associate professor and department chair of political science, University of Texas at Arlington, U.S.) has published numerous articles on women in the political process, the U.S. presidency, and effective pedagogy in journals such as *Women & Politics*, *State and Local Government Review*, *Congress & the Presidency*, and *Judicature*. Current research includes an exploration of the relationship among civic engagement, local policy, and political recruitment, as well as an examination of the politics of school-related volunteer organizations and their role in educational policy.

Mary T. Duarte, PhD, is currently an associate professor of history at Cardinal Stritch University, Milwaukee, Wisconsin. Recent publications include an upcoming chapter "A Favored Witness to History, Queen of the Belgians Louise-Marie" in *Revolution, Reform, and Rebellion: The Role of Agency and Memory in Historical Understanding*, and "Returning to the Continent—British Travelers to France, 1814" in *Acta Iassyensia Comparationis*, February 2016. Her current research focuses on the early letters of the Queen of the Belgians Louise-Marie and mother-daughter relationships with regard to ruling.

Anna Fligel, PhD and philosopher, is a specialist in the history of philosophy, political philosophy, and social ethic; she is also an Italian interpreter. She works as a lecturer at the University of Lodz. In her research, she focuses on contemporary political philosophy, especially liberal thought, and global justice theories, Italian political philosophy. She is an author of many articles in these areas, as well as one book *Benedetto Croce. Absolute Historicism* (Lodz 2007).

Mirjam Höfner, MA, is a research assistant of Dr. Sylvia Schraut in the Department of Modern History at the University of the Bundeswehr (Munich). She is interested in women and gender history. The PhD project "Mothers for Germany" is a sub project of the Bavarian Research Cooperation ForGenderCare, funded by the Bavarian State Ministry of Education, Cultural Affairs and Science and, in particular, by the University of the Bundeswehr (Munich). It focuses on the discursive link between care work and political participation of women at the beginning of the twentieth century (1890-1918) and in the aftermath of the Second World War (1945-1960).

Nathalie Reis Itaboraí is a graduate in communications (Universidade Federal de Juiz de Fora), has a master's degree in sociology (Instituto Universitário de Pesquisas do Rio de Janeiro, IUPERJ), and a PhD in sociology (Instituto de Estudos Sociais e Políticos, Universidade do Estado do Rio de Janeiro, IESP/UERJ). For almost two decades, she has been researching about the sociology of the family, gender and class inequalities, and the relationship between public and private life. She has completed two courses in the Economic Commission for Latin American and Caribbean (ECLAC) about care politics and gender indicators, and participated in several national and international congresses, including the Brazilian Political Science Association (ABCP) and Latin American Sociological Association (LASA). She has worked as teacher in some Brazilian universities; she currently works as editor in Universidade Federal de Juiz de Fora. She is the mother of three children.

María Moreno is the postdoctoral research associate for Ecuador in the project "Latin American Racism in a 'Post-Racial' Age" in the Department of Sociology of the University of Cambridge. The project aims to understand racism, antiracism, and racial inequality in Brazil, Colombia, Ecuador, and Mexico. María's previous research considered the participation of indigenous women from Latin America in local, national, and global spaces of activism. By examining the connections between processes of globalization of indigenous and women's rights, development agendas, local politics, and gender dynamics in indigenous organizations, her research highlights the connection of ethnicity, gender, and power in indigenous organizations in Ecuador, and for Latin American indigenous leaders and professionals working in national and global arenas of indigenous activism. María earned her PhD from the University of Kentucky's Department of Anthropology, supported by a Fulbright Foreign Student Scholarship and a Lambda Alpha Anthropology Honor Society grant.

Pınar Melis Yelsalı Parmaksız is an associate professor at Ankara University, Faculty of Political Sciences. Yelsalı Parmaksız received her PhD in Turkish studies from Leiden University in 2009 with the thesis titled *Modernization and Gender Regimes in Turkey*. Her main areas of interest are gender and modernization in Turkey, social and political theory, feminist methodology, and memory studies. She has published many articles on related subjects in journals and collected volumes. She has published the following books: *Neye Yarar Hatıralar? Türkiye'de Bellek ve Siyaset Çalışmaları* [*What Is the Use of Memories? Studies of Memory and Politics in Turkey*] (2013) and *Türkiye'nin Modernleşmesinde Kadınlar* [*Women in the Modernization in Turkey*] (2017).

Edyta Pietrzak, PhD, is an anthropologist and a political scientist. She is an associate professor at the Lodz University of Technology. She is the author of the following books: *Towards a Global Civil Society. Transgressions of the Idea* (2014), *Axiology of Public Life* (2011), *Freedom, Equality and Sisterhood* (2008), *Subject, Person, Identity* (2007), and *Women Talk about Their Life* (2006). She is editor of the journal *Civitas Hominibus*, and an expert in the EU social programs. Her research focuses on the issues of citizenship, public sphere, and women studies.

Sarah A. Schoellkopf, PhD, graduated from Connecticut College with a double major in Hispanic studies and sociology in 1997. She interned with Las Madres de la Plaza de Mayo during her junior year in college and then returned after graduation with a Fulbright Student Grant in 1998 to continue her previous research. She has subsequently organized lecture tours of the United States for the Las Madres and the Línea Fundadora. At the University of California at Berkeley, Dr. Schoellkopf received her MA in 2002 and her PhD in 2008 in Spanish and Portuguese. In the San Francisco Bay Area, she has taught at UC Berkeley, at various area businesses, at several community colleges, and at several independent schools. She is also on the board of several nonprofit organizations.

Beth Anne Shelton (professor of sociology, University of Texas at Arlington, U.S.) has research interests in time-use patterns, gender, family, and the intersection of work and family. Her most recent research focuses on women's unpaid work outside the home and how it reflects modern ideas about motherhood, family and work. With Rebecca Deen, she recently published "Bake Sales for A Better America: The Role of School Volunteers in Civic Life" in the *International Journal of Interdisciplinary Social Sciences* as well as a paper titled "Are Stay-at-Home Mothers Really at Home?: U.S. Mothers' Volunteer Work in Schools" in *Stay-at-Home Mothers: Dialogues and Debates*, edited by Elizabeth Reid Boyd and Gayle Letherby and published by Demeter Press.

Tuba Demirci-Yılmaz currently works as an assistant professor at the Department of Sociology, Faculty of Economics, Administrative and Social Sciences at Altınbaş University in İstanbul. She received her PhD in Ottoman History from Bilkent University in 2008 with the dissertation titled, *Body, Disease, and Late Ottoman Literature: Debates on Ottoman Muslim Family in the Tanzimat Period* (1839-1908). Her research focuses on various aspects of gender, the making of gender regimes, the history of family and social policy, feminist movements, feminist history writing, and women's lives in the Middle East in general and in Ottoman and republican Turkey in particular.